Digital Capitalism

Digital Capitalism

Networking the Global Market System

Dan Schiller

The MIT Press
Cambridge, Massachusetts
London, England

First MIT Press paperback edition, 2000
© 1999 Massachusetts Institute of Technology

This book was set in Sabon by Achorn Graphic Services, Inc.

Printed and bound in the United States of America.

Library of Congress Cataloging-in-Publication Data

Schiller, Dan, 1951–
  Digital capitalism: networking the global market system / Dan Schiller.
    p. cm.
  Includes bibliographical references and index.
  ISBN 0-262-19417-1 (hc: alk. paper), 0-262-69233-3 (pb)
  1. Information society. 2. Electronic commerce—Social aspects.
3. International economic integration. 4. Information superhighway.
5. Internet (Computer network)—Social aspects.
6. Telecommunication—History. I. Title.
HM221.S355   1999
303.48′33—dc21   .   98-41544
                                                            CIP

For Sunie, Lucy, and Ethan

Today more than ever, reason needs to be wide awake.
—José Saramago, "On Communication"

Contents

Acknowledgments

This book took shape as a result of collaborations, both formal and informal, which it is my pleasure to acknowledge. Its guiding themes were inspired by Brian Campbell's generous invitation to speak in Vancouver about the political economy of the Internet. At that meeting, I also had the pleasure and benefit of renewed interchange with two acutely observant high-tech analysts, Rod Hiebert and Sid Shniad. Another segment of the work, first drafted long ago in Philadelphia, benefited from the insight and knowledge of Pamela Tate. Michael B. Katz gave that initial text a critical but sympathetic reading. More recently, David Noble at Harvey Mudd College created an intellectually charged context for discussion of some of the same questions.

Other themes found their origin in articles written for *Le Monde Diplomatique*. For their encouragement—and the inspiration I take from their journal—I thank Ignacio Ramonet, Alain Gresh, and Philippe Riviere. Also important was the invitation proffered me by Carlos Blanco Aguinaga and Jose Monleon to attend what proved to be a very stimulating meeting at the University of Complutense, Madrid. Acknowledgment is due to the Association for Computing Machinery, for use of material published in Dan Schiller, "Net Makeover," *netWorker* 1(1), 1997, 39–44.

Closer to home I found other, no less indispensable, sources of help. I thank my fellow department members, Michael Cole, Susan Davis, DeeDee Halleck, and especially Ellen Seiter and Yuezhi Zhao; other colleagues at the University of California at San Diego, Michael Bernstein, George Mariscal, Page duBois, Tom O'Neil, and Don Wayne; my students, Maribel Castaneda Paredes, Meighan Maguire, and Dr. Lora

Taub; and, hardly least, five talented UCSD bibliographers and librarians, Patricia Cruse, Larry Cruse, Sam Dunlap, James Jacobs, and Elliott Kanter. Sandy Dijkstra got this book off to a running start. My colleague Phil Agre (now at UCLA) allowed me to test my formulations in cyberspace, via postings on his Red Rock Eater news service.

Richard B. DuBoff, Edward S. Herman, and Robert W. McChesney have been stalwart friends of this book at every point; I only hope it merits the support they have shown me. Herbert I. Schiller and Anita R. Schiller were equally helpful weekly discussion partners; albeit at a longer distance, Zach Schiller played a pivotal role in guiding my thinking.

I cannot recount the contributions that Lucy H. Schiller and Ethan D. Schiller have made to this work. Nor is a book proper thanks for the caring support, critical advice, and overall good cheer that I received from Susan G. Davis. You are my anchors and my stars.

Laramie, Wyoming
December 7, 1998

Introduction: The Enchanted Network

We have all heard the prognostications: the Internet will vault us into global brotherhood, revitalize our children's education, usher in an era of robust direct democracy—and, ultimately, create the conditions for the development of what the chief executive officer of Microsoft hails as a "friction-free capitalism."[1]

These predictions depend on a pair of related assumptions. The first assumption is that the Net comprises an informational cornucopia, the fruits of which will yield what former U.S. House Speaker Newt Gingrich calls (in a curious image) "a world that is bathed in information."[2] The second foundational assumption is frankly millenarian: that society, by exploring the Net's swelling cybercircuits and overstocked data warehouses, will shed its savagery and somehow morph into a kinder, gentler place.

Are these assumptions valid? What evidence exists that information is actually passing into a realm apart from prevailing economic relationships and institutional structures? Are dearth and domination truly disappearing into the maw of cyberspace? Are the social and moral inadequacies of the established media—publishing, film, musical recording, television, and telecommunications—giving up the ghost before a cybercornucopia?

This utopian vision—Internet as salvation—expresses ancient yearnings. Historical detoxification through scientific knowledge: the truth—information?—will make us free.

Hopes that a wired future will prove blissful are generally conditioned today by fears that our system of schooling is inadequate, that civic commitment has flagged, and that social groups are polarized and economically unstable.

I argue that we should be skeptics about the potential of cyberspace. Knowledge carried through the Internet is no less shaped by social forces than it is elsewhere. Far from delivering us into a high-tech Eden, in fact, cyberspace itself is being rapidly colonized by the familiar workings of the market system. Across their breadth and depth, computer networks link with existing capitalism to massively broaden the effective reach of the marketplace. Indeed, the Internet comprises nothing less than the central production and control apparatus of an increasingly supranational market system.

"Capitalism has always been an international system," writes the economic historian Richard B. DuBoff, "but *globalization* now implies an internationalizing of financial and economic flows that is far more integrated and puts new constraints on domestic policy options."[3] In this book, I show that the Internet and, indeed, the greater telecommunications system with which the Internet has intertwined comprise a leading edge of this epic transnationalization of economic activity.

In addition to broadening the effective reach of the marketplace, cyberspace is making feasible what Edward S. Herman calls a "deepening of the market"—both for commercial home entertainment and for education, which has long been exempted, at least in part, from commercial imperatives. Networks are directly generalizing the social and cultural range of the capitalist economy as never before. That is why I refer to this new epoch as one of *digital capitalism.*

The arrival of digital capitalism has involved radical social, as well as technological, changes. In this book I trace these metamorphoses through three interlinked realms. As is shown in chapters 1 and 2, the telecommunications system has been given an overarchingly new social purpose as it is subjected to *neoliberal,* or market-driven, policies. This metamorphosis empowers transnational corporations and concurrently aggravates existing social inequalities. In chapter 3, I show that cyberspace offers uniquely supple instruments for cultivating and deepening consumerism on a transnational scale, especially among privileged groups. Finally, in chapter 4, I show that digital capitalism has already begun to prey on education, placing some of the most sensitive processes of social learning at the mercy of a proprietary market logic.

. . . .

In order to make this a book for the informed general reader, a few preparatory remarks about the history and structure of the Internet may prove helpful. Digitization—reconciling telecommunications with the computer logic of 1s and 0s—comprises a sweeping and multifaceted tendency. Its general object is to increase the economic efficiency of networks by allowing them to be shared more thoroughly and effectively among many users. In an era of ever-accelerating demand, today's digital networks are built to accommodate greater traffic than their predecessors—plain old telephone service networks—can manage. Increased network capacity in turn rebounds back on the movement toward service integration: hitherto distinct services can be bundled together on high-capacity, or *broadband*, digital networks to realize gains in cost efficiency. The Internet offers a particularly important instance of this drive to establish more capacious digital networks. To understand why requires a brief excursion into its underlying technology.

In general, a network is a set of computers interconnected at both physical and logical levels. At each of these two levels, the Internet breaks with established practice. On the physical level, networks are established when computers are linked through telecommunication media such as copper telephone lines, optical fibers, or satellite relays. The Internet makes crucial use of this physical telecommunications infrastructure but soups it up with additional equipment. Specialized *switches* and *routers* encode messages into digital form, break them down into individual *packets* of data, assign an address to each packet, establish a transmission path for each separate packet to traverse, and recombine packets into complete messages at destination points. Chapter 1 examines how this technology differs from that used in older telecommunications systems.

On the logical level, computer networks, and the new capabilities that they layer onto the telecommunications system, also are structured by software, which endows them with the capacity for specific service applications, or *functionalities*, such as file transfers. Specifically, networks employ *protocols*, software programs whose joint use permits interconnected computers to exchange messages of different kinds. In the most basic sense, the Internet came into being because an expanding group of computer systems acquired the capacity to communicate by deploying a common set of protocols known as TCP/IP (subsequently, additional key protocols were also incorporated). From the perspective of its end users, the Internet may appear to be a unified system, but it is actually a gigantic assemblage of cooperating computer networks, a so-called *decentralized network* of networks. What motivated this increasingly widespread decision to interoperate computer systems? This vital question also is addressed in chapter 1.

The true uniqueness of Internet technology (TCP/IP) is that it may be used to establish fluid and versatile links between previously noncommunicating islands of computer functionality. On this foundation, a cascade of applications binding together an increasingly supranational Internet community suddenly became possible. Corresponding networks were built for highly specialized purposes in the United States, France, Britain, Japan, Australia, and other nations. Then, once the decision was taken to separate out the U.S. military's privileged network from its fledgling civilian counterpart, a hitherto restricted subscriber base became free to mushroom. A relatively informal system of computer addresses was devised. A succession of protocols permitting new kinds of intercommunication—the World Wide Web was far and away the most important—added explosively to the resultant surge in usage.

Because the Net bridged isolated pockets of characteristically more limited computing activity, users rapidly found uses for it. Indeed, it unexpectedly became sufficiently ubiquitous to force aside other prospective systems of network interconnection. By offering a ready means of adjustment to the main trend, the Internet *became* the main trend.

How and why this came to happen, and to what effect, comprise the unifying themes of this book. My aim is not to explicate the Internet's engineering but to uncover its dominant social patterns and directions. From this perspective, cyberspace not only exemplifies but today actually shapes the greater political economy of which it has become a critical part.

The networks that collectively comprise cyberspace were originally created at the behest of government agencies, corporate military contractors, and allied educational institutions. However, over the past decade or so, many of these cooperating networks have begun to serve end-users located principally in and around corporations. This shift in end-users suggests that the underlying logic of the Internet is also being transformed.

"Built to one set of economic principles," an authoritative report emphasized in 1996, the Net has commenced on a "transition to another set of
economic principles."[4] As it comes under the sway of an expansionary
market logic, the Internet is catalyzing an epochal political-economic
transition toward what I call digital capitalism—and toward changes
that, for much of the population, are unpropitious. What, then, are the
chief causes and primary features of digital capitalism, and what does
this millennial shift to digital capitalism entail? It is these questions that
I seek to grapple with here.

Digital Capitalism

1

The Neoliberal Networking Drive Originates in the United States

The architects of digital capitalism have pursued one major objective: to develop an economywide network that can support an ever-growing range of intracorporate and intercorporate business processes. This objective encompasses everything from production scheduling and product engineering to accounting, advertising, banking, and training. Only a network capable of flinging signals—including voices, images, videos, and data—to the far ends of the earth would be adequate to sustain this open-ended migration into electronic commerce.

To create such a system meant that the foundations of the world's electronic information infrastructure had to be recast. The new network system, within which the Internet loomed largest by the mid-1990s, required a sweeping metamorphosis of the structure and policy of existing telecommunications.

To set about this task, computer companies and leading telecommunications carriers allied themselves with the few thousand transnational enterprises that comprised their primary customer base. This partnership was animated by a shared political axiom: that corporate capital's ownership and control of networks should be put beyond dispute, even beyond discussion.[1] This neoliberal freedom to fashion networks into instruments of enterprise should remain unalloyed.

Neoliberalism comes by its name because its adherents' primary aim—paring unwanted state oversight and regulation of the economy to gain more unfettered freedom of action for private firms—resuscitates the liberal economic policy of Victorian Britain. Markets should be left alone to obey their presumed natural logic: so goes the laissez-faire doctrine that was reenshrined as domestic orthodoxy during the 1980s and assumed global preeminence during the 1990s. Because the best economic outcomes were produced by negotiations among individual economic actors who were unencumbered by extraneous obligations, government regulation must be minimized.[2] Paradoxically, however, to actualize something approaching such a free-market regime in telecommunications today (just as in Britain during the 1840s), unremitting political intervention was necessary. Thus, as we will see, the evolution of networking comprised as much a political as an economic work in progress.

During the 1990s, a top-to-bottom overhaul of worldwide telecommunications drove toward completion. Two features of this transformation stand out, as we will see in chapter 2. First, the network system-building boom was of a magnitude that the world had never seen. Old networks were upgraded to support novel services, while capacious new systems sprang up at every level, from local loop to global grid. Equally significant, however, was a second feature of the emerging regime. Policymakers the world over simultaneously abandoned public-service policies for market-driven tenets and acceded to the integration of networks on a transnational scale. National welfarist controls over this critical infrastructure dropped away, while disparities in access widened.

This tumultuous transformation was triggered inauspiciously, by an obscure series of piecemeal changes beginning in the United States in the 1950s.

Liberalization of U.S. Network Development

During the mid-1950s, near the beginning of the digital computer era, U.S. government agencies and educational institutions possessed perhaps three-quarters of the nation's several hundred computer installations. Throughout the 1960s, however, the not-for-profit orientation of early computing shifted. By the mid-1960s, manufacturers, banks, insurance companies, utilities, and retailers were operating two-thirds of a greatly enlarged base—some 35,000 installations—of computing facilities.[3] Many computer applications sought to rely increasingly heavily on telecommunications to make data-processing power available more broadly throughout business organizations. Originating as discrete islands of computer *functionality* (as different classes of service, or discrete applications, are sometimes called) in payroll, accounting, inventory, and other administrative areas, disparate networks soon began to unfurl into other fields: sales, credit authorization, customer service, production scheduling, and research and development. In 1960, a mere thirty-one U.S. computer systems permitted *online use,* meaning that these computers might be accessed via remote terminals connected by telecommunications links. These early online applications were limited to such areas of *transaction processing* as airline ticketing. A scant six years later, however, one survey showed that more than 2,300 online systems had been installed by U.S. businesses. Through an uneven but continuing process, to which we return momentarily, more and more corporate services began to be placed online.[4]

Anticipating this rapid buildup of network applications as early as 1947, one trade association—the American Petroleum Institute—created a Central Committee on Radio Facilities. The head of this curiously named unit declared that "practically every division or branch of the petroleum industry can well be served by one or more adaptations of radio to effect economies in operation, increase safety, or raise efficiency."[5] Oil companies were far from unique in sensing the industrial potential of telecommunications. An interindustry trade group, the Microwave Users Council, was established in 1954. Growing corporate dependence on early computer-communications networks in turn prompted the largest U.S. companies from every economic sector to undertake a long march through the nation's regulatory arena.

The Long March
Throughout the twentieth century, the telecommunications system had become subject to extensive governmental oversight. Federal and state regulation served several ends. Foreign ownership of this strategic industry, to begin with, was deemed inimical to U.S. national sovereignty. Far-reaching precautions were taken, therefore, to ensure that the telecommunications industry remained in U.S. hands. Legislation strictly limited foreign ownership of U.S. telecommunications companies, which contributed to forestalling, within a vital sector, the corporate economy's trend toward transnationalization.

Because they were classed as public utilities and common carriers, tele-communications companies faced an array of additional obligations during the welfare-state era. Specialists refer to these mandates as *exit, entry,* and *operating controls.* State public utility commissions—in partnership with a transcendent national agency, the Federal Communications Commission—monitored the prices carriers sought to charge, the services they sought to provide, and the technologies they sought to utilize. Under the terms of prevailing policy, the industry adhered to an overarching norm of nondiscrimination: comparable service for every subscriber. Established policy also placed a premium on long-term industry stability, end-to-end network responsibility, and nationwide residential telephone service.

Business network users, allied with entrepreneurial industries emerging around a cluster of constitutive technologies—computers, aerospace, and military electronics—found these regulatory mandates increasingly inhibiting. Why were they not free to build networks just as they pleased? As early as 1957, business users began to lobby, as the Automobile Manufacturers Association put it in an obscure proceeding, for "the same latitude in the use and implementation of our communications facilities that we enjoy in the use and implementation of the many thousands of other tools, facilities and services necessary to the conduct of our business"[6]— including, preeminently, the computer. Between the mid-1950s and 1970, business users elaborated a policy agenda around a general objective: freedom to develop corporate network systems and services as they preferred.

Through a series of highly technical proceedings at the Federal Communications Commission and elsewhere, these users insisted that they had the right to

• Build wholly proprietary systems, using microwave and other nontraditional technologies, for internal corporate data and voice communications;

• Lease from the existing telecommunications carriers *private-line* circuits to interconnect specific branch plants and offices on a full-time, or *dedicated,* basis;

• Rely on an emerging class of competitive long-distance carriers, whose chief strategy in turn was to supply business users with specialized network services;

• Attach independently furnished computers and other specialized instrumentation (including, by the late 1960s, these burgeoning private and competitive voice and data networks themselves) to the nation's existing public telecommunications network (PTN);

• Obtain preferential pricing policies for the specialized telecommunications services and equipment on which they were pinning a growing share of their operations; and

• Prevent any extension of regulatory oversight to computer services that involved use of communications facilities—that is, networks.

This obtuse agenda demanded nothing less than an autonomous sphere of corporate network applications that was essentially free of regulatory oversight and was parasitic on the existing telecommunications network. Business users and their allies wanted to unburden both in-house proprietary systems and a new generation of competitive carriers of the billions of dollars worth of historical costs that were factored into the rates and rules attaching to the existing national telecommunications network—to cut free of the nation's historical commitment to universal telecommunications service. They sought systematic discrimination in favor of their own special-purpose networks and against the general-purpose public system on which ordinary telephone users relied.

I document below some of the consequences of this lengthy embrace of discriminatory policies. Even at the outset, however, it must be noted that this astonishingly successful campaign for domestic liberalization destabilized and reoriented the entire U.S. telecommunications system. As one insider acknowledged, networking technologies have "developed in a kind of golden nest over the past thirty years. . . . Special policies were crafted that not only insulated this entire sector from virtually every kind of public process or control, but also provided it with substantial public benefits, both directly through significant government funding, and indirectly by subjecting other related sectors like telecommunications to regulations designed to foster the development and growth of computer networking."[7]

Regulators embraced the fiction that computer networks—which in fact made *increasing* use of the existing telecommunications infrastructure—could be treated as if they existed independent of that infrastructure. Proliferating network systems were therefore freed by regulators to be configured and reconfigured as needed in support of business users' objectives. The unregulated suppliers of these systems, chiefly computer companies, were effectively licensed to metamorphose from vendors of electromechanical business instrumentation (tabulators, typewriters, cash registers, calculators, and like machinery) into pioneers of next-generation network equipment and services.

Creating a liberalized networking sector required fiendishly complex operational details and consumed an entire generation's regulatory attention. Reduced to its essentials, however, it amounted to a straightforward and deliberate anachronism: regulators would simply draw a line, as if *computing* and *telecommunications* constituted clearly differentiable domains—which of course they no longer did. On the telecommunications side of the line, the existing rules of public service would continue to apply. However, on the computing side, established exit, entry, and price controls would be relaxed and progressively abandoned. So long as network applications were categorized by regulators as *data-processing* services, they could be pursued freely.

At first, this prodigal exception was reserved for business users, computer companies, and their offspring, pioneering network service providers. But the boundary line, of course, was unstable—not only because it was episodically subverted by specialized technical innovations but also because it existed chiefly as an artifact of the regulators' imagination. Through a series of proceedings that began in the mid-1960s, the Federal Communications Commission therefore drew and then redrew the line. As it did so, a greater and greater share of the burgeoning network industry was included on the liberalized computing side of the line. A critical watershed was reached in 1980. In its *Second Computer Inquiry*,[8] the FCC then decided that even regulated telecommunications companies, the core of the nation's telecommunications infrastructure, would be permitted to establish subsidiaries that could bypass existing regulatory strictures. Though at first this comprised a selective exception, it too was soon generalized. What had originated as a specialized networking industry endowed with exceptional market freedom was now set to expand comprehensively into the greater telecommunications system.

As a result of these decisions, the domestic telecommunications industry convulsed. Until the early 1970s, the nationwide telecommunications network continued to be run by AT&T, which was the sole provider of long-distance service and the overall network manager (in cooperation with its own local service subsidiaries and a couple of thousand smaller providers). However, the FCC authorized a chain of new entrants, including both satellite companies and terrestrial carriers like MCI and Sprint. Momentum increased to open additional segments of the telecommunications market, beyond long distance—equipment supply, data services, satellite and international services, and ultimately local telephone service—to "competition." The AT&T divestiture, the largest corporate shakeup in world history, comprised only the most spectacular by-product of this transition to a neoliberal development policy.

With the benefit of hindsight, what should have been plain at the time is now painfully clear: even if it should entail the sacrifice of the bluest of blue-chip companies, the U.S. policymaking establishment was determined to grant business users maximum freedom to exploit information technology networks as a private matter. In fact, neither of the two unquestioned titans of the information industry in 1980 retains that luminary status today: an ensuing orgy of creative destruction has instead left IBM chastened but still strong and AT&T in questionable condition.

Of course, no one could have predicted these results. Liberalization was embraced first and foremost as a reflex of political intervention by leading banks, insurance companies, retail chains, automobile manufacturers, oil companies, aerospace firms, and other corporations, all of which sought to reorganize their business operations around networks. Around 1970, short-term lobbying to secure piecemeal regulatory changes shaded into long-term strategic planning. At about that point, corporate executives and government bureaucrats recognized that the stakes in this arcane area of policy were huge—that continued U.S. corporate stewardship of the exploding information technology industry might renew waning U.S. global political-economic power. Thus the impact of liberalization quickly began to extend beyond the theater of U.S. domestic telecommunications. This outward-rippling expansion led toward a comprehensive restructuring of the world's information infrastructure, which is examined in detail in chapter 2.

Innovating Network Technology

This ongoing process of liberalization prompted a multifaceted push into network technology development. Today's paramount network innovation—the Internet—emerged here, at the margin of the existing telecommunications order, in the newly authorized, expanding zone of liberalized development.

The Internet's emergence had nothing to do with free-market forces and everything to do with the Cold War military-industrial complex. In fact, "[f]or nearly the first ten years of its existence," writes one insider, "there was a single, cohesive, technical community through which the U.S. Department of Defense controlled every aspect of the Internet's funding and evolution."[9] The Internet's direct ancestor was the Arpanet, which in 1969 inaugurated a radical new system for routing digitized messages between interconnecting computers. Conventional telecommunications systems used a technology, perfectly appropriate for voice communication, called *circuit switching.* To connect calls, circuit switching established a dynamic link between the caller's and the recipient's phone lines; for the duration of their conversation, that link remained in place. The *packet switching* around which the Arpanet was structured, in contrast, imposed a procedure more appropriate for data interchanges. Every message was broken up into dozens of *packets,* assigned a destination address, and sent along one of a series of multiple paths across the network. Once the packets arrived at the recipient's site, they were reassembled in a split second in their original order, and thus the original message was reconstituted and received as sent. Circuit switching reserved network capacity on an exclusive basis for each conversation; packet switching allowed it to be shared effectively among multiple users.

The Arpanet was built to military specifications to allow previously independent computers to share resources. Packet switching was designed to provide *hardened* communications facilities, so that, its proponents apparently believed, even a nuclear attack would not prevent messages from getting through because packets could simply bypass damaged portions of the network.[10] Ahead lay the daunting technical challenge of interconnecting disparate *networks* of computers, which might be operating according to very different standards. By the early to mid-1970s, military sponsorship resulted in the invention of the *protocols,* or instruction sets, that made feasible such network intercommunication. The Transmission Control Protocol (TCP) and the Internet Protocol (IP) constituted the requisite suite of software instructions that, as the 1970s drew to an end, used satellites, mobile radio circuits, and fixed terrestrial lines to tie together with increasing effectiveness an expanding set of military networks.

Despite this expansion, what we now know as the Internet continued to be housed within the secretive netherworld of the garrison state. One of the Internet's primary features stems from its unique—and, in its original military context, unlikely—ability to further the goal of information sharing by facilitating common use of once-unbreachable individual domains. Its distinctiveness, and its attraction, lay mainly in its unparalleled ability to span between hitherto isolated computer resources.

Commercializable demand for information sharing, as we have begun to see, had been building up to torrential levels in at least three distinct ways: intraorganizationally, chiefly though not only within transnational corporations; interorganizationally, again mainly between and among such companies; and, finally, between corporations and individuals. In each case, however, enhanced forms of information sharing depended on improved means of network interconnection. Only through fluid new links between the disparate networks that were proliferating could new forms of information sharing be extended.

What we know as the Internet engaged this raging demand for information sharing by offering an unprecedentedly tractable technology for network interconnection. Internet technology had been created to work with the full variety of extant and prospective digital networks. Equally important, it did not hostage present-day need to some remote future vision: just deploying TCP/IP brought new forms of information sharing suddenly within reach. The Internet's astonishing versatility—its still rapidly evolving capacity to support novel as well as established forms of intercommunication—only added to its popularity.

The Internet was and is built by utilizing a set of commands, or protocols, that enable computers to set up an electronic space—cyberspace—with its own specific rules and functions. Although it was developed within the U.S. military-industrial complex, this foundational technology lies in the public domain. The rights to use it were made freely available, at first to a select group of cooperating universities and other military contractors and then more widely. The result, as Robert H. Reid declares, was that "nobody owned the network. Virtually nobody made money from it directly. And almost every piece of software that governed or accessed it was free."[11] The Internet thus resulted "as much from the free availability of software . . . as from anything else."[12] Had a proprietary ethic been applied to it, in contrast, there can be little doubt that the Net would have been stunted during infancy.

During the 1980s, the National Science Foundation began to expand the use of this strategically important system beyond military applications. A new "backbone network" sponsored by the NSF provided high-capacity circuits to carry great loads of data traffic between five university-based supercomputer research consortia, also established via NSF sponsorship. The NSF also permitted existing regional and university computer centers to use Internet technology to physically connect to this backbone. Some 200 networks quickly did so.[13] Traffic rapidly grew, to the point that the military portion of the network was split off, while the NSF continued to develop its new civilian counterpart.

As this civilian NSFNET was further upgraded, its base of users was deliberately enlarged beyond computer scientists in universities, government agencies, and think tanks. Increasingly diverse communities of researchers found reasons to use NSFNET. File transfers—exchanges between one computer host and another—brought them hitherto inaccessible programs and data, and remote access distributed computer processing power to dispersed locations. As early as 1973, however, three-quarters of all traffic on the originating Arpanet comprised email.[14] Email was the NSFNET's paramount offering because it permitted researchers to communicate conveniently and informally with distant colleagues. Throughout the 1980s, efforts to increase the utility of email interchanges and the other services helped spur additional network interconnection, both among U.S.-based interuniversity systems and between networks being constructed around universities in other countries.[15]

The Internet, a term that came into use during the mid-1980s, denoted the decentralized set of networks—some 3,500 by late 1991—that connected to the NSFNET backbone. These individual networks, each run and funded on its own, developed informal organizational means of cooperating with one another to direct traffic and set policy. Rapid-fire innovation continued within this loose-knit system to enhance underlying network capabilities, to develop means of interconnection for personal computers, and to establish and improve standards for the representation of information on the Internet. In 1989 the *hyperlink* technology that tied together Internet sites and documents was created at a European physics laboratory, and in 1992 a simple *graphic interface* to this electronic web (Mosaic) was developed by programmers at the University of Illinois.

The seeds of a market-driven approach to networking were sown early. The ongoing liberalization of U.S. network development freed the initial corporate sponsors of Internet technology (principally Bolt, Baranek, and Newman, a military contractor and consulting firm) to exploit its commercial applications. Outposts of market activity quickly materialized, particularly after the publicly funded technology of packet switching was spun off in the early 1970s. Private vendors such as Telenet now sought to furnish corporate users in dozens of cities with access to data services, such as remote access to computer facilities. Proprietary online subscription services, such as those provided by CompuServe (established in 1979), Prodigy (1982), and America Online (1985), emerged in this same space. Initially authorized by the Federal Communications Commission in 1973, such *value-added* or *enhanced* data services existed at—indeed, helped to constitute—the deliberately nebulous, and constantly receding, boundary of U.S. regulated telecommunications.[16] The originators of Telenet also voiced a proprietary attitude toward Internet technology, in an early attempt to impose draconian intellectual property standards on the Net.[17]

More portentous still was the hothouse growth, beginning in the early 1980s, of *local-area* data communications systems. The dominant technology for local-area networking was called Ethernet, a combination of hardware and software for linking workstations into office networks that was built around an "open," or nonproprietary, standard and offered publicly available documentation. Public ownership spurred the standard's wide diffusion; by 1998 Ethernet systems produced by about 100 vendors claimed $15.5 billion in annual sales.[18] Corporate America was likewise the major site for local-area network applications. Gulf Oil, for example, was using email over a local-area network by the mid-1970s; and major vendors, like Xerox and Digital Equipment, were elaborating models for local network services.[19] By 1996 a dense warren of 1.3 million local-area networks, inhabited by perhaps 100 million users, honeycombed businesses and other organizations worldwide.[20] Although Internet technology was not integrated on a significant scale in local-area networks until the mid-1990s, the growth of these specialized intracorporate systems engendered a spiraling need for increased interconnectivity—for comparable computer resource sharing *beyond* immediate local settings. Local network proliferation therefore comprised a critical prerequisite for the eventual takeoff of the Internet as a decentralized network of networks.

The politics of telecommunications network liberalization, meanwhile, put an increasing premium on market-led development. This neoliberal economic policy was already crowding out parallel public-service initiatives. During the early 1980s, for example, the U.S. Postal Service was pressured by would-be private rivals to withdraw its proposal for a nationwide electronic messaging service called ECOM (Electronic Computer-Originated Mail). On the other hand, the rapid enlargement of NSFNET was contingent on the decision to permit commercial as well as university-based networks to interconnect with NSF's backbone network. The NSF's backbone itself was furnished under contract to a partnership between two corporate spearheads of the liberalization trend, IBM and MCI.

By 1992, the interconnection of disparate networks via the NSFNET had grown to the point that 5,000 systems, to which an estimated 4 million users had access, were making use of Internet technology (TCP/IP).[21] The not-for-profit system's growing mass and escalating momentum were now such as to draw a full-scale entrepreneurial intervention. Thus an effort commenced to restructure the Internet on starkly neoliberal lines.

In February 1994, the NSF announced that four Network Access Points (NAPs) would be built so that a new class of Internet operators might interconnect directly with each other to exchange traffic. The purpose of the scheme was to cede provision of the Internet backbone network directly to commercial carriers. Little more than a year later, the NSFNET backbone was indeed supplanted by the NAP architecture, and the latter in turn became the Internet.[22] Additional NAPs, directly owned and privately controlled by corporate vendors, were likewise established.

Before turning to assess the further developments that propelled Internet technology into more intimate relation with the existing telecommunications infrastructure, we must first survey how networks evolved into a critical business necessity. This subject claims priority for two reasons. First, as already mentioned, today's Internet is simply inconceivable as a historical outcome absent prior development of inhouse corporate networks on a gargantuan scale. Second, this mushrooming information technology sector came to comprise the leading edge of the larger economy, which in turn lent irresistible momentum to the reconstruction of the world's information infrastructure.

The Evolution of Corporate Networking

Corporate reconstruction around networks was not limited to any sector but was economywide. The installed base of computers in the United States rose from 5,000 in 1960 to around 180 million by 1997 (95 percent of which were PCs).[23] Banks took a leading role. Between 1972 and 1985, the 1,000 largest U.S. banks increased the proportion of their operating expenses dedicated to telecommunications from 5 to 13 percent, and finance became the sectoral leader of overall corporate information technology spending. Citicorp's Global Telecommunications Network, the largest private system in the world, by the late 1980s linked offices in ninety-four nations, transmitted 800,000 calls each month, and supported $200 billion in daily foreign-exchange trades. Merrill Lynch, the largest U.S. securities firm, was then spending $400 million on telecommunications each year, well above the average for leading firms across all sectors.[24] By 1997, however, Merrill was spending this amount just in the U.S. domestic market, and the company's annual outlay for information technology overall had leapt from $800 million in 1993 to $1.5 billion.[25] Networked automatic teller machines proliferated; the number of U.S. ATMs increased from 95,000 in 1993 to 165,000 in 1998, while these bank-owned systems began to handle more transactions (11 billion annually, or 1.2 million every hour) than human tellers did.[26] The enormous cost of system upgrades needed to furnish networked financial services itself helped fuel a massive bank-consolidation drive.[27]

Financial network applications harbored further profound political-economic consequences. They allowed exponential increases in the trading volumes of securities-market, foreign-exchange, and other speculative instruments,[28] so that stateless capital flows acquired the ability to overwhelm the national monetary policy objectives of even the largest economies.[29] As economic historian Richard B. DuBoff stresses,[30] indeed, finance helped pioneer globalized capital circuits.

Economy-Wide Network Investment
Despite the role assumed by finance, however, information technology investments were never confined to this single sector. Overall expenditures on telecommunications by a diversified list of top 100 business users at the end of the 1980s ranged from an annual low of about $20 million to a high of $1 billion, with a yearly mean between $50 and $100 million.[31] Throughout every area of economic activity, leading companies sought to integrate networks into core activities of production, distribution, marketing, and administration. By 1986, in consequence, more than one-third of all U.S. spending on capital facilities for telecommunications occurred *outside* the sphere of common carrier investment, and the resulting private networks—of which there were by now literally thousands—were growing by 30 to 40 percent a year.[32] Rapidly evolving was an operational business infrastructure, mastery of which served to endow particular companies with widely remarked competitive advantages.

Manufacturers from Boeing to General Motors raced to establish network systems, hoping to enhance their strategic capabilities by sharing corporate information resources inhouse among thousands of employees and, increasingly, also with customers and suppliers. To speed products to market, pharmaceutical and electronics manufacturers built supranational research and development facilities at multiple sites, linked by networks.[33] Rather than waiting until oil exploration ships returned to port, the American Petroleum Institute harnessed advanced satellite technology to transport oil-drilling site data collected at sea, thereby shaving a month off the time needed to analyze the data.[34] Extending just-in-time technologies innovated by automobile manufacturers, merchandisers like Target and Kmart used computerized inventory management systems with point-of-sale scanners and bar-coded merchandise to pare expenses and keep shelves stocked.[35] Wal-Mart proved especially adept at exporting its data systems to support its rapidly growing worldwide operations.[36] 7-Eleven, the third-largest retailer in the world, likewise relied on a succession of specialized computer systems to link thousands of stores and supply depots.[37] Call centers, staffed by 1,000 to 2,000 employees wearing headphones and facing computer screens, bulked up in Britain and the United States as a new way of selling everything from life insurance to household goods.[38] "Building on its Lexis-Nexis database unit," on the other hand, "the Anglo-Dutch publisher Reed Elsevier rushed to place its 1,800 academic and trade journals (the company is the world's largest publisher of scientific periodicals) online."[39]

General Electric, a diversified industrial and financial company, began to convert its entire supply chain from paper to electronic networks, a move its executives boasted would annually save hundreds of millions of dollars.[40] Chrysler, on the eve of merging with Daimler-Benz, introduced a digital manufacturing system that it hoped would cut months off vehicle development time.[41] GM actually diversified substantially into communications by acquiring the satellite company Hughes Electronics. Its global rival, Toyota, envisioned a parallel metamorphosis, and by 1996 telecommunications furnished $820 million in annual revenues from some thirty-six investments made by the Japanese "motor" company (later, it decided to sell off these units).[42] Whirlpool, one of the world's two biggest makers of home appliances, networked its 2,000 product engineers to ensure that appliances manufactured in its thirty-five factories around the world could be built to a limited set of standard technology "platforms."[43]

We must not impute any overarching rationality to these reengineering projects. The waste they created, wrote the *Wall Street Journal,* was "staggering." According to a 1996 study, fully 42 percent of corporate information technology initiatives are abandoned prior to completion.[44] On the other hand, however, the economic impact of corporate reorganization around networks was indisputably large.

Between 1984 and 1993, the percentage of U.S. workers using computers doubled, from one-fourth to nearly one-half. In 1996, 7.4 million people worked in the U.S. information technology industry, while industries that were major users of information technology employed about half the workforce.[45] Computers, telecommunications equipment, and software accounted for nearly 12 percent of overall U.S. capital stock by the mid-1990s.[46] The share claimed by the information technology sector in U.S. gross domestic product increased disproportionately, from 4.9 percent in 1985 to an estimated 8.2 percent in 1998.[47] Such statistics, of course, take no account of the transnationalization of corporate production and the attendant corporate investment in network gear outside national borders.

Both in absolute terms and as a proportion of total corporate capital investment, network applications occasioned a spectacular increase in capital expenditures that showed no signs of letting up. Two points about this trend stand out. First, in keeping with the transnational structure of corporate capitalism, information technology investments were accelerating worldwide. Second, however, these investments remained disproportionately great in the United States, which in 1995 accounted for some 40 percent of global information technology consumption. "There is no doubt," wrote an analyst, "that U.S. companies are now far more computer intensive than most of their major multinational rivals."[48] (Private telecommunications networks, correspondingly, were also far less visible in Europe and Japan.) Intel's then CEO even chided Asian economic leaders, declaring that the economic crisis there might turn into long-term economic stagnation if they continued to underinvest in information technology.[49]

Steadily increasing from previous decades, dramatically so after the 1974 to 1975 recession, U.S. corporate outlays for information processing and related equipment moved ahead of factory machinery and mobile equipment to become by the mid-1980s the largest single category of U.S. capital equipment spending.[50] Between 1970 and 1996, indeed, the percentage of all U.S. corporate capital investment allocated to information technology climbed steeply, from 7 percent to around 45 percent (and with additional growth expected).[51] Investment in computers and software by 1995 comprised three-quarters of the overall increase in corporate capital investment,[52] while two years later software itself became America's third-largest manufacturing industry.[53] Inclusive of computing and telecommunications, information technology was proclaimed (by the

American Electronics Association) the United States' largest industry.[54] Domestic information technology hardware expenditures alone totaled $282 billion—17 percent more than U.S. purchases of new motor vehicles and parts, 49 percent more than outlays for new homes, and 168 percent more than commercial and industrial construction. There was evidence, claimed *Business Week*, "that high tech may now have a larger multiplier effect in the U.S. than traditional manufacturing industries such as autos."[55] Business analysts began to write of a "new business cycle"—a new alternation of boom and bust, with attendant novel vulnerabilities—based no longer on housing and autos but on information technology.[56] Information technology investment, finally, and network applications in particular, comprised the pivot of a restructuring of big capital—both industrial and financial.

Corporate Mobilization of Internet Technology

Corporate applications of Internet technology—intracorporate and business-to-business—comprise the true fulcrum of Internet system development. Corporate networks are the guiding hand of technical experimentation within cyberspace and comprise the leading site of its creative ferment.

Intranets, which apply Internet technology inhouse, are the latest manifestation of some thirty years of mounting corporate investment in proprietary information systems. An estimated nine-tenths of Fortune 500 companies launched intranet projects in 1997, at a cost of billions of dollars.[57] Indeed, sales of the server software that was needed to "publish" material on the Web indicated that inhouse intranet development "will significantly outpace Internet growth."[58] Growth of intranet applications helped to propel unexpectedly large increases in corporate demand for dedicated, high-capacity (1.54 Mbps) T1 circuits, priced at several thousand dollars a month; in the United States, the number of T1 lines in use was projected to more than double between 1994 and 1998 from 850,000 to nearly 2 million.[59]

Protected by "firewalls" that employ both hardware and network security software, intranets may either permit access to the open Internet or be cordoned off from it. Even when they allow employees to access Internet resources, however, intranets refuse or strictly limit reciprocal access to corporate computer systems by open Internet users. But intranets were rapidly extended to form *extranets,* which allow corporations to expand their shielded activities by linking up with collaborators. Cutting-edge network applications (voice and video) were also expedited within these inhouse corporate systems, ahead of their appearance on the open Internet.

The Internet decisively increased corporate abilities to widen the sphere of information exchange. From the beginning, military computer networks attempted to neutralize the disadvantages of incompatible computer systems. Arthur L. Norberg and Judy E. O'Neill show persuasively that the Arpanet—which pioneered the packet-switching technology on which the Internet was subsequently to build—began as what its military sponsors called "a fundamental attack on the problem of hardware and software incompatibility."[60] Incompatibility in turn was deemed a problem by military agencies because disparate computer systems prevented far-flung computer researchers, addressing common tasks, from sharing data, programs, techniques, and knowledge about computing.[61] From that day to this, advances in the technology of networking have steadily increased the ability of computer users to work together by sharing hardware and software resources.

During the early stages of network development, the leading computer vendors succeeded in locking in business, as well as military, clients to incompatible hardware and software systems. Local-area networks and distributed data-processing systems, which were established by companies during the 1980s and early 1990s, admittedly constituted a critical advance over their precursors, the mighty but highly specialized stand-alone systems configured around mainframes. They dramatically deepened the process of workplace computerization by permitting office employees to share resources of various kinds: both hardware tools—such as printers—and software files (programs and data).

Yet these *legacy systems* had only a limited ability to interconnect with each other and with the greater telecommunications network. The practical range of so-called *groupware,* for example—which is used for sharing information across an office or a department—was substantially restricted by the exigencies of operating distinct local-area networks. Managers thus began to perceive that their existing networks both imposed extra costs and resulted in significant practical limitations.

Intranets were promoted as an encompassing alternative to legacy systems and, in fact, comprised a further step in the tradition of extending the sweep of collaborative work processes among dispersed employees. They held out the promise of a considerable increase in the scope of computer-mediated interaction among groups of workers. The goal of networking remained, however, "to connect computing systems, and through the systems the . . . [employees], so that . . . duplication of effort [could be] avoided through the sharing of resources and improved communication" and so that new kinds of collective labor could be applied to business processes.[62] *Collaboration software,* sold by vendors to facilitate anything from real-time coordination of complex projects to group presentations and training, quickly became a booming corporate Internet market.[63] Intranets harmonized and expanded inhouse access to information that was stored on multiple corporate networks, thus permitting corporate information systems managers "to cut across the proprietary polyglot of systems and networks that they must manage."[64]

Via these proprietary systems, corporate databases were made more generally available (on server computers) to employees within a single building, on campus, or, through a further extension, across the world. Groupware applications were given added flexibility to accommodate rapidly shifting organizational imperatives: monthly sales figures, benefits packages, video seminars and training programs, phone books, blueprints, compliance data, and other corporate information resources were posted online; information was available to larger pools of staffers, while managers also gained new abilities to monitor their work.[65]

Intranets did not entail any wholesale leveling of corporate hierarchies. To the contrary, different classes of employees were typically assigned distinct levels of access to shared corporate databases. Companies thus devoted growing energy to managing intranet content and controlling intranet access. Bankers Trust, a $9.6 billion holding company, was hardly unique in warning employees that management monitors all Internet communications (including email, as is widely customary) and that any visit they make to an external Web site using the bank's system may be tracked.[66]

As islands of corporate activity were linked, considerable cost savings sometimes resulted, even while the work that went into existing business functions was strategically reorganized. Motorola, under project deadline pressure, posted high-resolution images of a new product (a cable modem) on an intranet. Step-by-step instructions for assembly, testing, packing, and shipping were thereby made available on the factory floor of its Mansfield, Massachusetts, plant. This intranet application was both faster and measurably cheaper than the company's earlier paper documentation system.[67] (This local willingness to innovate, however, did not forestall Motorola's economic reverses and fall from investor grace in 1997 and 1998.) British Telecom's intranet granted its staff immediate access to information needed to handle customer inquiries more promptly. Around half its employees, some 65,000 people, made use of the system, which was said to have saved the company 740 million pounds in 1997—comprising "the single most successful systems investment the company has ever made."[68] At Microsoft, by spring 1997 almost every employee had found reasons to use the company's intranet, MSWeb—which published more than 690,000 corporate documents for use by some 20,000 workers.[69]

By extending its intranet, Holiday Inn gave customers online access to its reservations network.[70] Benefits were thereby derived by its newly self-serve customers, and the hotel chain decreased paid employee labor. Off-loading paid employee labor onto suppliers and customers became a characteristic tendency of extranets that further extended the operational range of corporate information systems.[71]

Many companies already leased point-to-point lines to connect to a limited number of external parties, typically customers or suppliers. Extranets functionally resembled these private wide-area networks, but they were held to be more efficient. Extranets were heralded for eliminating the need to purchase dedicated lines between particular sites, as they depended instead on already shared facilities within carrier networks.[72]

But their potential impact was much greater. Because extranets ran on general Internet protocols, they again extended the reach of sponsoring companies. Both the market posture and the organizational basis of such enterprises depended, as Moschella relates, on this movement toward "external forms of automation, using computers to reach customers, suppliers, investors, and other key third parties."[73]

With extranets, authorized outside partners thus gained access to internal corporate data via the Internet using their normal Web browsers rather than proprietary software. This in turn meant that a given company could invite as many collaborators as it chose, while the cost of setting up the new link remained relatively small—because each partner was typically already accessing the Net. Security issues remained considerable; standardization of encryption and directory services was far from fully satisfactory.[74] Nor was the U.S. government easily able to reconcile corporate demands for free commercial access to state-of-the-art encryption systems with demands by the FBI and other enforcer agencies that encryption should remain a responsibility vested in themselves. *Virtual private networks,* however, used *tunneling* protocols to transform the open Internet into a more secure channel, access to which was further delimited via deployment of user-authentication software.

Ford's system connected 120,000 workstations at offices and factories worldwide to thousands of proprietary Web sites with information regarding markets, competitors, and part-suppliers' efficiency. As a product-development system, Ford selectively opened its intranet so as to "let[] engineers, designers, and suppliers work from the same data" and updated that data hourly. Ford hoped to link its 15,000 dealers to its intranet and to move toward building cars on demand, thereby saving billions of dollars in inventory costs.[75] Some 90 percent of the transportation conglomerate CSX's customers likewise already dealt with the company over the Internet.[76] Caterpillar, a manufacturer of agricultural machinery, hoped to compress product-development time on design projects by asking outside experts and employees to use collaborative engineering techniques within carefully demarcated areas of its corporate information system. Sharing of real-time computer-aided design and manufacturing applications, videoconferencing, and common consultations with historical data files were among the prospective applications.[77] ITT, a large industrial conglomerate, deployed networks to turn 600 engineers in twenty locations around the world into a design group capable of working on projects almost around the clock.[78]

Intranets and extranets together comprised the leading edge of business-to-business *electronic commerce,* which in turn easily outshone other applications of the Net in the mind's eye of corporate America. Companies linked up on the Internet, among other things, "to streamline their supply chains and automate run-of-the-mill sourcing functions."[79] Costly printing and mailing of industrial catalogs were supplanted by corporate Web sites featuring descriptions, color pictures, and even sounds. Often, business buyers could purchase goods immediately by making only a few keystrokes to send information directly to a vendor's computer, thereby eliminating what one writer calls "whole layers of workers."[80] For more than a decade, business-to-business trading systems had already existed as proprietary (Electronic Data Interchange) networks that allowed buyers and suppliers to exchange purchase orders or invoices electronically. The existing industry, however, "has now turned to the Internet to extend its reach and make it easier and cheaper for small firms to use." The French retailer Carrefour, for example, tested an extranet developed by a U.S. company to permit its Italian buyers to select from among dozens of competitive suppliers of more than 1,000 products (stock control units) for its stores worldwide.[81] Companies such as Ford Motor, Home Depot, and American Express likewise pioneered use of an electronic purchasing system called *open buying* that aimed to standardize the transmission of purchasing data and thereby eliminate a vast array of dedicated machines and special phone lines. Fully one-third of the $6 billion in annual sales garnered by network-equipment producer Cisco Systems, in a widely cited example, came through the Internet. By adding credit checking, production scheduling, product support, and customer-service operations onto the Net, Cisco boasted that it would be able to handle a 50 percent growth in sales without adding a single employee to its 150-member sales staff.[82] Cisco also advertised on the Net to recruit prospective employees from around the world.[83]

Again, electronic commerce was not limited to any one sector. In addition to manufacturers and retailers, finance capital jumped on the cyber-bandwagon. The number of online accounts at brokerage firms and mutual fund companies doubled between 1996 and 1997, with a further surge during early 1998 to 192,000 a day. The share of individual investor trading comprised of online transactions grew to as high as 25 percent during 1998.[84] In addition to Charles Schwab, the well-known brokerage firm that commanded a significant proportion of current online accounts,[85] numerous specialized online trading services sprung up. E*Trade, for example, vaulted into Internet stock trading via high-visibility television advertising.[86] Giant banks also rapidly moved to implement Internet services. Wholly circumventing brick and mortar branches, Citibank moved to introduce Web banking in Britain—to those with annual incomes of at least $49,000.[87] Morgan Stanley, Dean Witter, Discover (a diversified financial services complex) contemplated an all-out attack on traditional commercial banking by establishing a direct banking business over the Internet, using its Discover brand name. Discover had 48 million credit-card holders, as well as an Internet stock-brokerage service.[88] A huge pool of financial information sites spread onto the Web to provide well-heeled Netizens with advice on speculative investments.[89]

On this terrain, Internet vendors of every kind vied to gain competitive advantage. Netscape, for example, by its CEO's admission, garnered the vast proportion of its revenue—as much as 75 to 80 percent—from business users.[90] And information technology spending as a whole was dominated by corporations, which collectively accounted for an estimated 88 percent of the domestic total in 1997.[91]

Taken together, the growth of these corporate systems and applications signified that, as one trade journal announced in summer 1997, "the Internet is becoming the primary platform for the essential business activities of computing, communications, and commerce." Internet business consultancies boomed, while soothsayers declared that, within just a few years, business-to-business electronic commerce was destined to account for hundreds of billions of dollars in sales.[92] In turn, initiatives that aimed to transform more limited legacy systems into integrated enterprisewide networks showed that corporate networks and the open Internet were becoming "inextricably intertwined."[93]

Underway throughout diversified corporations, in fact, was a multisectoral effort to utilize the Internet as the basis of a new, decentralized, global information infrastructure. Only a thoroughgoing modernization of underlying telecommunications systems could sustain such a comprehensive, economywide move into electronic commerce. But this in turn would require a broader and more drastic political-economic change than we have chronicled so far. The liberalized zone of market-driven network development, which had already begun to encroach on the world's telecommunications systems, would have to become primary.

The Internet and the Telecommunications Infrastructure

By the late 1990s, telecommunications companies had spent some forty years retrofitting themselves to carry computer data. A host of specialized equipment and services—first in switching and network management and then beyond—testified to the carriers' integral reliance on computers. As regulatory liberalization gave them incentive to do so, carriers had long since also begun to move beyond the sole activity of transporting voice calls. Multifunctionality across the network became an operational reality: faxes and computer data comprised a large and growing share of carrier traffic volume. Indeed the Internet itself was largely laid over the telecommunications network, and, as the Net expanded, it placed increasing demands on this established infrastructure.

The Internet, however, concurrently disrupted these processes of gradual transition. Established telecommunications carriers, which were often the largest organizations in their home countries, received a series of nasty jolts.

Telecommunications Systems at Risk

It became plain that the Internet would comprise a progressively more important channel for the full range of established telecommunications services, including conventional voice service, the carriers' traditional bread-and-butter market. The titans of telecommunications, which had spent two decades crafting their own strategic plans for data carriage, unexpectedly had to jump atop the Internet bandwagon. With its decentralized structure, its unfamiliar data-traffic patterns, and, above all, its independent economic basis, the Internet posed grave problems of assimilation.

Some experts believed that the Internet's unrestrained growth would eventually lead to a system crash of biblical proportion. Network dependence among major corporations had grown acute, and—when a single line of incorrect software code could accidentally trigger a ramifying failure of electronic switching systems—portents of catastrophe were easy enough to find. When AT&T's specialized, high-speed business-data network went down for a day in April 1998, for example, credit cards became useless and electronic inventory systems failed at half of Wal-Mart's 2,400 U.S. stores, Southwest Airlines lost control of cargo tracking, and 1,200 Wells, Fargo ATMs shut down.[94] The very next month, a paralyzed communications satellite knocked out much of the nation's pager network. Technicians redirected some 25,000 U.S. satellite dishes so that they could again pick up signals transmitted via a replacement satellite.[95] Signaling recognition of its mounting vulnerability to such network failures, General Motors disclosed that it expected to spend a staggering $360 million to fix its year 2000 problems—so named, because existing software has been written in a way that might cause it to misread *2000* as *1900,* triggering prospectively crippling malfunctions in factories, engineering labs, and offices across the world. Citicorp reported that its costs for year 2000 corrections might total $600 million,[96] and U.S. firms expected to spend the almost incomprehensible sum of $50 billion fixing year 2000 glitches.[97] A top-level presidential commission pondered how to counteract potential deliberate attacks mounted against "critical infrastructures" linked by networks in energy, banking, transportation, human services, and telecommunications.[98]

The undoubted fact of such vulnerabilities notwithstanding, the Internet's surging growth suggested a deeper, if perhaps a less easily grasped, societal danger: the terms on which Internet development has been predicated directly threatened the operating principles, and the vast sunk costs, incarnated in the carriers' existing networks.

According to a report cited by then-FCC chairman Reed Hundt, by September 1997 the construction of new network capacity aimed at Internet traffic was outstripping that for voice channels by a ratio of three to one. MCI and Sprint each already carried more data than voice traffic.[99] Just three years before, 85 percent of traffic carried by undersea cables had been voice, and 15 percent was data; by late 1997, it was a fifty-fifty split.[100] Studies submitted to the FCC by local U.S. telephone companies suggested that some 5 to 10 percent of the minutes on the public, switched telephone network represented Internet traffic and that

that proportion was destined to increase rapidly and overtake residential voice traffic within just a few years. As Internet traffic surged, indeed, some said that data transmission was likely to account for no less than 95 percent of the traffic on public networks by 2005.[101] In Europe, likewise, it was projected that corporate network data traffic would be five times greater than corporate voice traffic by 2003.[102]

The Internet's legion of applications placed the existing telecommunications industry at immediate risk.[103] Internet fax-service comprised the first significant usurpation. WorldCom's UUNet, for example, deployed its global Internet backbone network to support a high-security fax service, with prices at 35 to 55 percent below those charged by the traditional voice carriers.[104] GTE and MCI soon matched the offering.[105]

Internet telephony portended a far more substantial danger. Though only recently quite poor, the quality of *voice over IP* services was rapidly improved on the open Internet. By 1997, it had become nearly indistinguishable from that of conventional telephony in some specialized contexts. Business users, who accounted for a disproportionate share of overall telecommunications demand, were the first to turn to IP telephony, adding it to their existing internal data networks primarily to realize cost savings.[106] Startup companies selling Internet telephony packages aimed at this emerging corporate market linked up with major vendors such as IBM.[107] One writer mused that Microsoft or Netscape might even choose to add Internet telephony capabilities to future versions of their office software packages. In any case, by 1998, AT&T, British Telecom, and Deutsche Telekom were experimenting with voice over IP.[108]

Catering to corporate demand, and extending it selectively into the consumer market, was a flock of telecommunications companies sporting unfamiliar names. Qwest Communications International (which joined the ranks of major carriers when it acquired LCI International in 1998 for $4.4 billion), ICG, IDT, and Level 3 were among the vendors that sought to broker IP telephone services at cut rates to individual consumers.[109] At a cost of billions of dollars, some of these retail suppliers (most notably Qwest) built freestanding networks using Internet technology; thus they were also able to act as wholesalers. Lacking immediate access to Internet "backbone" networks, in turn, some major telecommunications carriers attempted to act as subcontractors for these specialized vendors.[110]

The goliaths were only beginning to collect appreciable sums from the Net. AT&T showed Internet and other online revenue of $79 million in the first quarter of 1998, when GTE posted Internet sales of $172 million; while MCI and WorldCom (which, as a condition of their 1998 merger, had to sell off MCI's Internet operation) together claimed Internet revenues of $475 million.[111] But Internet traffic was growing furiously, and Internet telephony alone seemed certain to steal an increasing share of PTN traffic.[112] "If you don't control network assets from voice to Internet in the future, you don't have a prayer of being a significant global player," became the new industry wisdom.[113] Big carriers, led by long-distance vendors, in turn began to move at full throttle during 1997 and 1998 to integrate forward into Internet services.[114] Overseas, selected public telecommunications operators—Deutsche Telekom was at the forefront—likewise moved to integrate Internet technology.[115]

As the flexible and capacious Internet was adapted for messages traditionally carried over conventional telecommunications networks, dramatic and contentious shifts began to occur in the political economy of telecommunications provision. "Packet-switched networks," thundered erstwhile FCC Chairman Reed Hundt, "will soon carry most of the country's bits, and that will change the economics, the structure, and just about everything else about the telecommunications industry."[116] It remained unclear, however, whether the Internet would swallow the existing telephone system—or vice versa. On the one hand, significant augmentation of the Internet's underlying technical architecture—packet switching—would be needed before all the service offerings afforded by circuit-switched networks could be integrated. On the other hand, leading telecommunications companies already were assimilating key elements of Internet technology into their existing networks.[117] Both competitive rivalry and consolidation through diversification therefore became typical. This dynamic and complicated process meant that the Internet's potential collision with the existing telecommunications industry was often exaggerated.

The goal was clear: higher-speed (*broadband*) data-traffic systems would accommodate existing voice services with video as well as data and would be offered first within and between big corporate computer networks and subsequently within the greater public telecommunication system. Let us begin our assessment of this metamorphosis by looking more carefully at how and why established telecommunications providers (Public Telecommunication Operators) began to supply Internet systems and services.

If You Can't Beat Them, Join Them

Across virtually all market segments, the logic of network system development was similar. Smaller companies that specialized in what were initially niche markets at the frontier of the liberalization process worked the new territory. When they succeeded, major traditional suppliers either snapped them up or rushed to develop comparable applications on their own. Actions by major telecommunications equipment manufacturers—Lucent had $26.4 billion in 1997 revenues, and Northern Telecom had around $15 billion—were illustrative of this general course.

Routers are the specialized machines that direct and manage network traffic, while *switches* encode signals and establish connections between network locations. Scrambling to find points of entry in the white-hot Internet market during 1997, four of the world's top five telecommunications equipment manufacturers bankrolled Juniper Networks. Juniper's ambition was to develop a qualitatively faster router switch—in competition with Cisco Systems (which had 60 percent of the router market and $6.4 billion in 1997 sales), as well as smaller vendors such as Bay Networks, Cabletron, and 3Com—to sell to the network operators that provide Internet "backbone" circuits.[118] For this same purpose, Lucent also acquired data-equipment supplier Yurie Systems for $1 billion (after having purchased Ethernet switch maker Prominet to pursue the market for inhouse corporate networks).[119] Northern Telecom placed an even bigger bet through its $7.27 billion takeover of Bay Networks. Yet another top traditional equipment manufacturer, France's Alcatel Alsthom (which became prominent following its acquisition of IT&T's extensive international facilities), sought to enlarge its presence in the U.S. market by purchasing DSC Communications for $4.4 billion.[120]

A second expression of the telecommunications industry's rapidly escalating involvement with the Internet was its concerted move into *systems integration.* Systems integrators are companies that contract to set up and manage business computer networks on an outsource basis. They patch together diverse network technologies and service offerings. Seeking maximum cost efficiency, they simultaneously contract to lease services from outside vendors, while also relying both on their own facilities and on network components owned by customers and installed on their premises. Systems integrators have thrived during the past decade of global merger fever; the U.S. market for these network management services was estimated at $27 billion in 1997, with further spirited growth projected. The increasing significance of system integrators offers evidence of an underlying shift in market orientation that I have already sketched. Carriers are unmistakably focused less on providing basic services to residential users and more on assembling and managing the specialized network capabilities demanded by sophisticated corporate users—including, pre-eminently, intranets.

As systems integrators were called "to resolve the increasing chaos caused by internet-working enterprises,"[121] the traditional carriers came into increasingly direct competition with a spate of outside rivals. Catering to the systems-integration market were specialized companies like EDS, consulting and accounting firms like Arthur Andersen, and computer vendors like IBM.[122] So carriers themselves decided that they had to give the systems-integration market top-level strategic attention. MCI entered the field by acquiring Canada's SHL Systemhouse at a cost of $1 billion in late 1995.[123] British Telecom inaugurated its Syntegra unit for the same purpose. Sprint paid $425 million in 1997 to acquire another specialized systems integrator, called Paranet.[124] AT&T in 1995 set up an internal network consulting and computer-outsourcing subsidiary to target this new market; this subsidiary, AT&T Solutions, had $218 million in revenues in the year ended 15 April 1998.[125] To boost its credibility with clients, AT&T Solutions said it would maintain its own parent company's voice, data, and image networking, network computing, and data processing—a system that included 120,000 desktop computers, as well as a massive mainframe operation.[126] Lucent, diversifying from equipment supply into systems integration, not only created a network-management service for corporate customers that owned sophisticated voice and data networks but went on to open a huge network-management center for phone-company clients as well.[127]

Yet another important channel of consolidation lay in direct forward integration by telecommunications suppliers into Internet service provision. Leading carriers' enormous annual investments in their networks (AT&T's capital spending comes to over $8 billion a year)[128] were reoriented to accommodate this strategic imperative. Beginning with marketing alliances with existing service providers,[129] carriers went on to supply Internet services themselves in two chief ways: as retailers and as wholesalers. Each is considered briefly below.

Internet service providers (ISPs) manage the retail link with Internet customers, providing connection to the system for a subscription fee and offering various other services. This market was worth around $6.5 billion in the United States by early 1998 and around $2.3 billion in Europe.[130] ISPs range in scope and orientation from huge local telephone companies like Bell Atlantic (and like the commercial online service AOL, which functioned more precisely as an intranet), to local, not-for-profit organizations; the average number of subscribers per ISP, though increasing, was still scarcely 3,000 in mid-1997.[131] Within this wider field lay a variety of carrier ventures, such as AT&T's online service startup. AT&T's WorldNet offered Internet access with an aggressive pricing strategy (since modified) that garnered 1.1 million customers by early 1998.[132] Through a deal with Internet search-service Lycos, AT&T also hoped to lure Internet users looking for telephone numbers to click through to its automatic dialing service.[133] EarthLink-Sprint combined Sprint's 130,000 Internet service subscribers with EarthLink's 445,000.[134]

Local telephone carriers' forward moves into retail Internet services, on the other hand, were initially sporadic and defensive. From spring 1996 to August 1997, the number of ISPs existing in the United States more than doubled to some 4,000.[135] This increase expressed something more than a simple effort to catch the coat tails of a high-growth market. Companies that chose to enter the ISP market (and their subscribers) were privileged—in the United States—to do so without having to pay anything like the full cost of doing business.[136] This vital point requires further explication.

Under federal regulation, U.S. ISPs had been classed as providers of an *enhanced* service. This designation conferred on ISPs a characteristically privileged status within the liberalized zone of network development. It exempted them from the interconnection, or *access,* charges levied on other systems that tie in with local telephone networks; it also meant that ISPs did not have to pay into the government's *universal service fund,* which provided subsidies to support telephone access in low-income and rural areas. As a result of this sustained federal policy, ISPs enjoyed a substantial cross-subsidy, which was borne by ordinary voice users of the local telecommunications network. Local telecommunications companies were in the forefront of those seeking to protest this arrangement because these local exchange carriers had to supply the vast majority of the circuits used to link personal computers with the Internet on what they believed were inequitable financial terms.

The effects of this ISP subsidy policy were not limited to the pocketbooks of the local carriers. As Nathan Newman has detailed, through this subsidy the Internet effectively cannibalized "past and present investments in the local phone infrastructure":

Local phone users, mostly lower-income users without a computer in the home, are seeing investments diverted to industry and higher-income Internet users that could have been targeted for upgrading the overall network or delivering new technology for schools, hospitals, or other public places serving the whole public. Instead, the specific private subsidies for the Internet industry have helped fracture planning for the overall local phone system and blocked the general upgrading of data traffic.[137]

The inequity of these arrangements extended even beyond the fact that publicly supported local telephone networks subsidized yuppie Netizens. Internet users displayed markedly different behavior than voice telephone users. Whereas ordinary voice telephone calls averaged just a few minutes in duration, Internet hook-ups tended to last at least three times as long, and heavy users left their computer connections to the Net on all day (or all night). Data carriage thus placed a strain on a telephone system engineered for voice calls, as local networks were filled to bursting with incompletely compensated Internet data traffic.

Exhibiting the same favoritism to new competitors that has typified the liberalization process over the course of its forty-year development, recent legislation—specifically, Section 251(c) of the Telecommunications Act of 1996—imposed yet a further onerous requirement. It mandated that local telephone companies that chose to modernize their networks in hopes of supplying customers with broadband Internet access had to make these new facilities available to would-be rivals at cut-rate wholesale prices.[138] Not surprisingly, under the circumstances, the local carriers were not exactly quick to enter Internet and other broadband service provision. Outside North America, in contrast, where local carrier charges continued to factor as a major item in Internet service pricing (an average of around two-thirds of total charges in OECD countries), existing carriers rapidly claimed a central role in furnishing such access. Deutsche Telekom's online service—Europe's largest—already claimed around 1.4 million subscribers in mid-1997, for example.[139]

The strain caused by these domestic U.S. policies increased further as ISPs began using the Internet to transmit voice calls.[140] Local exchange carriers' own primary service markets now stood to take a direct hit from arbitrarily privileged rivals. In April 1998, the FCC signaled what the *Wall Street Journal*—an organ of neoliberal policies—labeled "a terribly significant and unfortunate shift" by suggesting that it might begin to impose universal service fees on those ISPs that provided Internet telephony services.[141] The FCC's trial balloon changed little; its hands-off policy persisted. Local exchange carriers such as Bell Atlantic, however, accelerated their plans to offer more widespread access to high-speed data transmission services,[142] a point we return to in chapter 3.

This brings us to the other major means by which carriers sought to diversify into Internet services. The relationship between layered Internet services and underlying network backbones is indirect, as established transmission facilities—dedicated circuits and switches—are souped up with specialized routers and other instrumentation. Following the NSF spinoff of the backbone network in 1995, a growing number of companies entered the market to provide wholesale Internet distribution services. They did so by interconnecting with each other at the Internet's officially designated network access points (NAPs) (and increasingly as well at privately arranged NAP sites). In the United States, thirty network service providers (NSPs) carried the traffic of the thousands of smaller ISPs.

There existed, however, a sharp differential between the leading wholesalers and the rest; a bare handful of companies dominated this market. *All* of the five leading backbone suppliers, which together handled perhaps 80 percent of U.S. Internet traffic (the rest being accounted for by twenty-five smaller companies) were, in fact, by mid-1997 owned by major telecommunications carriers. Some, such as internetMCI or Sprint IP Services, were developed inhouse concurrent with the growth of the Internet. Others became acquisitions: GTE Internetworking was the fruit of GTE's takeover of BBN, while WorldCom's UUNet—itself already a leading backbone in its own right—acquired what had previously been the fifth major wholesaler, ANS (which had operated as a captive unit of America Online). During its negotiations to purchase MCI, WorldCom sold the former's Internet operation to an overseas carrier, Cable and Wireless, even as the merged MCI-WorldCom remained a major provider of wholesale network service, not only in the United States but also in Europe.[143] A laggard in this area though still the leading U.S. carrier, AT&T confirmed its importance in 1997 by announcing that it would begin offering its 10 million corporate customers access to a high-speed Internet backbone, at some 580 points around the United States. AT&T experienced pressure to introduce its own backbone, when BBN—with which it had previously contracted to host a majority of its 2,000 corporate Internet customers—was acquired by GTE.[144]

Thus the Internet positively seethed with strategic potential. By mid-1998, the established telecommunications industry was certain to enter a widening range of additional Internet markets, including billing, domain name registration, directory, and other services.[145] Telecommunications carriers looked to their ISP relationships with millions of customers, as well as to their growing control over underlying facilities—physical lines and switches, and the specialized routers and software that logically define the Internet, as well as private network access points—as sources of leverage over future system development.

Not long ago, interconnecting backbone networks used to exchange messages at NAPs via unbilled *peering* arrangements, whereby the different vendors simply agreed to allow each others' traffic to transit their own networks. Peering arrangements of this kind contributed greatly to the Net's vaunted open culture. Today, in contrast, some major backbone operators will interconnect only with other operators who, like themselves, also interconnect at all of the system's major network access points. That is, they are beginning to choose—and to refuse—to peer, in light of their own strategic and economic considerations. And might not network service providers likewise begin to insist on levying new fees on interconnecting Internet service providers as their wholesale market power concentrates down into just a handful of carriers? One authority on the economics of the Internet notes that these major backbone providers "are in a position to declare themselves the Internet, and it could mean the costs of access are going to go up sharply."[146] If the backbone suppliers successfully impose new costs on Internet service providers, in turn, the latters' ranks are likely to thin rapidly—in one projection, to fewer than 100 within five years. Similar moves by telecommunications carriers were also evident in Europe, where pricing pressures and costly technology upgrades put the squeeze on "Internet small fry."[147]

I do not seek to imply, however, that the established leaders of the telecommunications industry will simply extend to the Internet their traditional domination over voice services. On one hand, shakeups, conflicts, and new strategic openings render any such outcome uncertain. Little-known WorldCom's 1996 takeover of MFS Communications, which in turn had just acquired another leading Internet wholesaler and service provider, UUNet Technologies, transformed WorldCom into one of the biggest supranational suppliers of advanced data services, with hundreds of local access points worldwide at which businesses might connect directly to its network. WorldCom's subsequent takeover of MCI vaulted this recently obscure company to the very topmost rank.[148] The third-largest U.S. long-distance carrier, meanwhile—Sprint—announced a much-ballyhooed remodel of its national network. A \$2 billion system that deployed Internet technology to integrate voice, video, and data traffic now became the company's strategic centerpiece.[149]

There were wild cards, as well. Qwest staged a multibillion-dollar foray into data services.[150] Its equally well-capitalized rivals included a nationwide pipeline operator, Williams Companies, and other unfamiliar new entrants—Level 3, IXC Communications—as the attempt to profit from new-built national and global IP networks diffused.[151] Then there was SITA, which spun off its international managed data network—the world's largest, supplying services to 420 airlines in 220 countries—offering managed data services to multinational companies outside the airline and aerospace industries.[152] These *green-field* providers, working out of the liberalized sector of network development, possessed advantages that continued to be denied to incumbents. Above all, they could realize the lowered costs of market entry afforded by new technologies, while eschewing from the start the legacy of universal-service provision with which established operators were burdened.[153]

Yet it cannot be emphasized sufficiently that this ongoing shakeup of the supply end of the telecommunications industry comprised a strategic response to a profound shift in demand. Corporate users of Internet systems and services never lost their primacy within the wider metamorphosis. It was essentially on their behalf that the carriers were impelled to increase their efforts to mesh unlike technologies and to roll out new IP networks, so as to offer comprehensive service packages with high-end features for preferred customers. By 1998, for example, MCI had gone further than most rivals in integrating its packet-switched data network and its circuit-switched voice network.[154] Its intention was to develop "pricing structures, technical solutions, and business arrangements to provide more robust and reliable service for applications that require it, and for users willing to pay higher fees."[155] Corporate demand to lock in predictable levels of service, with priority access to network bandwidth, meanwhile, increased for good reason.[156] In part, business users were looking for improved guarantees that underlying networks wouldn't seize up and crash and thereby prevent "mission critical" corporate data from continuing to slide serenely across the globe.

The open Internet remained largely a U.S. system. Some 60 percent of the Internet's host computers in early 1997 were located in the United States;[157] the Net relied on English as its lingua franca; and its very architecture still forced *intra*-Asian traffic to transit to network exchange points located in the United States before being routed back to Asian destinations.[158] Its system of bestowing the top-level domain names needed to give users workable Internet addresses was likewise still dominated by the United States. Despite these decided skews, however, the Net's supranational orientation was deepening with each passing month. We are now in a position to see that its increasingly transnational orientation placed the Internet suddenly at the forefront of the more encompassing neoliberal policy trend that swept through global telecommunications.

2

Going Global: The Neoliberal Project in Transnational Telecommunications

The telecommunications industry has been forced to sit up and take notice of cyberspace. But the Internet is only a leading element in the hurricane of destructive creativity that has cascaded through global telecommunications. At stake in this unprecedented transition to neoliberal or market-driven telecommunications are nothing less than the production base and the control structure of an emerging digital capitalism.

As business users' dependence on network systems grew more concerted, more multifaceted, and more extensive, an unparalleled telecommunications boom was triggered. Capital investment surged forward; the number of worldwide installed main telephone lines has grown *eightfold* since 1960, and increased by nearly 60 percent just between 1990 and 1997—from 520 to 800 million.[1] Cellular phone systems added hundreds of millions of additional units to the worldwide base. This system-building frenzy is the subject of much of chapter 2. First, however, it must be set in the context of a general—and, indeed, a spectacular—economic shift: the rapid consolidation of transnationalized capitalist production.

Transnationalized Production

Hobsbawm remarks that "when we consider how logical Marx's prediction of the eventual spread of the industrial revolution to the rest of the world seemed, it is astonishing how little industry had left the world of developed capitalism before the end of the era of empires, and indeed before the 1970s."[2] Between 1973 and 1993, however, transnational corporations (TNCs) from the developed countries grew in number from 7,000 to 26,000; at the later date, the world's 100 largest nonbanking

TNCs held no less than $1.4 trillion worth of foreign assets.³ In 1995, overseas affiliates of U.S. transnationals, which led the larger trend, enjoyed $1.8 trillion in in-country sales, more than three times the value of total U.S. exports.⁴ Ford, Toyota, and Daimler-Benz—like their counterparts in virtually every economic sector—vied to outdo each other in "globalizing" their productive operations.

For this was indeed a global economic shift, albeit a highly uneven one. Transnational companies invested on an immense scale in new plants, offices, and factories, above all in the already developed countries of Western Europe (the European Union accounted for over half of total sales by U.S. companies' foreign affiliates in 1995⁵) but also throughout the poor world.⁶ While capital flows of every kind surged, annual foreign direct investment (FDI) in less developed countries thus tripled between 1990 and 1995 to $112 billion. Moreover, 38 percent of all FDI outflows went to developing countries in 1993 to 1995, compared to just 22 percent over the 1983 to 1992 period.⁷ Despite sharp, but selective, retrenchment in the wake of what began as an Asian economic crisis,⁸ the trend was apparent: developing countries were becoming proportionately more significant hosts for manufacturing and other industry. The largest fraction of total private capital flows to developing countries went, however, to a mere handful of nations, with China and Mexico leading and African countries lagging severely; still, even the poorest countries were included within the orbit of foreign ownership.⁹ Foreign direct investment flowing into Latin America reached an all-time high of $50 billion in 1997.¹⁰

The transnationalization of corporate enterprise in turn carried over into the organization of production. By the mid-1990s, transnational companies generated some two-thirds of total world exports of goods and services. In turn, around a third of these export flows occurred as intrafirm transfers¹¹—transactions between units of a single parent company. To sell into markets worldwide and to gain access to cheap labor pools wherever they might be, top corporations grew intent on reconfiguring their operations as transnational production chains. TNCs, as an authoritative report summarized, were "reorganizing their cross-border production activities in an efficiency-oriented, integrated fashion, capitalizing on the tangible and intangible assets available throughout the corporate system."[12]

Accelerating cross-border corporate mergers and acquisitions can be expected to further expedite innovation of such production chains. The volume of worldwide corporate mergers and acquisitions expanded dramatically during the mid- to late 1990s. In 1996, global mergers and acquisitions were worth a total of $1 trillion, and the pace increased sharply during the two subsequent years; during just the first six months of 1998, deals worth $1.318 trillion were announced.[13] "In the U.S.," remarked one foreign banker, "buying and selling companies is just like selling sacks of potatoes."[14] Initially, in truth, the lion's share of this activity did come from the United States—"We are in the midst of the greatest wave of mergers in American history," remarked *Fortune*[15]—but European and Japanese combinations soon also accelerated.[16] Especially noteworthy, within this larger process, was that the value of cross-border mergers and acquisitions doubled between 1988 and 1995 to $229 billion; during 1996 it increased further to $275 billion, moving up yet again to $320.5 billion in 1997.[17] In addition, cross-border production and marketing agreements between firms also proliferated. During 1995, nearly 4,600 such agreements were concluded globally, compared with 1,760 in 1990.[18]

The economic debacle that began in East Asia and ricocheted across the world did little to reverse this cross-border consolidation trend. Indeed, the Asian meltdown arguably granted it both additional impetus and scope. By insisting in 1997 and 1998 that, in return for bailout "aid," Thailand, Indonesia, and South Korea had to approve radically increased levels of foreign investment in overextended domestic industries, the International Monetary Fund conveyed the cross-border takeover boom into hitherto-sheltered East Asia—just as a huge transfer of ownership to foreign hands had also occurred in the wake of Mexico's financial crisis during 1994 and 1995.[19] Six of the fifteen largest foreign acquisitions by U.S. companies between January 1996 and late 1997 were of companies located in poor countries.[20] U.S. acquisitions of Asian business properties reached a value of $8 billion in the first half of 1998, double that of the previous record year, with European buyouts at $4 billion, also at record levels.[21]

Sophisticated network systems in turn comprised the increasingly essential infrastructure for engorged transnational corporations, pursuing export-oriented, regionally or even globally integrated production strategies.[22]

Corresponding to the ongoing buildup of transnational production chains, therefore, was a powerful pan-corporate attempt to subject worldwide telecommunications policy to United States–originated, neoliberal regulatory norms.

Transnationalized Networks and the Export of U.S. Neoliberalism

Neoliberalism required sweeping application if it was to serve the needs of companies whose offices and factories increasingly spanned across borders. Implementing a global telecommunications grid under direct corporate control could occur, however, only as a result of direct political intervention. The organizational structures of international telecommunications regulation expressed the preference for national sovereignty that typified a prior age. They had to be overturned. Intense pressure to reshape this organizational firmament, in both bilateral and multilateral contexts, became a consistent hallmark. In telecommunications, it was first introduced throughout the developed market economies (the states comprising the Organization for Economic Cooperation and Development, or OECD), and subsequently more generally by U.S. governmental agencies, alongside independently organized equipment suppliers and business user groups.

The carryover from domestic to supranational policy venues was direct because the business telecommunications users that spearheaded the U.S. domestic drive for policy liberalization were mainly transnational enterprises. As costs for transoceanic circuits plummeted, international telephone calling volume correspondingly rose—from under 4 billion minutes in 1975 to over 70 billion in 1996.[23] Most significantly, already by 1984 some 1,000 transnational computer-communications systems were in operation, "the overwhelming majority of them established by transnational corporations from developed market economies to service their worldwide affiliate network."[24] The initial establishment and preservation of these transnational private networks gained a critical beachhead for the advancing U.S. neoliberal model. Through these systems began to course a substantial proportion—exactly how much is not known—of international telecommunications traffic volume. Estimates that transnational business demand generated 20 percent of the world's $600 billion in 1996 telecommunications revenues (and fully 33 percent of the carriers' profits) took inadequate account of the huge business—still increasing as the stampede to Internet services accelerated—the carriers lose to these inhouse corporate systems.[25]

Business users wished, understandably enough, to harmonize and mesh their offshore operations—actual and prospective—with the customized telecommunications applications they were developing in the United States. Gathering force after the early 1970s, as postwar prosperity flagged in the face of resurgent international economic competition, declining growth rates, and chronic overcapacity, were United States–based transnational corporate demands for customized service offerings and, more broadly, for a more permissive global telecommunications regime. Through global telecommunications liberalization, big banks, for example, glimpsed the possibility—and profitability—of around-the-clock global trading in an unfolding array of instruments, from foreign exchange to futures contracts, government debt, and beyond. But the demand was, once again, general across the span of transnational enterprise. As early as 1981, a top AT&T executive responded to this reorientation by declaring that "there really is no longer a 'domestic market' separated from international dealings. Large customers increasingly expect to deal with their international telecommunications and data in a systematic, unified way. International systems solutions to communications needs are increasingly demanded."[26]

Telecommunications network applications accordingly began to undergo uneven transnationalization. Toll-free telephony, for example, originated in 1967 in the United States. By 1996, some 10 million domestic toll-free (or *freephone*) numbers earned an annual $12 billion for U.S. carriers. Indeed more than two-fifths of all traffic carried on AT&T's domestic network was by now comprised of toll-free calls. This commercialization of the domestic telephone system introduced mounting pressure for analogous services elsewhere; by 1997, freephone service was set to permit consumers worldwide to place orders to centralized customer support locations.[27] Attesting to their own changing orientation, the major U.S. carriers hawked telephone service to prospective customers in many languages: by 1995, MCI was marketing in nineteen languages, and AT&T in no less than 140.[28] But transnational network applications went beyond banking and sales.

Across a correspondingly lengthening range of productive and distributive activities, the reorganization of capital thus initiated a reciprocal re- organization of labor. Networked business processes substantially increased management's ability to disperse both the object and the subject of labor—jobs and workers—so as to maximize profits. The array of labor processes, and the types of job categories, that could be reconstituted around networked production chains burst through prior constraints. Transnationally networked production thus harbored profound consequences for global labor markets and for the worldwide division of labor. This became especially evident in the wake of the embrace of capitalism by both China and the erstwhile Soviet bloc countries, when hundreds of millions of people were summarily thrown into the labor market. This "vast *labor pool* that global capitalism has tapped into . . . is the new leviathan," observed *Business Week* chief economist William Wolman and Anne Colamosca.[29]

High-technology corporate operations could move—and, as we saw, in fact were moving—beyond the developed market economies: "any value-added activity can be located, at least in principle, in any part of a TNC system."[30] For example, of the fourteen "megafabs" in development before the Asian economic debacle in 1997—high-technology semiconductor fabrication plants costing at least $1.5 billion each—four were scheduled to be located in poor countries (China, Korea, and Taiwan), while the Celtic fringe—Ireland, Scotland, and Wales—would play host to three others.[31] IBM, Microsoft (10 percent of whose worldwide workforce of 22,300 was of Indian origin), and Cisco Systems (the world's top vendor of networking equipment, which supplied the instruments that routed most Internet traffic) set up software research and development laboratories in India to tap into the technical talent available there.[32] Data-entry jobs became subject increasingly to relocation; Morton Bahr, president of the Communications Workers of America, asserted, for example, that it is "very easy to move [telecommunications] billing and accounting across the border" from high-wage to low-wage areas.[33] Offshore corporate back offices produce an increasing range of services—including database management, accounting, ticketing, subscription processing, insurance claims, and software development—which were used as inputs in "domestic" U.S. production and were intended to serve domestic demand.[34] Offshore animation factories in South Korea, Taiwan, and the Philippines produce *The Simpsons, Ninja Turtles,* and other shows.[35]

On one hand, therefore, as a direct consequence of its reliance on networks, transnational corporate management enjoyed new flexibility—though certainly nothing approaching absolute freedom—in deciding where and for how long to locate any particular production process. On the other hand, this same restructuring demanded that ever-increasing priority be accorded to telecommunications. Of the $16 billion in direct capital investment expected during 1997 in Mexico, where the minimum wage had slipped to about $3.30 a day, about $5 billion—nearly a third—was to be channeled into telecommunications.[36]

Worldwide sales of telecommunications services grew, correspondingly, at a rate (during 1995, 7 percent) far above that of global gross domestic product.[37] The unprecedented transborder system-building boom that ensued, however, bespoke not only changing economic and organizational structures but also a sweeping political victory. It climaxed a long series of policy changes won market by market and ultimately multilaterally by transnational business users and transnational network suppliers.

Of special early import was the 1984 privatization—in Margaret Thatcher's Britain—of the United Kingdom's national carrier, British Telecom, and the authorization of a competitive carrier, Mercury (now owned by Cable & Wireless). These measures permitted the United Kingdom to offer itself as a hospitable site for the information system operations of major U.S. firms needing access to European markets.[38] By 1997, no less than 120 rival companies competed in all segments of the British telecommunications market, which in turn had become the main hub for Continental Europe.[39] Pressure correspondingly ratcheted up on adjacent countries to liberalize their own policies.

Not surprisingly, transnational corporate competitors of the United States–based companies that led the initial push to liberalize readily recognized that their reliance on a restricted basket of high-priced "plain vanilla" offerings elsewhere placed them at an increasingly severe competitive disadvantage.[40] At the same time, in the wake of the continuing liberalization of the U.S. market that led to the AT&T divestiture of 1982 to 1984, the leading U.S. carriers also enlisted in the campaign. The campaign for further global liberalization gained momentum.

During the 1980s, a politics of neoliberal telecommunications reform took hold in dozens of nations. Particularly noteworthy (and still largely undocumented) was the success of Internet-expansion policies that, as Rutkowski boasts, were "implemented over more than a decade through some of the most extensive and effective bilateral and multilateral regulatory forums and initiatives in U.S. history."[41] Before 1989, nonetheless, only nine countries had undertaken to follow in the wake of U.S. liberalization by privatizing an existing telecommunications system operator. With the exceptions of Japan and Britain, these comprised a scattering of much smaller and more vulnerable economies, within the immediate range of Anglo-American pressure: Belize, Jamaica, Gibraltar, Canada, and Chile.

With the collapse of Soviet socialism, however, the scale of the neoliberal project in telecommunications rapidly expanded and gained devotees within scores of countries. In "respectable" circles, indeed, dissenting voices became all but inaudible. Across much of the world, telecommunications structures and policies of long standing were fundamentally revised—as European Telecommunications Commissioner Martin Bangemann declared—so as to "release the forces of the market" by eliminating existing state monopolies in telecommunications services and network infrastructure operation.[42] In a vital development, the European Union agreed in 1994 to open basic voice telecommunications—the core domestic service offered by its members' national public telecommunications operators (Posts, Telephones and Telegraphs, or PTTs)—to competition in 1998.

Similar efforts also began to bear fruit elsewhere. Neoliberal policymakers took over the ostensibly multilateral International Telecommunication Union, while other key organizations—the World Bank and the

International Monetary Fund—continued to do the bidding of U.S. state agencies. In the context of the debt crisis of the 1980s, unprecedented support developed among national elites in Latin America, the Caribbean, and Africa for the neoliberal doctrine that economic development should be driven by the market rather than the state. Nationalistic anti-imperialism waned to its twentieth-century low point, and privatizations of state telecommunications systems occurred in Mexico, Venezuela, Peru, and Argentina. Though limited initiatives got underway in Malaysia, Singapore, and Korea, liberalization throughout Asia, in contrast, remained more restrained.[43]

As a consequence of these initiatives, no fewer than forty-four public telecommunications operators were privatized between 1984 and 1996, with a total capitalization of $159 billion, about one-third of which came from outside the home countries involved. By value, 11.5 percent of these privatizations took place in Latin America and the Caribbean, 31.3 percent in Western Europe, and 54.3 percent (almost exclusively reflecting Japan's huge privatization of NTT) in the Asia-Pacific area.[44] Telecommunications privatizations accounted for fully 44 percent by value of the 547 infrastructure privatizations that occurred overall between 1984 and 1996.[45]

A wholesale methodology was elaborated under the zealous eyes of the United States–based banks, law and accounting firms, advertising agencies, and management consultants that had positioned themselves to catch the privatization wave.[46] "Underwriting telecom," explained the *Wall Street Journal* in 1996, "is the hottest area among large investment [banking] houses, reaping each of them revenue of more than $100 million annually."[47] At the peak of the European boom in the mid-1990s, banks were skimming about 3 percent of the value of each privatization.[48] Demand for these stock issues was nearly insatiable, as an unparalleled buying spree uprooted previously sacrosanct national telecommunications operators.[49]

Marketing initial public offerings of shares in Deutsche Telekom, or France Telecom, or Spain's Telefonica, or Telecom Italia to unprecedented numbers of first-time stock purchasers, the stewards of the privatization process deftly bruited a supposed "people's capitalism." Thereby they succeeded, again and again, in enlisting formidable middle-class support for the new regime.[50]

Gaining the acquiescence of employees proved more difficult. A solicitous International Telecommunication Union declared that such employee support "can be critical in helping the government obtain labour acceptance of the privatization process. Privatising . . . is often perceived as a prelude to large-scale redundancies. Having employees take part in the privatization process as investors can be used to overcome resistance." Special discounts were therefore sometimes offered to employees; in the case of Telefonos de Mexico, the tranche devoted to employees was fully underwritten by a $325 million loan.[51] Even so, in many countries employees remained actively opposed to privatization, not least because of the punishing job losses it indeed often inflicted.

Trading in telecommunications stocks, however, enjoyed a mighty surge; shares of the Brazilian telecommunications operator, Telebras, contributed as much as 50 to 60 percent of the daily stock market volume in that country. Additional privatizations and new equity offerings continued to be scheduled, as national telecommunications providers in Turkey, Australia, China, Brazil, Poland, Portugal, Korea, Switzerland, and India looked for tens of billions of dollars of additional investment capital throughout 1997 and 1998.[52]

More important, political support for liberalized system development had consolidated among corporate capital and upper-income strata almost everywhere. During 1996 to 1997, even as the Internet was exploding into general view, this growing political commitment to globalizing capital in telecommunications and, of course, beyond became newly emboldened. A series of multilateral policy directives now took direct aim at the social welfare objectives, international interconnection and rate-setting principles, and sovereign national networks that had defined the previous era.

Neoliberal Telecommunications Provision

Extraterritorial Corporate Charters

As 1996 drew to a close, a World Trade Organization meeting in Singapore outlined an agreement to eliminate trade tariffs on $500 billion worth of computer and software products—roughly equivalent to world trade in agriculture—by the year 2000. The twenty-eight governments that signed the Ministerial Declaration on Information Technology Products in Singapore accounted for 84 percent of global telecommunication equipment exports and 88 percent of PC sales—but only 20 percent of global population.[53] Giant windfall profits to the U.S. companies that supplied a major part of global trade in this sector were predicted.[54]

Two months later, on 15 February 1997, the WTO concluded a second colossal trade accord. The organization had been under fierce pressure since the previous April when the United States had gambled that by walking out of the talks, some prospective signatories—especially less developed countries—might be induced to offer further concessions. The U.S. stance proved to be justified. In the end, the WTO agreed to open basic telecommunications markets within some seventy countries accounting for 94 percent of world telecommunications markets—around $600 billion in overall annual revenue—and just over half of world population. New or improved offers came in by the dozen, from countries such as India, Pakistan, South Korea, Indonesia, the Philippines, Singapore, Malaysia, Hong Kong, South Africa, Ghana, Brazil, and Mexico. Asian nations, in particular, seemed to display a new willingness to accede to the liberalization program.

One trade journal reported that, as the talks headed toward closure, U.S. industry advisors "scrawled the slogan 'wildly enthusiastic' on pieces of paper, flashing the signs at U.S. negotiators."[55] They had cause to be exhilarated by the outcome. Transnational telecommunications carriers obtained commitments allowing foreign investment—at levels that varied but often ran as high as 100 percent—in existing national service providers that had long been sheltered from outside control. Large telecommunications suppliers, more generally, would be permitted to acquire, establish, or hold significant stakes in telecommunications companies worldwide; the way toward predictable transnational expansion was thereby cleared. As the U.S. Trade Representative put it: "American companies will now be free to offer cellular service in Mexico, satellite-delivered Internet access in Japan, intra-Europe and domestic long distance in Germany, hand-held satellite telephony in Korea, international business networks in Singapore, and video-conferencing in the United Kingdom. In all these technologies, our companies are the world leaders, and in all these technologies our companies will be free to compete."[56]

Business users, for their part, gained assurances of a harmonized multilateral operating framework affording predictable market access to equipment and services—binding agreements that WTO member countries were legally obligated to apply. Signatories had approved "enforceable regulatory principles based upon the framework for competition" that had previously been established by the United States.[57] The *New York Times* was quick to explain what this meant: "The agreement, for the first time, empowers the WTO to go inside the borders of the seventy countries that signed it to review how quickly and effectively they are deregulating a key part of their economies. . . . And if the WTO finds evidence of foot-dragging it can, in theory at least, authorize penalties."[58]

This extraterritorial corporate charter—which came into force early in 1998—carried drastic implications for systems of national telecommunications provision, particularly throughout the poor world. Glaring disparities in provision and access had historically marked these PTO systems. Throughout most of the world, the needs of rural inhabitants and of poor people in general were long simply ignored. Telecommunications service existed mainly in urban enclaves, and chiefly at the behest of corporations and upper-income strata. As a contributor to meaningful social reconstruction, therefore, the older system of national provision must be classed a failure.

Notwithstanding this judgment, national telecommunications systems emerged from the ashes of colonialism with significant social welfare features. Often wrested painfully from ITT or another foreign owner, these state-run systems functioned in themselves as bastions of sovereignty. It was symbolic that, in many of the world's capital cities, postal or communications ministries were physically situated near the seat of state power. Their policies, furthermore, were not merely a reflex of capital's demands. Business users had to pay a premium for the privilege of gaining access to affiliates, suppliers, and customers within and between diverse national networks. Following a cross-subsidy principle, long-distance, and especially international, calls were priced high—sometimes at several times their cost—in order to underwrite rudimentary domestic telecommunications services, and often other state functions as well. Equally important, domestic telecommunications systems were among the largest of national employers, public or private, and thus it was of wider significance that they frequently accommodated collective bargaining rights of some kind. Telecommunications provision could boast, indeed, of being one of the world's most heavily unionized economic sectors: the Postal, Telegraph, and Telephone International Union claims 4.6 million members.

In the post-WTO liberalized environment, the transnational orientation of national telecommunications systems was dramatically strengthened, even as their characteristically limited social-welfare features were targeted for attack. Strong pressure was exerted on system operators "to police and protect the newly established market freedoms."[59] The "market discipline" that was so loudly heralded, however, actually comprised a form of preferment that discriminated systematically in favor of the rate policies and service offerings demanded by transnational business users.

Where protected national carriers had earlier subsidized local service through high-priced international service (in Israel, to choose a comparatively advanced economy, international telephone calls generated 30 percent of total industry revenue, while in the far weaker Philippines international business accounted for 52 percent of revenues),[60] now *rate rebalancing* came into vogue. Rate rebalancing, aimed at decreasing prices for international calls, was prompted and steered in no small part by U.S. regulators, who carried out a series of unilateral actions to force it on the world.

One such measure was the FCC's authorization of callback services, which, akin to Internet telephony suppliers, used the liberalized U.S. market (the United States accounts for over a quarter of all international telephone traffic) as a lever with which to exact concessions from correspondent nations. Callback operators, most of whom were based in the United States, allowed customers in, say, Japan to place international calls using AT&T's lower-priced network—thereby bypassing Kokusai Denshin Denwa, Japan's higher-priced international carrier. Callback companies in effect provided overseas customers with a dial tone from the United States, where decades of liberalization had produced some of the cheapest international call charges in the world. Two dozen countries tried, without success, to intercede against these United States–based callback operators; the FCC refused to rein them in.[61] Rates duly began to plummet, either in response to, or in preemptive anticipation of, entry by callback operators; in France, for example, international charges were expected to drop by about 40 percent just during 1997.[62]

Attempting to spur an even deeper and more general worldwide price decline, U.S. regulators then sought to use the instabilities engendered by callback operators and Internet telephony vendors as a pretext for jettisoning the entire international accounting rate system. These accounting rates fixed the terms for dividing up international calling revenues among the world's telecommunications operators. A product of the era of national monopolies, the system established a stable system of transfer payments among carriers of outgoing and incoming calls. But the FCC now imposed preemptive benchmarks on the amounts U.S. carriers could remit to foreign carriers for international calls to their countries. The International Telecommunication Union gave the initiative the appearance of multilateralism. But its claim that the prospective benefits of liberalization would outweigh the roughly $10 billion in annual accounting rate revenues received by developing countries, in the form of hard foreign-exchange earnings, rang hollow.[63] At the time of writing, nevertheless, the accounting rate system verged on a "melt-down."[64]

Money lost as a result of sharp rate declines for international services has been made up by reciprocally increased charges for local household phone service—hence, "rebalancing."[65] In poor countries, the inequity of rebalancing was especially extreme. In Indonesia, even before the ravaging economic crisis took hold there during 1997 and 1998, the consequence of rebalancing was that a group of perhaps 300,000 overseas callers was privileged over a general population of 190 million—most of whom continued to lack ordinary telephone service.[66]

Neoliberal policies thus subjected social need to a calculus of principled indifference. Yet their results were complex, at least inasmuch as disparities in access to telecommunications are concerned.

System Building and the Social Fracture
The sheer scope and the changing geographic pattern of contemporary global investment in telecommunications made it easy to claim that the entire world was—at last!—getting wired. During 1996, fixed-line tele-

phone networks added 50 million lines worldwide (compared with 45 million in 1995 and 38 million in 1994), while mobile communications systems accounted for an additional 52 million new subscribers (from 33 million in 1995, 19 million in 1994).[67] Some $166.4 billion in telecommunications investment was made during 1996.[68] Low-income countries (with GNP per capita of less than $765 in 1995 dollars) saw a nearly fivefold increase in their main telephone lines between 1990 and 1996 to 79.7 million; cellular subscriptions grew from practically none to 7.5 million over the same interval.[69] Rapid market growth, though occurring throughout poorer regions, was especially noteworthy—in some instances even after the economic collapse began there—in Asia.[70]

Incontestably the most spectacular system building occurred in China. During August 1997, China's Ministry of Post and Telecommunications celebrated the instalment of its 100 millionth telephone line—a 100-fold increase over a mere twenty years. As much as three-quarters of this growth occurred after 1990. Over this period, China installed an estimated 73 million phone lines—more than all the rest of the less developed countries together, and the equivalent of adding France's national system every two years. At an additional cost of tens of billions of dollars, moreover, China hoped to install as many telephone lines in the succeeding three years as existed in 1997 in the United States.[71]

It was surely significant that no less than three-quarters of the capital required by China's telecommunications growth was sourced domestically—and that, in sharp contrast to the position of WTO signatories, self-sufficiency in this strategic industry continued to comprise an acknowledged goal. "Some sixteen joint-venture manufacturers—many majority-Chinese owned—make a complete array of equipment, from integrated circuits to digital public exchanges."[72] With the surge of neo-liberal capitalism in the wake of the Cold War, however, less-favored countries had scantier maneuvering room than China.

However, in many of them—Mexico, Hungary, perhaps South Africa—the terms on which telecommunications systems were privatized still yielded significant extensions of access. In Hungary, for example, fixed and wireless telephone installations doubled the number of phone customers in the four years after 1993.[73] Argentina almost doubled its teledensity (number of main telephone lines per 100 inhabitants) from 9.5 to 17.7 between 1990 and 1996.[74] In India, Indonesia, Iran, Pakistan, Vietnam, Morocco, the Philippines, and Thailand, the number of main telephone lines more than doubled between 1990 and 1995, while in Egypt, Turkey, Bolivia, and Honduras came gains almost as large.[75] Dozens of other countries could claim less significant—but still undeniable— expansion. Assuredly, these were cases where liberalization improved access to telephone service throughout a broad swath of the domestic population.

Yet inequalities of provision remained severe. Households that continued to be definitively unable to afford telephone service in 1996 comprised practically half of the worldwide total (676 million out of 1.466 billion households); an additional 244 million households were only marginally more likely to subscribe.[76] If telephone subscribership was diffusing throughout middle classes worldwide, then these strata still made up at most a fraction of total population. At the end of 1996 (the last date for which generalizable data exist), one-quarter of countries still possessed less than one main telephone line per 100 inhabitants, and over 950 million households lacked a telephone.[77] There were 100 residential main telephone lines per 100 households in the high-income countries that harbored perhaps one-sixth of global population; while in the low-income nations where more than half of the world's people lived, there were just seven telephones per 100 households.[78] The ITU hoped, surely overoptimistically, that the percentage of households that could afford telephone service in 1995 was .8 percent in Tanzania, 19.7 percent in Morocco, 6.7 percent in the Philippines, 20.5 percent in Brazil, and— the uppermost limit in the poor world—45.4 percent in Mexico and 60.2 percent in Malaysia.[79]

The ITU's hopes were attached to real gains. Nonetheless, over three-fifths of all main telephone lines still were installed in just twenty-three developed countries, housing less than 15 percent of the world's population.[80] The International Telecommunication Union quixotically sought to define *universal service* as existing when everyone in a country lived within five kilometers of a phone.[81] As the millenium drew near, telephones remained, for most people, "exotic objects"—as in the shanty-town of Mangueira, Brazil, where a homeowners association aspired to reach the point where every ten households might share a single telephone line.[82]

Even starker differences in the pattern of provision of next-generation networks and network services portended that global inequality was shifting into a new register. In 1997, an estimated 84 percent of mobile telephone subscribers, 91 percent of all facsimile machines, and fully 97 percent of all Internet host computers were in developed countries. It was symptomatic that the Internet's predominant language—English—was spoken by a mere 15 percent of the world's people.[83]

The social fracture was being reconfigured, therefore, even as the networked economy expanded its reach. Increasing inequality of condition could be traced even into the affluent heartlands of developed capitalism as corporate shareholders successfully wrested away as profit the lion's share of a generation's worth of productivity gains. By one estimate, a median income U.S. family of four in 1996 had income 3 percent below that of a similar family in 1989—and a mere 1.6 percent above the income of such a family in 1973.[84] The upper 5 percent of U.S. households increased its share of national income from 15.5 percent in 1981 to 21.4 percent in 1996, while the bottom 80 percent lost ground. The average U.S. CEO thus made 209 times the pay of factory workers in 1996—up from 42 times as much in 1980.[85]

In turn, leading consumer products companies like Disney and General Motors undertook to develop "two-tier marketing" plans, polarizing products and sales pitches to reach "two different Americas"—rich and poor. The corollary was growing stratification of access to telecommunications: "Nobody puts as much effort into dual marketing as the telecommunications industry," stated *Business Week*.[86]

On one hand, the number of U.S. households installing telephones underwent its fastest growth since 1945, as Internet-enabled PCs and fax machines induced an unprecedented number of high-income earners (upward of 15 percent of households) to pay for extra lines. Upper-middle-class neighborhoods were systematically planned and built by developers according to a formula that translated square-footage into additional telephone lines. A tract of million-dollar house lots in one California community received an allocation of ten telephone lines per unit.[87] Upper-income apartments in New York City, similarly, came outfitted with multiple telephone lines; a handful of *cyberbuildings* boasting *express-lane* Internet access were even equipped with the highspeed (T-1) telephone lines that ordinarily were reserved for large corporate users. For as little as $75 per month in extra charges, inhabitants who could afford to pay a minimum of $350,000 for a condominium—or $2,100 monthly for a one-bedroom apartment—could avail themselves of (shared) T-1 access.[88]

Carriers, not surprisingly, began to place an unrelenting marketing emphasis on *power users*—high-value residential customers who spend lavishly on a basket of telecommunications and information services, typically including (on an annualized basis) $650 on cellular; $500 on local wireline phone service; $400 on long distance; $375 on cable, pay-per view, and video on demand; $250 on paging; as well as hundreds of additional dollars on online access, newspapers, magazines, and fiction.[89] Evidence mounted that the corporate-sponsored build-out of high-capacity networks was systematically evading poor neighborhoods in order to concentrate on well-off suburban residences and business parks.[90]

The new strategic focus was glaringly evident in the industry's advertising campaigns. No longer pitched to the masses "as an upstart David to AT&T's Goliath," for example, "MCI plans to reposition itself as an integrated communications service for more affluent consumers. Using targeted prime-time TV ad buys, it will try to reach well-educated professionals, ages 30 to 50." " 'We're going to change our focus from being omnipresent to the entire market to talking to the top third of the consumer market that represents opportunities in cellular, Internet, and entertainment,' " declared MCI ad chief John Donoghue.[91] Motorola's Iridium system, following on the wildfire success of its $1,300 black StarTAC conventional cellular handset,[92] targeted global executives with worldwide satellite telephone service, planning to charge $3,000 a phone and $3 a minute. Even before it moved to acquire access to millions of cable television households by acquiring TCI, AT&T had already "refined" its marketing strategy to focus on "the top tier of high-spending consumers of communication services. . . . The 20 percent of people who account for 80 percent of the company's $6 billion in annual profit and who use everything from cell phones to Internet services."[93]

On the other side, in the U.S. local telephone rates increased at a rate 56 percent above inflation between 1984 and 1991. The $4 billion pay telephone industry gained FCC approval to charge whatever rates it liked (though it found that demand dropped sharply when service was priced above fifty cents)—and was freed of the obligation to maintain pay phones in unprofitable locations.[94] More than one in five homes in New York's poorest communities had no telephone at all; prepaid phone cards and public telephone arcades were the emerging media of "choice" for the bottom half of the population. While four-fifths of affluent families owned a personal computer, similarly, just one in ten of low-income families did.[95]

"Market discipline" exhibited reciprocally punishing effects on prevailing employment and working conditions throughout the worldwide telecommunications industry. Where, before, staffing policies at public telecommunications operators had often supported relatively high levels of employment, now the talk was all of "excess" workers and downsizing. Number of employees per line began to be used as a supposedly neutral statistical support for comparisons between "lead-edge" and laggard system operators. Layoffs and outsourcing of an increasing range of high-tech operations to nonunion shops became regular features on the liberalized landscape.[96] An ongoing trend toward increased automation (via remote diagnostics, testing and repair, and computerized call centers) accelerated where market conditions permitted.[97] Setting a global example, the first and largest "competitive" carriers spawned by U.S. liberalization—MCI and the long-distance unit of Sprint—practiced aggressively antiunion employment policies and were intolerant in principle of collective bargaining rights.[98] Shniad and Richardson sketch the changed picture:

Telephone jobs were once characterized by a relatively high degree of job security, by work that was carried out at a reasonable pace, by wages and benefits that were relatively good, and by the existence of clearly defined job ladders and transfer rights, all of which practically guaranteed that workers' skills would be enhanced and that their income would grow over time. These attributes helped to create and maintain a stable workforce within the telephone companies. All of them have been undermined.[99]

National system operators themselves adhered increasingly to the new market logic in preference to the older welfarist ethic of public service.

Nowhere were these effects of neoliberal telecommunications more palpable than in the historical source and center of the global liberalization trend, the United States. Here, the business press reported that the Regional Bell companies that had been spun off by the old AT&T were drawing "praise from Wall Street for cutting employment, 'reengineering' their companies, and diversifying into new businesses." With AT&T itself, these seven giant providers of local telephone service had an employee head count of 967,000 in 1984, at the moment of the AT&T divestiture, but this figure had declined to 755,000 by early 1996.[100] AT&T itself cut 123,000 jobs just between 1991 and 1995—30 percent of its global labor force—comprising the largest corporate reduction in the world over that interval.[101] Demoralization not surprisingly became widespread. Bell Atlantic found that its early retirement program was so popular that it unexpectedly had to open negotiations with its union "to prevent a crippling exodus of line installers, technicians, clerical workers, and other employees."[102] The expanding "competitive" sector of the industry somewhat offset these job losses, of course, but as mentioned above, it refused to recognize collective bargaining rights.

In turn, as one newspaper report declared, "the high-quality phone service that once helped define American prosperity can no longer be taken for granted." One of the regional Bell companies (Nynex, now part of Bell Atlantic), for example, "let its network deteriorate in parts of Brooklyn and the Bronx, where corroded wires lead to scratchy lines and service outages. It also cut nearly 14,000 jobs from its payroll since 1994, which left it unable to cope with the swelling demand for phone lines in 1995 and 1996." During the second half of 1995, in the areas served by nine major local exchange carriers, no less than a quarter of all customers complained of a service problem—usually quality or billing—and in some areas the percentage was higher. Nynex's service record became so poor that in 1997 the New York Public Service Commission ordered it to refund $110 million to customers for shoddy service and improper business practices. This was on top of $70 million in fines levied on the company during 1996. Nynex missed 142,300 appointments with customers during the last three months of 1994, up 30 percent from the year before. And there were 212,800 customers whose phones were out of service for more than twenty-four hours during the quarter—a 39.8 percent annual increase.[103] Customer complaints to California state regulators, likewise, more than doubled over a five-year period (1990 to 1994).[104] Pacific Bell, recently absorbed by SBC, planned to shut all its public offices throughout California, at the expense of the more than half a million customers—including many poor and elderly—who paid bills, filed complaints, or reviewed rates in person.[105] Proposals to hike rates for directory assistance calls and for emergency cut-in services became routine.[106]

During the first half of 1997, the FCC received a record 12,000 complaints from telephone subscribers about *slamming*—the practice by which competitive telephone companies sign up new customers without their permission.[107] A Senate investigation estimated in 1998 that at least a million people a year were being slammed.[108] *Cramming*, as the practice of billing customers for services they didn't order, also mushroomed—and not only among marginal outfits. Pacific Bell, for example, employed a sales incentive plan that was said to pressure employees to sell services that customers didn't want.[109] Phone scams, deceptive billing practices, and outright fraud grew rife.[110] Customers responded by adhering to a market logic of their own, as a growing number signed up for telephone service with one company, failed to pay their bill, and then repeated the process with a competitor. (During 1996 about 3 percent of total U.S. telephone industry revenue—some $6 billion—was lost to unpaid bills, an increase from the 1 percent common during the 1970s.)[111] The deluge of complaints from telephone customers was disregarded, except insofar as it could be coopted for opportunistic purposes by politicians working hand in glove with the neoliberal program.[112]

Virtually by definition, liberalization of telecommunications system development produced an unaccustomed volatility. System builders were forced to mortgage project plans to intolerant capital markets. When wireless companies that had promised to pay $10.2 billion for 493 spectrum licenses auctioned by the FCC encountered unexpectedly lackluster interest on the part of investors, and their stock prices duly plunged, they came back to the agency demanding that it either give them more time to pay or else actually reduce the extent of their obligations.[113] The agency obliged—thus the free market in action!—but there could be little confidence that its action had taken the wireless companies out of harm's way.

Investors simply remained unconvinced that five or six rival wireless vendors in each U.S. city all could succeed. Thus the market itself refused to sanction economic competition, at least on the scale envisioned by regulatory true believers.[114]

No one specific effect of liberalization may generalize to the entire world. Nevertheless, the price paid for accelerated system development under liberalized conditions was overarching, as market-driven policies targeted the social service features of the old regime, up to and including the idea of national control over telecommunications. Even in the United States, approval of the WTO accords by regulators meant that long-standing limits on foreign investment in domestic telecommunications were relaxed (though the FCC employed a legal loophole to retain its power to intervene in the case of a purported "foreign investment threat").[115]

To be sure, neoliberalism's global attack on the industry's public-service character was often resisted by the telecommunications workers who set up and repaired the switches and phone lines needed to make the system work. Strikes and demonstrations provoked by market-led telecommunications initiatives—privatizations above all—broke out from 1996 to 1998 among telecommunications workers on at least three continents, in places as diverse as Colombia, Israel, Lesotho, the Philippines, Peru, and Puerto Rico. Some of these strikes prompted large worker mobilizations.[116] But sometime rivalries among contending unions, and the ascendance of neoliberal orthodoxy among middle-class consumers and stockholders, weakened attempts to widen popular resistance. Employee militance had far to go before it could constitute an effective counter to neoliberalism's global project.

On the other side, the U.S. Trade Representative frankly underlined who neoliberalism's real beneficiaries were intended to be: under the terms of the WTO agreement carriers would have "the right to use their own facilities and to work directly with their customers everywhere their customers go—providing seamless end-to-end services, not handing calls off to monopoly providers elsewhere."[117] Private carriers and business users, that is, had acquired unprecedented freedom to cooperate in reintegrating telecommunications into the workaday operations of transnational capitalism.

As the pioneer of a greater networked economy that was utterly dependent on powerful computer-communications systems, the United States played an aggressive role in crafting this result.[118] Reed Hundt, outgoing chairman of the U.S. Federal Communications Commission and a self-styled admirer of U.S. Federal Reserve Bank Chairman Alan Greenspan, spoke before the U.S. Chamber of Commerce: "The FCC was instrumental in the successful completion of the World Trade Organization agreement on telecommunications. We proposed and adopted rules here that made it clear to foreign countries that we would not tolerate the market-distorting effects of closed markets around the world."[119] Still, perhaps the WTO agreement is best understood as a victory not for the United States but for transnationalizing capital in general—though one that therefore privileged the United States–based enterprises that comprise the largest proportion of TNCs worldwide.

The WTO pact, as Cynthia Beltz of the American Enterprise Institute (a neoliberal thinktank) explained, acted principally "to prevent the rollback of liberalization commitments once they are made." It established a framework for action by representatives of nation states. "But," observed Beltz, "it cannot move beyond what individual countries are willing to pursue." "Getting countries to live up to their commitments is always hard," she declared, "and in telecommunications the transition path will be particularly difficult," owing to the agreement's sanction of "loopholes" that permitted national authorities to try "to safeguard public service responsibilities such as universal service or to protect the 'technical integrity' of the public telecommunications system." "Given the institutional limits of the WTO," in sum, "we should not expect too much too soon from its rulemaking revolution."[120]

However, as Beltz was apparently relieved to announce, this would not matter much: "The most powerful forces pushing for liberalization did not even have seats at the negotiating table," and "competition in international telecommunications will continue to intensify in the next few years irrespective of what happens with the WTO rulemaking revolution."[121] The eggs needed to make the neoliberal omelette already had been broken. A generative locus of change had been created within the complex of big capital, and network suppliers as well as users had become intent on developing supranational systems and applications. Absent radical intervention, therefore, "marketplace developments" would largely set "the de facto rules of the game for the new telecommunications environment."[122]

Transnational Network Systems: Train Wreck on the Supply Side?

A year before the WTO deliberations concluded, legislation was passed in the United States that, by permitting convergence between once separate communications industry segments, opened the greater communications market to unparalleled domestic consolidation. Within a year, there had been $103 billion worth of mergers and acquisitions in U.S. telecommunications, and the pace of dealmaking continued to heat up: 136 deals, worth $120.5 billion, were announced during the first six months of 1998.[123] After the WTO pact was finally reached, it also promised "to uncork a flood of deals, as telephone companies—big and small, domestic and foreign—scramble to find partners and build alliances across borders."[124]

From the demand side, of course, business users had already long been intent on achieving "international systems solutions"; coherent business applications otherwise had to contend with the restrictions and the fragmentation imposed by discrete national networks. During the second half of the 1990s, moreover, corporate users' demand surged for additional bandwidth, or information-carrying capacity, to support Internet applications and other services. To accommodate this demand required ever-more capacious network systems. In spring 1997, the leading manufacturer of such high-capacity transmission circuits reported that its core optical fiber offerings were sold out for the next two years.[125] A consultant estimated that the worldwide market for fiber-optic cable would almost double between 1997 and 2001, from less than 35 million "cable-fiber kilometers" to nearly 66 million.[126] Suppliers, long alerted to their leading users' ambitions, raced to consolidate their systems by transnationalizing their operations and diversifying to support an extended array of service offerings. They knew that telecommunications network integration can generate considerable economies of scale and scope—that is, that a supplier can achieve lower unit costs by furnishing a basket of different telecommunications services including local, long-distance, cellular, and now

Internet access. Furthermore, they reasoned, consumers would prefer to purchase all forms of service from a single provider.[127]

This is not to suggest that the reshaping of telecommunications was inspired solely by rational system development strategies. Equally integral to the restructuring process were financial considerations. "Deal-makers flush with junk bonds" and like instruments, reported the *Wall Street Journal*, were "storming the staid phone industry, where some of the biggest mergers in history have been hatched, prodded by investment bankers seeking to top one another's deals and fees."[128] In any particular case, it might be virtually impossible to decide—absent insider knowledge—where bonafide strategy gave up pride of place to arrant speculative chicanery. The prerogatives of finance capital thus indisputably infused the neoliberal development of the global information infrastructure.[129]

It is not feasible to give an exhaustive tally of the whirlwind of dealmaking that commenced—dealmaking that may "strain, if not exhaust, the capital available."[130] Rather, I will single out a few key examples of the emerging alliances between would-be transnational carriers and aspiring national and regional affiliates.

Big Deals

British Telecom's initial purchase of a 20 percent ownership interest in MCI, approved by the U.S. FCC in 1994, kickstarted the transnationalizing trend. It was soon followed by European Union authorization for Deutsche Telekom's and France Telecom's initiative to create a continental "supercarrier," which would in turn gain approval from the United States to acquire a 20 percent interest in Sprint. By 1997 Global One, the name given to this joint venture, maintained an international network with more than 1,200 points of presence in sixty-five countries.[131] AT&T, meanwhile, pursued its own alliance (called WorldPartners) with several other carriers.[132] By 1997, international service sales contributed several billion dollars to AT&T's total annual revenue, and AT&T had undertaken dozens of joint ventures with foreign partners; the company had built up a presence in over 100 countries.[133]

In November of 1996, BT raised the ante, making a $21 billion bid to acquire the 80 percent of MCI that it did not own. The $43 billion postmerger company would have claimed a presence in seventy-two countries (often through joint ventures), a net income that would rank it sixth in the world on the basis of profit, and 43 million customers. MCI and BT were explicit about their prospective merger's global orientation, boasting in an advertisement that theirs "will be the . . . least nationalistic communications company ever seen."[134]

They spoke too soon. MCI announced unexpectedly high losses from entering local service provision in the United States. The merger, BT's top shareholders insisted, should be renegotiated. An interloper with strong Wall Street backing, WorldCom, made a last-minute rival bid for MCI. (Backed by its own roster of banks and lawyers, GTE also entered the fray with a contending offer.) WorldCom's $37 billion takeover offer was based almost entirely on its stock, whose inflated value reflected not only its earnings and assets but also investment analysts' exceptionally favorable opinion. Were the good offices of speculators a sufficient anchor for such a critical infrastructure?

Speculative ambitions attached, in turn, to strategic system-building objectives. A nonunion company catering mainly to business customers and claiming a powerful Internet presence, WorldCom's success in stealing away MCI offered a telling comment on the nature of these objectives.

By joining MCI's long-distance network to the business-dominated local service subsidiaries it established or acquired to serve nearly 100 U.S. cities, WorldCom reduced its dependence on access to existing Bell Company networks. (In the two years following passage of the Telecommunications Act of 1996, no less than $15 billion was raised on Wall Street to underwrite growth of more than a dozen such "competitive local exchange carriers.")[135] This would allow the combined company to bypass the expensive access charges that were imposed by regulators on long-distance carriers interconnecting with local networks. By sidestepping this existing system, of course, WorldCom's pursuit of business users would contribute to its deterioration.

An analogous strategy in Europe—where WorldCom was spending billions of dollars to complete a fiber network to connect financial centers and where it already carried 10 percent of Continental Internet traffic— promised to pose analogous threats in that region. Without handing off traffic to any other carriers, WorldCom will route traffic from any of five major European cities—Brussels, Frankfurt, London, Paris, and Amsterdam—over its own network to a roster of U.S. destination cities.[136] Bypassing incumbent carriers on both sides of the ocean, WorldCom's newly established transatlantic submarine cable facilities and urban business networks will allow it to link directly some 4,000 business structures in Europe with 27,000 such buildings in the United States.[137]

Soon after the WorldCom-MCI deal had been consummated, AT&T and British Telecom responded by creating yet another joint venture to provide specialized services to transnational corporate users.[138] The intended beneficiary of the herculean reorganization of telecommunications that is underway remained transnational corporate capital. Transnational companies, as the director of Korea Telecom declared, were intent on achieving access "to an increasingly sophisticated, seamless communications network, enabling them to conduct business around the clock and around the world:

Users are demanding cheaper, simpler ways of dealing with their worldwide communications, one-stop shopping for international networks, one bill for domestic and global services, payment in one currency, and ideally, one inexpensive contract for everything.[139]

Large companies, agreed David C. Moschella, looked forward "to an increasingly interoperable and fully supported global information management capability."[140]

Global alliances in telecommunications were in turn chiefly a response to this imperative. Of one such hook-up, a candid industry analyst declared: "The opportunity specifically being addressed here is the selling of . . . services to multinational businesses": "It's not about selling telecom services to consumers; they are targeting the top 2,000 corporations in the world." (AT&T, the largest international carrier, actually serves some 3,700 transnational customers.)[141]

As they girded to clash in dozens of domestic markets, transnational telecommunications companies took on leading local businesses as partners; in Mexico, for example, MCI allied with Banamex, the largest domestic bank, while AT&T teamed up with the conglomerates Alfa and Visa-Bancomer.[142] Like thirty other companies worldwide, Mexico's established PTO, Telmex, partnered with Global One, the joint venture between Deutsche Telekom, France Telecom, and Sprint. A newcomer,

Qwest Communications, forged an agreement with Bestel, itself a joint venture of GST Global Telecommunications and Grupo Varo's Odetel.[143] SPC, yet another new Mexican telecommunications company, cut a deal with Lucent to set up a national wireless network.[144] Mexican telecommunications offered not just another new market for MCI and AT&T, in particular,

> but also the missing link needed to complete their proprietary networks in Canada and the U.S. With Mexico, both companies will have uniform networks that span all North America—the world's most lucrative call corridor. Some 1,000 multinational corporations in Mexico could use North American network services.[145]

Integrated transborder networks constituted the carriers' top strategic objective because only through this means could their most favored customers create integrated, network-based production systems. Global cross-border merger and acquisition activity in telecommunications reached a record $17 billion in 1997 (a 15 percent increase over 1996), with more than half the total accounted for by European groups in the run-up to full liberalization slated for 1998.[146]

The race to forge alliances engendered bewildering about-faces. Telefonica was left suddenly stranded, without a global partner, after the collapse of the BT-MCI negotiations; it subsequently signed on with MCI-WorldCom.[147] France Telecom, which already possessed interests in phone operations from Belgium to Argentina, sought to acquire a stake in Infostrada, a venture with Olivetti and Bell Atlantic that intended to compete with the erstwhile PTO, Telecom Italia—only to find itself replaced by Germany's Mannesmann, while Bell Atlantic also negotiated to leave the venture.[148] Italy's PTO, meanwhile, took a 44 percent stake in France's new fixed-line competitor, Bouygues-STET.[149] In what had been for decades a comparatively placid field, fractious quarrels sometimes broke out, both directly among partners[150] and between corporate management and outside investors.[151] AT&T's alliance with Telecom Italia, for example, suffered an embarrassing collapse in the wake of a management disagreement.[152]

Mighty inflows of capital surged into what had been a relatively discrete sector. Eyeing Germany's $60 billion phone market and its 36 million residential customers, dozens of would-be competitors stormed into service provision.[153] The industrial conglomerate Daimler-Benz, for instance, joined with German retailer Metro and RSL Communications of the United States to offer long-distance services to companies and high-income individuals, in competition against Deutsche Telekom.[154] Mannesmann, with Deutsche Bahn, AT&T, AirTouch, and Unisource, created an alliance to build a network based on the German railway's phone lines.[155] Cegetel, perhaps the leading "domestic" competitor of France Telecom, comprised a partnership between Generale des Eaux, British Telecommunications, Mannesmann, and SBC.[156] Even national carriers whose size placed them in the second and third ranks, such as those of Denmark or Malaysia or Portugal, plunged into significant offshore investments.

Great unevenness again characterized the pattern of this investment. Of the $95 billion raised worldwide for telecommunications privatizations in the four years to early 1998, a mere $1.7 billion was directed at Africa, and most of that was for South Africa. The ITU concluded that, even on the most favorable assumptions, fewer than one in fifty Africans would have direct telephone access by 2000.[157]

In some countries, as the boom ran its course, newly privatized phone companies were permitted to retain a service monopoly for a period of years simply to entice foreign investors.[158] (Adherents of privatization made no bones that corporate control over this critical infrastructure remained their foremost goal, even preceding "competition.")[159] Elsewhere, again in hopes of luring sufficient capital, the small, impoverished countries that came late to the privatization party had literally to give away the store. Guatemala promised, on one hand, to open its market to immediate competition in local, long-distance, paging, cellular, and most other telecommunications services. On the other hand, the winning bidder for the nation's existing telecommunications operator, Guatel (whose sale was to be superintended by J. P. Morgan), was paid off with a guarantee that there would be no government oversight of rates. These benefices were enough to bring fourteen foreign telecommunications companies into negotiations.[160]

In the wake of double-digit currency depreciation, meanwhile, suddenly overextended Southeast Asian telecommunications operators found their capital investment plans in tatters. Telekom Malaysia and Pilipino Telephone Corporation, for example, cut back on planned expansions.

The Indonesian PTO's joint ventures with U.S. West, Cable & Wireless and France Cables et Radio likewise failed to lay as many lines or produce as much revenue as expected.[161] Other Asian operators were forced to make onerous concessions, as in South Korea, which met demands by investors to relax already loosened restrictions on foreign ownership of telecommunications providers.[162] Indonesia's PTO, 21 percent of whose shares were in foreign hands by 1998, cut its capital spending and, desperate for revenue, became a candidate for additional privatization. But market conditions remained too poor to permit such action during 1998.[163] Brazil, wobbling unsteadily from the effects of the spreading economic crisis, likewise lifted all foreign ownership limitations on some about-to-be-privatized operators.[164] Only China, after toying with the idea of a limited liberalization, balked.[165]

New Media Systems

Transnational alliances between erstwhile national capitals were particularly quick to cluster around new telecommunications media and not because of some intrinsic or arcane technical attribute. The costs of new telecommunications infrastructure systems in most cases simply exceeded what could be undertaken even by pooling domestic capital sources. Transnational carriers in a position to bankroll the new systems thus often could condition their offers of support on a license to bypass the social responsibilities that attached to established network facilities.

Investment in mobile communications systems was the fastest-growing form of foreign investment in telecommunications; according to the staid International Telecommunication Union, the extent of such investment was "staggering."[166] Five of the eight mobile telephone licenses awarded by Taiwan in 1996 went to U.S. firms partnered with domestic companies (the other three went to Hong Kong–based and German-based consortia).[167] Airtouch, a U.S. telecommunications firm, by 1998 maintained cellular businesses in eleven countries and reached several million international customers.[168] BellSouth entered Latin American wireless markets in 1989 and by 1997 served a pool of customers in ten countries in the region.[169]

Analogous opportunities were afforded by new satellite communications systems, which required extensive transborder coordination of spectrum assignments and operations. From the dawn of the space age in the late 1950s until around 1980, global satellite services (whose underlying technology remained essentially a U.S. military fiefdom) were provided via international consortia, of which by far the most significant was Intelsat. National PTOs played a preponderant role.

During the 1980s, however, satellite provision underwent a metamorphosis. Privately owned and operated systems began to be authorized. Akin to other existing nonprofit international satellite consortia, Intelsat, with its unmatched satellite fleet and billion-dollar revenue, was slated for privatization in 1998.[170] Commercial applications, making use of new generations of satellite technology, forced their way forward. Even the Indian space program, which invested $2 billion, beginning in 1964, in a persistent attempt to achieve national self-reliance in satellites and rocketry, seemed to be giving in to the pressures for opening up ownership and control of this strategic sector to foreign investors.[171]

By 1998, there were some 180 commercial communication satellites in geosynchronous orbit and a total of 530 satellites of all different kinds (in addition to hundreds of thousands of pieces of detritus—space junk left behind by rockets and shuttles).[172] Yet the world stood on the threshold of an unparalleled boom in satellite system and service development. U.S. satellite makers planned to build and launch 1,700 satellites (mostly low- and medium-earth orbit models) over the decade beginning in 1998, worth a projected $121 billion—a rate of investment that would approach the level of U.S. federal highway spending.[173] A handful of mainly United States–led consortia, headed by aerospace manufacturers, planned to ring the planet with next-generation multisatellite systems. An increasing number of these ventures planned to provide global coverage for high-speed Internet services, prospectively supplanting established terrestrial networks. Eleven different satellite industry segments, including manufacturing, launching, and service applications, were projected to drive the industry's growth from around $38 billion in 1997 to a stupefying $171 billion projected for 2007.[174]

Just two of the new consortia (Skybridge and Teledesic) won control from 142 countries of more than twice the spectrum used by all of the United States 1,561 television and 12,199 radio stations combined.[175] Teledesic partnered moguls Bill Gates and Craig McCaw with Boeing; Motorola subsequently dropped a separate project in order to join the group.[176] Skybridge brought together Loral, Alcatel Alsthom of France, and Japanese investors.[177] Lockheed Martin struck a deal with InterSputnik that garnered it fifteen scarce orbital slots, and then sought to purchase Comsat, the U.S. affiliate of Intelsat, for $2.7 billion.[178] Iridium comprised a consortium of telecommunications and industrial companies anchored by its prime contractor, Motorola, but also including strategically placed African, Chinese, Middle Eastern, Korean, Japanese, Italian, Thai, German, and U.S. interests.[179] Globalstar's major investor was again Loral Space & Communications—which acquired additional discounted ownership shares in 1998 from two hardpressed South Korean partners.[180]

Submarine cable system development evinced analogous tendencies. Transoceanic cable projects had long involved numerous nations' public telecommunications operators. Now, however, ownership structures were opened to permit private investment and operation. The Fiber-Optic Link Around the Globe (FLAG) system, at a cost of more than a billion dollars, tied together U.S., Japanese, and Middle Eastern interests in a 28,000 kilometer system with landing points in Europe, Egypt, India, Malaysia, China, and Japan.[181]

It was all a far cry from the preceding era of national flag carriers. The telecommunications industry was frenziedly chewing up erstwhile national networks and spitting them out again as units in prospectively integrated transnational corporate systems. Alex J. Mandl, former president of AT&T, expected that within a few years the shakeout would culminate in a mere four or five telecommunications behemoths with worldwide reach, alongside hundreds of regional and niche firms.[182]

In the face of surging demand for transnational, multimedia Internet services, system builders of every kind raced to gain (or at least not lose) advantage by constructing advanced networks. Predictably enough, this system-building boom soon raised the question of whether global telecommunications—akin to many other industries, from automobiles to semiconductors—might be headed toward a market glut, that is, a state of secular overcapacity. When, in October 1997, Motorola announced that it alone would build 500 or more communication satellites over the decade beginning in the year 2000, at least some industry analysts seemed chagrined. An Arthur D. Little consultant questioned whether demand for so many satellites could be justified.[183] And, immediately following the

Asian financial debacle of 1997, the region's mobile telecommunications operators were said to be heading for a shakeout.[184] During the first half of 1998, reflecting these worsening conditions, two hitherto separate satellite ventures (Celestri and Odyssey) each merged with a different partner.[185] By fall, 1997, Corning—a market leader—reported that, in the face of surplus capacity to produce optical fibers, it had cut back its growth projections. Further advances in the technology, however, promised to increase available capacity even more.[186]

Internet development needs to be situated within this vortex. This was not merely because, as one industry conceded, there existed "a direct correlation between the deregulation of the telecommunications infrastructure of a region and the growth of Internet and Intranet use within that region."[187] Nor was it only because the overarching patterns of market development in telecommunications—transnationalization and business user paramountcy—held good as well for the Internet. Even more important was that the Internet already had become a vital policy wedge, offering perhaps the sharpest tool in the arsenal of those who sought to widen and deepen the scope of digital capitalism. To chart the uses of this new function requires that we return to the political dimension of change and to the United States, which comprised digital capitalism's historical source and center.

Freeing the Flow of Electronic Commerce: Digital Capitalism's Proprietary Frontier

Contemporary network system development, as we have seen, is no mere reflex of economic action; it proceeds by means of concerted political intervention as well. As the Internet bore down on the established telecommunications industry, U.S. political intervention intensified yet again.

Unilateral U.S. Government Initiatives

Over the course of a single week in 1997, two rival branches of the United States government arrived at a remarkable political consensus concerning the proper guidance of cyberspace. At first sight, this may seem farfetched. What common ground was there between the (conservative) U.S. Supreme Court ruling striking down key provisions of the Communications Decency Act (CDA) (*Reno v. American Civil Liberties*

Union, No. 96–511) and the (liberal) White House policy document "The Framework for Global Electronic Commerce"?[188]

The two pronouncements in fact converged with ramifying force on a single theme: rather than continuing to be subject to governmental oversight, the development of Internet systems and services should be left as much as possible to the market.

When the Supreme Court ruled that laws to regulate free speech violated constitutional protections, its verdict reached beyond the limited object of protecting minors from indecent communications. Jerry Berman, of the Center for Democracy and Technology (which opposed the CDA), was moved to declare that the Court had handed down nothing less than "the First Amendment for the twenty-first century."[189] Rather than simply celebrating this redemption of civil liberties, however, we may ask: How could the most reactionary Court in a hundred years persuade itself to find for the most unrestrictive possible interpretation of the Internet's legal status? What were the implications of its decision to render the Net freer of government restraint than the other electronic media—telephony and television broadcasting?

The Court's ruling (in most important respects, a unanimous one) was sweepingly comprehensive: it "makes it unlikely that any government-imposed restriction on Internet content would be upheld as long as the material has some intrinsic constitutional value," reported the *New York Times.*[190] "The Framework for Global Electronic Commerce" built on the Court's formal edict. In principle, said the president in a message accompanying the report, the Internet should be accorded "minimal regulation"; it should be "a place where government makes every effort . . . not to stand in the way."[191] The same conclusion had, in truth, already emerged as a specific and considered goal of other government agencies, such as the FCC—which produced a staff report on the Internet earlier in 1997.[192] And, in this respect, basic consistency had marked the evolution of the report on electronic commerce itself; an earlier draft had declared, for example, that "unnecessary regulation could cripple the growth and diversity of the Internet."[193]

Two sensitive issues—user privacy and encryption standards—continued to obstruct the comprehensive application of this laissez-faire policy.[194] But these issues portended only limited exceptions to what, by consensus, was locked in as a guiding orthodoxy: that the Internet should undergo market-led development to the maximum possible extent. This doctrine, in turn, was actually but the latest expression of a policy that has been pursued by U.S. leaders with extraordinary consistency and vigor for over half a century. "The U.S. government," declared the report on electronic commerce,

supports the broadest possible free flow of information across international borders. This includes most informational material now accessible and transmitted through the Internet, including through World Wide Web pages, news and other information services, virtual shopping malls, and entertainment features, such as audio and video products, and the arts. This principle extends to information created by commercial enterprises as well as by schools, libraries, governments and other nonprofit entities.[195]

With great clarity of purpose, supporters of the free flow of information have used this tenet as a prime mover of U.S. political and economic interests over the decades.

Behind the doctrine's apparent high purpose lay blatant attempts at self-aggrandizement. U.S. news agencies, film distributors, and broadcasters and, later, satellite networks, information providers, and communications companies of every kind—with the larger consumer economy just behind them—relied on it to justify rapid postwar expansion into global markets. While Western Europe and Japan turned to rebuild their shattered economies, the free flow of information spearheaded an informal brand of domination, which linked dozens of newly independent but economically impoverished states to a political economy directed chiefly by extraterritorially minded U.S. government agencies and businesses. As Herbert I. Schiller summed up the doctrine's import, over twenty years ago: "Freedoms that are formally impressive may be substantively oppressive when they reinforce prevailing inequalities while claiming to be providing generalized opportunity for all."[196] Has this opportunistic use of a noble idea now been transcended?

In a word, no; the doctrine remains pivotal. But the emergent policy consensus recast the free-flow policy to meet the exigencies of a new medium—the Internet—within the substantially altered setting of a post–Cold War transnational political economy. "Ultimately," concluded an understated editorial in the *Economist,* "the Internet could breed a new approach to regulation, less paternalistic and more trusting in market forces."[197] Cynthia Beltz cogently identifies the Internet's role as the leading edge of neoliberal policy change:

U.S. negotiators seeking to open global telecommunications markets could not have asked for a more effective ally than the Internet. It is a global medium that didn't require a multilateral agreement to advance traditional U.S. trade objectives. It is dramatically reducing the cost and increasing the speed with which services can cross national borders. The speed with which the Internet has surged onto the scene has also disarmed many that might have otherwise opposed or tried to manage its entry. Telecommunications providers around the world have been left scrambling to get on the Internet bandwagon, while regulators have been left wondering what just passed them. While they figure that out, the Internet is being used to interject competition and provide telecommunication services that bypass the excessive rates charged in Asia and Europe.[198]

Never before has a functioning medium made such a hash of geopolitical boundaries. By annihilating traditional territorially anchored controls,[199] the Internet has been configured to comprise what one legal analyst terms a "universal jurisdiction" that endangers every lesser sovereignty.[200] In prospect, in cyberspace is an increasing abandonment of the erstwhile system of country codes and area codes through which conventional telephone networks exchange messages. Instead, Internet addresses denominated by "generic top-level domain names" such as *.com* and *.edu*—and, almost surely, many others still to come—act as spearheads of supranational interchange, which are deliberately indifferent to the physical location of interoperating machines.[201]

Nor do electrons pulsing across the Internet distinguish message content or mode; what originates and culminates as speech, image, or sound is reduced in transit to a common digital bitstream. In turn, this process of *convergence* allows older legal distinctions to appear freshly problematic. *Speech* and *commerce,* to take the most salient examples, become increasingly entangled. Where the Internet is concerned, rulings that are ostensibly about the former cannot but harbor portentous consequences for the latter. There is no question that the U.S. Supreme Court's decision to overturn the Communications Decency Act marked a victory for civil liberties. Yet the same verdict simultaneously rendered a camouflaged preferment (by granting expansive assurances of nonintervention) for electronic commerce. Thus, the property-right concept of freedom of speech that had informed the free-flow doctrine through earlier decades was in the process of being greatly strengthened.

Emboldened intellectual property laws, as we will see momentarily, only bolstered this result.

The Court's decision relied, just the same, on a highly questionable point of fact. Writing for the majority, Justice John Paul Stevens asserted that arguments that sought a basis for restricting First Amendment liberty in the regulatory history of broadcasting were unfounded. "The Internet . . . has no comparable history," he stipulated, that would serve to justify extending to it the more limited protection that has typified U.S. law's treatment of broadcasting. Precedents drawing "on the history of extensive government regulation of the broadcast medium; the scarcity of available frequencies at its inception; and its 'invasive' nature" relied illicitly on "factors [that] are not present in cyberspace":

Neither before nor after the enactment of the CDA have the vast democratic fora of the Internet been subject to the type of government supervision and regulation that has attended the broadcast industry. Moreover, the Internet is not as "invasive" as radio or television. The District Court [whose opinion the U.S. Supreme Court here upheld—DS] specifically found that "communications over the Internet do not 'invade' an individual's home or appear on one's computer screen unbidden. Users seldom encounter content 'by accident.' "[202]

Despite the farfetched claim that the Internet has not been regulated by any government agency (think of the early role of the U.S. Departent of Defense) and therefore should remain forever free of oversight, and despite the debatable question of whether clicks with a computer mouse yield fewer unbidden encounters than clicks with a TV remote control, the vital question (which is discussed at length in chapter 3) is whether the Internet indeed may be distinguished from broadcasting.

Much of the Internet's importance has stemmed from its increasing versatility and, in particular, from its impressive ability to support and extend a range of once discrete media services. There can be no doubt that these already encompass broadcasting,[203] as we will see later. The president himself tacitly acceded to this critical point in heralding the Net's unfolding applications: "Within a generation, we can make it so that every book ever written, every symphony ever composed, every movie ever made, every painting ever painted, is within reach of all of our children within seconds with the click of a mouse."[204] As this welter of *multimedia* services and genres began to flourish on the Internet, in turn, the critical distinctions on which Justice Stevens placed his—and

our—faith were likewise put in question. As the torrent of technical innovation proceeded, finally, the Internet's incorporation of media services
including both broadcasting and telephony could be used as an Archi-
medean point against whatever forms of government oversight seemed
most onerous.

The Court's decision gave added proof that Internet deregulation was
not the outcome of any technological imperative; rather, it comprised a
continuing political choice. Joseph Farrell, then outgoing chief economist
at the Federal Communications Commission, affords an especially clear-
eyed view of the motivations that informed this choice:

> One serious barrier to deregulation will be the culture of entitlement . . . that
> encrusts our telecommunications policy. It will therefore be crucial to reduce the
> scope of that culture. . . . One likely strategy may be to start by deregulating
> "new" services, to wall them off from the culture of entitlement.[205]

The Electronic Commerce policy document's major author, Ira Maga-
ziner, agreed: "If there's ever an arena that should be market driven, this
is it."[206]

Viewing the judiciary's ruling and the administration's policy on electronic commerce as sides of the same coin, corporate interests were quick
to offer accolades.[207] In truth, they had lobbied for exactly such a result.
In the later stages of the judiciary's review of the Communications Decency Act, for example, the U.S. Chamber of Commerce had argued "that
the law presented a threat to the country's ability to compete globally in
an age of new communications, an argument that very likely got the attention of the free-market conservatives, including Justices Thomas and
Scalia, who joined Justice Stevens's opinion."[208]

This deregulatory ambition, again, harbored an explicitly extraterritorial element: to discourage other nations from imposing restrictive regulations of their own on cyberspace.[209] As the *Los Angeles Times* noted,
"The report, in many ways, is intended to set an international agenda
for the Internet. The document advocates that other governments adopt
a similar approach toward taxes and content regulations in an effort to
make electronic transactions across national borders as seamless as those
that now occur between states."[210]

The release of the report was carefully timed, therefore, for audiences
both at home and abroad. Not only did it piggyback on the Supreme

Court's CDA ruling; it also tried to set the agenda for a series of upcoming international negotiations. The object lesson was slated, for example, for a Paris-based OECD meeting at which the question of government regulation of the Internet was to be addressed.[211] President Clinton also suggested that the administration hoped to petition the World Trade Organization "to turn the Internet into a free-trade zone within the next twelve months."[212]

A concerted and multifaceted strategic initiative actually was underway. On one side, all federal department and agency heads were placed under presidential instructions to "review their policies that affect global electronic commerce and . . . make sure that they are consistent with . . . this report."[213] On the other side, U.S. state agencies prepared to mount a full-court press in negotiations to establish a comprehensive electronic free-trade zone. The directive called for aggressive, coordinated engagement across a range of intergovernmental organizations, whose warrants cover everything from tax issues to telecommunications policy and from technical standards making to intellectual property laws.

The United States kept up the pressure to keep the Internet free of foreign tariffs, trade barriers, and other restrictions. Late in 1998, for example, the administration agreed to keep the global network largely unregulated, a condition of financial aid for developing countries' Internet access projects.[214] After considerable jockeying, likewise, the World Trade Organization agreed to keep products delivered electronically over the Internet (though not physical goods ordered on the Net and shipped across borders) duty-free for at least another year.[215] Considerable diplomacy, however, was required to obtain this result. Trying to deflect charges (by European and Australian governments and other bodies) that the United States remained intent on global domination of the Internet, senior U.S. policymakers struggled to give more than lip service to the comity of nations.[216] Through mid-1998, at least, their success was notable. No countertrend toward robust multilateral oversight and regulation of the Internet had yet materialized—in a field where each succeeding month saw fresh applications corrosive of existing national media structures and regulatory controls.

International political and diplomatic struggles of Internet policy, to be sure, became more intense, especially between the United States and the consolidating European Union. However, regarding the transcendent neoliberal tenet that sought to ensure inviolable private property rights in—and over—cyberspace, harmony reigned. Intellectual property rights comprised a telling case in point.

Because digital networks had been created, as we have seen, to accommodate unprecedentedly fluid exchanges of information among dispersed users, they paradoxically posed new threats to information property holders. Extending intellectual property law to the digital world meant something much more, however, than simply bringing private property rights up to date, as adherents tried to claim. It portended more, even, than enclosing and policing cyberspace in the interests of specialized corporate information proprietors like Time-Warner or News Corporation. In the emerging era of digital capitalism, *all* major businesses were becoming informationally oriented—through research and production processes as well as through the outright sale of information products and services. The president of the database company Oracle even wondered whether "patents and intellectual property will actually become components of greater value to a company than real estate or plant and equipment."[217] "Intellectual property" summarized the economist Lester C. Thurow, lay "at the center of the modern company's economic success or failure."[218] "Adjusting" intellectual property laws to take account of the peculiarities of cyberspace, therefore, involved nothing less than a radical shift in society's overall treatment of *information in general.*

The prospective use of computer networks to further the goal of information plenitude, on the other hand, constituted industry's worst nightmare. Apache is a server (or publishing) software program created and released in 1995 by a group of programmers working informally together in their spare time. Distributed for free, Apache was taken up by major companies, including Kimberly-Clark, McDonald's, and Texas Instruments. By 1998, it was in place at nearly half of the Web sites on the Internet—more than double the share garnered by Microsoft or Netscape for their competing proprietary server programs.[219] In the view of adherents of electronic commerce, such palpable demonstrations of the hacker slogan "Information wants to be free" constituted subversive infringements on the rights of enterprise. The U.S. Commissioner of Patents and

Trademarks, Bruce Lehman, claimed summarily that the "National Information Infrastructure will not realize its full commercial potential"—a possibility he evidently deemed so inimical to national purpose that it didn't require further comment—"unless copyright protections are extended" to digitized computer networks.[220] From liberal economist Thurow's perspective, "The days of the low-cost sharing of private knowledge are over":

The Industrial Revolution began with an enclosure movement that abolished common land in England. The world now needs a socially managed enclosure movement for intellectual property rights or it will witness a scramble among the powerful to grab valuable pieces of intellectual property, just as the powerful grabbed the common lands of England three centuries ago.[221]

Thurow's argument may be faulted for proclaiming that we may save a kernel of social justice by preemptively privatizing the existing information commons. Nevertheless, there is no gainsaying the force of the current trend "toward stronger and more enduring intellectual property rights, and fewer limitations on the rights of copyright-holders vis-à-vis public-good uses of information."[222] As a U.S. National Research Council study put it, "The sponsors of new proprietary rights explicitly contemplate a level of systematic commercialization . . . that is unprecedented."[223]

Social goals above and beyond profitmaking thus were to be suppressed or at least harshly restricted and contained. And, critically, as the Electronic Commerce initiative suggested, this transformation needed to occur *globally*. U.S. attempts to inaugurate the new intellectual property regime commenced even before the release of the E-Commerce framework document, for example, at the World Intellectual Property Organization (WIPO) meeting in Geneva during late 1996. Unlike the concurrent deliberations at the World Trade Organization, however, the WIPO negotiations—where the official U.S. position progressed through daily consultations between Bruce Lehman and a business trade group called the International Intellectual Property Alliance—did not culminate in an unequivocal victory for propertied interests. Efforts therefore continued unabated to work toward an "intellectual property regime" that would privilege business over any other social interest.[224] In April 1998 alone, U.S. authorities announced trade sanctions against Honduras for "overt and unacceptable" piracy of U.S. videos and TV signals while, prompted by complaints from recording and movie industry trade groups, across the globe in Hong Kong, police seized $90 million worth of illicit compact disks.[225]

More important, domestic U.S. policy as usual continued to press beyond the norms of prevailing practice. In December 1997, President Clinton signed into law "The No Electronic Theft Act," which made it a criminal offense to possess or distribute multiple copies of online copyrighted material, for profit *or otherwise*.[226] With strong support from the publishing, movie, and music industries and, once more, from the Clinton administration, during mid-1998 the U.S. Congress worked to pass legislation that would expand copyright protections to online content, while extending the term (to ninety-five years from first publication) of corporate copyright protection.[227] Defenders of democratic information access worried that the bills conferred well-nigh absolute power over digital information to copyright owners. Even customary "fair use" of copyrighted materials by librarians, students, and educators could be deemed illegal.[228]

This continuing mobilization again drew on economic as well as political power. As the Internet's transformation into a medium of electronic commerce gained momentum, online companies demanded greater control over Web content—over who linked to their sites, how they linked, and how their content was displayed and made available. Broadcast Music Inc. (BMI), representing music publishers and recording companies, began to use a so-called robot program to regulate the use of its musical properties on the Internet. The program combs the Web to discover sites likely to contain music files; after further review, sites utilizing sound clips without BMI's permission are notified that a license is required. "While BMI says it will initially focus on commercial Web sites for licenses," wrote a *Wall Street Journal* reporter, "it also plans to target smaller sites in the future."[229]

Like BMI, trade groups such as the Association of American Publishers and the Recording Industry Association of America (RIAA) acted as an advance guard for the more general corporate effort to regiment the uses of information. Indeed, the RIAA succeeded in shutting down three Web sites and had plans to obtain court orders against hundreds of others to protect its members against so-called copyright infringement on the Web.[230] Its dedicated vigilance was triggered by awareness of a rapidly increasing threat. Customers can buy CDs from online record stores for delivery through the mails or, using new services such as the one that was introduced in September 1997 by AOL, obtain CD-quality audio computer files directly over the Net.[231]

The online ticket-selling service Ticketmaster likewise attempted to block users of a Microsoft Web site from linking freely (that is, clicking through) to its own site. Ticketmaster wanted Microsoft to pay it for the privilege of routing users to its service, on the theory that Microsoft's site otherwise would gain uncompensated value from its link to Ticketmaster's. Ticketmaster claimed that Microsoft had "wrongfully appropriated and misused Ticketmaster's name, trademarks, and Website."[232] At issue was that Microsoft's link cut through directly to a ticket-buying page—and bypassed Ticketmaster's own carefully sequenced prior content (several screens of Ticketmaster promotion and advertising). A Microsoft executive, Frank Schott, declared that the software giant was rising only to defend "free navigation and linking back and forth": "It's outrageous that they're trying to change the basic rules of the Web," he complained.[233] Was Microsoft, then, an information democrat? Hardly. Its own click-through service routed users to advertisements sold by Microsoft rather than by Ticketmaster.

Foretastes of what unregulated supranational flows of proprietary electronic commerce may entail were already apparent. The World Trade Organization ruled in 1997 that Canadian laws seeking to protect Canadian periodicals against competition from *Sports Illustrated* and other U.S. magazines violated the WTO's free-market global trading protocol. The U.S. Trade Representative, Charlene Barshefsky, praised the decison—which came as a response to a U.S. complaint—and peremptorily dispatched efforts to protect national cultures: "WTO rules prevent governments from using 'culture' as a pretense for discriminating against imports."[234] In fact, the foreign (read: U.S.) share of Canadian cultural markets stood at 95 percent for movies screened, 84 percent for musical recordings sold, 83 percent for magazines sold at newsstands, 70 percent for music played on radio stations, 70 percent for books sold, and 60 percent for English-language TV programming.[235] Canada ultimately gave ground in the dispute, although the United States remained officially dissatisfied.

Perhaps an even more significant instance of encroachment stemmed directly from the Internet's own runaway growth. Between 1981 and 1990, a French interactive computer system run by its PTO, France Telecom, became the largest public computer-service network in the world.[236] Using 6.5 million subsidized terminals called Minitels (at $10 a month), about 40 percent of the nonretired French population (or 20 percent of the overall population of 57.5 million) accessed the state-controlled network at home or at work, to make secure, online purchases worth billions of francs each year from some 25,000 vendors—banks, mail-order houses, travel agents, railroads, agricultural advice services, and others. Chat services abounded. Not insignificantly, 2 million subscribers to the system were domiciled in eleven other countries, mostly in Europe, though the system's dominant language was French. As recently as 1995, U.S. analysts counseled that the Minitel network compared favorably with the Internet: "Developers of tomorrow's information highways," they stressed, "might profitably peer toward . . . France."[237]

By the mid-1990s, however, Minitel traffic began to stagnate, while such service growth as there was stemmed mainly from users with PCs equipped to access Minitel services—PCs that, in an increasing number of cases, also were linked to the Internet. By mid-1997, the threat to France's system had grown obvious.[238] Declaring that "The Minitel . . . could end up hindering the development of new and promising applications of information technology," France's Socialist premier, Lionel Jospin, ordered that $244 million be spent to ready the nation for a full-scale embrace of the Internet. Otherwise, he reckoned, the growing technology gap between the Minitel and the state-of-the-art Internet system "could soon have dire repercussions on competitiveness and employment."[239] The eminently functional Minitel system thus had to give up pride of place before the Internet's success. Outrun and encircled, even France—one of the world's largest and most powerful economies—stepped back from independent network development on a national and, indeed, a more limited transnational scale.

The bellicose triumphalism of U.S. free-flow advocates, in this context, recalled the tone of their antecedents throughout the postwar Pax Americana. David Rothkopf, who served as Deputy Undersecretary of Commerce during the first Clinton administration, then became managing director of Kissinger Associates, the corporate consulting company run by the former Secretary of State. In an article entitled "In Praise of Cultural Imperialism?" Rothkopf left no doubt as to his own answer: "For the United States, a central objective of an Information Age foreign policy must be to win the battle of the world's information flows, dominating the airwaves as Great Britain once ruled the seas." The United States, he conceded, already dominates the "global traffic in information and ideas"—and this was a desirable outcome because "Americans should not deny the fact that of all the nations in the history of the world, theirs is the most just, the most tolerant, the most willing to constantly reassess and improve itself, and the best model for the future." Such language was not idiosyncratic. Robert Kagan, erstwhile coeditor of the conservative (Murdoch-financed) *Weekly Standard,* suggested in 1998 that "the truth is that the benevolent hegemony exercised by the United States is good for a vast portion of the world's population."[240] An opposing interpretation of U.S. behavior better caught the underlying reality. The United States, a critic observed, "demands to have its way in one international forum after another. It imperiously imposes trade sanctions that violate international understandings; presumptuously demands national legal protection for its citizens, diplomats, and soldiers who are subject to criminal prosecution, while insisting other states forego that right; and unilaterally dictates its view on UN reforms or the selection of a new secretary general."[241]

Within this context of U.S. unilateralism, moreover, the information and communication sector indisputably is assigned a privileged role. As Rothkopf relates,

it is in the economic and political interests of the United States to ensure that if the world is moving toward a common language, it be English; that if the world is moving toward common telecommunications, safety, and quality standards, they be American; that if the world is becoming linked by television, radio, and music, the programming be American.

At the end of the day, he insisted, "It could not be more strategically crucial that the United States do whatever is in its power to shape the development of [the global information] infrastructure, the rules governing it, and the information traversing it."[242] Having reached the nub of his argument, Rothkopf observed—accurately—that the United States "is the world's only information superpower."[243] The question was, how could U.S. leadership over "the infosphere" be preserved throughout this portentous historical moment?

Extending the Transnationals' Political-Economic Supremacy into the Next Century

Unprecedented telecommunications investments are being made. Small wonder, then, that—as we have seen—ownership of foreign *infrastructure* facilities (preeminently, but not only, in telecommunications) by U.S. corporate affiliates abroad began a steep climb.[244] The issue, Rothkopf related, was not simply how to garner the lion's share of these expenditures for U.S. companies. It was also, and even more profoundly, about establishing

the foundations of a system that will dictate decades of future choices about upgrades, systems standards, software purchases, and services. At the same time, new national and international laws will be written, and they will determine how smoothly information products and services may flow from one market to another.[245]

And, finally, Rothkopf couched the question that brings us back to the Internet: "Will steps be taken to ensure that Internet commerce remains truly free?"[246] Mainstream analysts were in broad agreement that those who hope to profit from new forms of online trade must offer principled opposition to any "external regulation designed to obstruct this flow."[247]

Concerning the Internet and, indeed, the encompassing digital capitalism that it served both to expedite and undergird, there thus existed a direct and massive interlock between the U.S. free-flow policy, U.S. corporate domination of global information markets, and the needs of transnationalizing capital—including, preeminently but far from solely, U.S. capital.

Companies headquartered in the United States already took in an estimated 62 percent of global information technology business, and that share was rising.[248] U.S. companies held fully 75 percent of global software markets and in this estimate claimed roughly the same share of the worldwide Internet economy.[249] Microsoft—more than half of whose annual software sales came from its subsidiaries in nearly sixty countries—targeted foreign markets for yet more intensive cultivation.[250] The last major European manufacturer of personal computers, giant Siemens of Germany, announced it would withdraw from this market early in 1998.[251] Following Fujitsu, NEC (Japan's largest PC maker) conceded defeat in its fight to maintain a proprietary PC system in its own home market and decided instead to sell machines built to Wintel standards. (NEC's market share in Japan had slid from as much as 70 percent to 35 to 40 percent.) "A similar pattern has been seen in telecommunications," wrote two *Financial Times* analysts, where in everything from advanced television systems to cellular telephony, Japanese companies have lost out to U.S. (and in some cases to European) rivals.[252] Significantly behind the United States (and even the United Kingdom) in shifting terrestrial TV broadcasting to a digital format, for example, Japanese authorities raced to accelerate the latter's domestic launch, hoping thereby not to lose out in supplying markets for a wide range of projected new services.[253] David Moschella provided a tart conclusion, even before the Asian financial firestorm confirmed it:

One of the paradoxes of our time is that it is often said that the twenty-first century will be dominated by Asia. But the twenty-first century is also called the "Information Age." Given the wide gap between U.S. and Asian information usage, it is difficult to see how both of these statements can be true.[254]

U.S. state agencies' overall effort was to interconnect the interests of U.S. information technology companies with those of transnational business, so as to advance both. This involved a dual strategy. On one side, U.S. policymakers hastened to unleash the U.S. vendors that already largely dominated global information technology systems and services from constraints that obstructed further market advances. On the other side, they attempted to free transnational capital to the maximum possible degree to bid for U.S. companies' business.

To a spectacular extent, the effort worked—both in telecommunications, as we have seen, and beyond. In the seemingly unrelated area of financial services, for example, during the 1970s the United States undertook to liberalize its own domestic banking system and financial markets. Long-standing legislative walls protecting banks, securities firms, and life insurers from competition with one another were torn down. Unrestrained rivalry produced both a series of market failures and a spate of consolidated financial services conglomerates. It also engendered a slew of specialized products reliant on sophisticated new technology. Only the giant, integrated companies could afford the advertising needed to build financial brands, and only they could pay for the information technology systems on which the new service offerings relied; the top ten banks in the United States today spend an average of more than $1 billion each year on technology.[255] Growth of financial conglomerates making use of advanced information technology to provide their customers with access to these new services in turn generated increasing pressure to roll out parallel offerings elsewhere around the world. As other countries moved to emulate the liberalized U.S. financial services market, U.S. information technology firms (even if not always U.S. banks) gained additional market leverage.

Japan's banks', insurers', and securities firms' "unprecedented rush to computerization," playing catchup with the U.S. deregulatory trend, was expected to result in spending of $11.3 billion on computer systems in 1997, with individual leading companies likely to spend as much as $1 billion each. "These financial titans are turning to U.S. technology," the *Wall Street Journal* explained, "because Japanese computer companies don't have the financial services technologies, or the experience in setting up networks, that American companies have honed in the free-for-all U.S. market." U.S. exports of computer software to Japan grew by more than one-third in 1996 and were likely to grow by another one-third in 1997, to $7.5 billion. United States–based systems integrators and specialized computer network consultants likewise looked to Japan's deregulated financial services markets—especially after bank failures there permitted them to snap up Japanese financial service companies at bargain-basement prices—for newfound market growth.[256]

Crucially, however, when considered at longer range, the ultimate beneficiaries of U.S. policy and, in particular, of the free-flow doctrine, were no longer solely U.S. interests. Between 1957 and 1966, the value of U.S. direct foreign investment (in constant 1957 dollars) doubled from $25.4 billion to $54.8 billion.[257] United States–based companies in turn then accounted for the great preponderance of overall direct foreign investment. Between 1980 and 1995, however, even as the value of such investment continued to surge (from about $514 billion to $2.73 trillion), its composition changed dramatically. Although more than tripling in value (to $705.6 billion), the U.S. proportionate share of the total declined from 42.9 percent to 25.8 percent. Concurrently, French companies increased their direct foreign investment from $23.6 billion to $200.9 billion; German corporations, from $43.1 billion to $235 billion; British companies, from $80.4 billion to $319 billion; and Japanese companies, from $18.8 billion to $305.5 billion.[258] Between 1980 and 1994, furthermore, the ratio of corporate foreign direct investment to gross domestic investment doubled (to something less than 4 percent), meaning that the economic significance of transnational capital underwent a secular increase.[259]

Although the United States remained the paramount source of transnational corporate investment, in short, virtually everywhere, big capital likewise overspilled domestic borders. Symptomatic was that

- By one ranking, U.S. companies in 1997 accounted for only fifty-seven of the world's top 100 companies, ranked by market value;[260]
- Especially since 1987, when the United States became a debtor nation, foreign owners rapidly increased their property holdings *inside* the United States: British and Japanese interests each account today for well over $100 billion worth of factories, plant, office buildings, and other productive investment in the United States;[261] and
- The United States information sector *itself* fell prey to further transnationalization: French and German owners hold a 20 percent interest in Sprint, the third-largest U.S. telecommunications operator, and non-U.S.-based corporations own half of the six major Hollywood film studios, several leading record company distributors, and a substantial sprinkling of book and periodical publishers.[262]

So times have changed and with them the import of the free-flow doctrine. As a senior fellow at the Council on Foreign Relations soberly notes, "The fears raised prematurely in the 1970s that multinational business would erode national sovereignty are far more strongly grounded today."[263] No matter how revanchiste or opportunistic their individual intentions may be, in the context of a transnationalized digital capitalism, the architects of free-flow policies necessarily advance an ethos fit for transnational business per se. United States–based businesses comprise only its largest class of beneficiaries. Wherever their headquarters may be located, these megacorporations share a common need for comprehensive cross-border exchanges of computer data, telephone calls, images and video streams. *That* need is ultimately what the free-flow doctrine works to sustain.

This critical point was readily apparent in the recommendations on the Internet promulgated by the Global Internet Project (GIP), a group of fifteen CEOs and senior executives of U.S., British, German, and Japanese software and telecommunications companies. Chaired by John Gerdelman of MCI, the group urged governments to "resist the temptation of superimposing on the new digital world regulatory frameworks that existed during the industry era." In particular, GIP sought to prevent key segments of the high-technology industry from being regulated for the first time and recommended positioning the Internet "in the vanguard of the deregulatory trend."[264] During 1997 and 1998, policies that emphasized market-led development of electronic commerce were declared as formal state commitments—not only by the United States but also by the European Union and by Japan's Ministry for Trade and Industry.[265] Japan not only endorsed the concept of unregulated, tax-free electronic commerce but also—probably for tactical reasons—joined the United States in opposing stricter European Union privacy regulations slated to come into effect in late 1998.[266]

Even where governments did not actively affirm the principle of market-led development, they could be made to back away from regulating or restricting the Net out of fear that, if they did, home-based companies would be "left behind."[267] (Think back, for example, to France's recent turn to embrace the Internet.) Continued access to the United States' gigantic domestic market—which, as we saw, led the corporate charge into electronic commerce—functioned as a reliable carrot for companies that could no longer find adequate room to grow within their own home markets. Unless such companies kept pace with the U.S. market leaders in innovating new forms of electronic commerce, they feared that they would soon find themselves at a profound competitive disadvantage.

A prominent economist and one-time policy advisor to the director general of the World Trade Organization's organizational ancestor put these points with impressive clarity. "The most potent force for the world-wide freeing of trade," wrote Jagdish Bhagwati,

is unilateral U.S. action. . . . Such ultramodern industries as telecommunications and financial services gained their momentum largely from unilateral openness and deregulation in the U.S. This in turn has led to a softening of protectionist attitudes in the European Union and Japan.

These developed economies are now moving steadily in the direction of openness and competition—not because any officials in Washington threaten them with retribution, but because they've seen how U.S. companies become much more competitive once regulation and other trade barriers have fallen. . . . Faced with the prospect of being elbowed out of world markets by American firms, Japan and Europe have no option but to follow the U.S. example, belatedly but surely, in opening their own markets.[268]

Depending on the circumstances, government regulation of networks may—or may not—symptomatize an authoritarian temptation. Universal telephone service, for example, is unthinkable absent the cross-subsidies that regulators once worked to stabilize. The *absence* of such regulation, in contrast, today virtually guarantees that business will fix the social purposes and policies of the medium. In this, the critical formative period of Internet's institutionalization, the system's stewards are insisting on carte blanche to direct its future development as they see fit. What may we expect of this reorientation?

"Almost every aspect of daily life," declares the U.S. "Framework for Global Electronic Commerce," stands to be affected: "education, health care, work and leisure activities."[269] Across this vast range, the prospect is for the primacy of intracorporate, business-to-business, and business-to-consumer network applications. (The consumer computing market (inclusive of PCs, modems, software, online services, and such) comprises but a fraction of the worldwide information-processing market—an estimated 7 percent of the $530 billion spent during 1995; three years later, business-to-business selling continued to outstrip other forms of electronic commerce by a wide margin.)[270]

Vital though they are, it is not simply conventional forms of cultural expression that are up for grabs. The "Framework for Global Electronic Commerce" leaves little doubt that U.S. policymakers have targeted a far larger market spectrum:

World trade involving computer software, entertainment products (motion pictures, videos, games, sound recordings), information services (databases, online newspapers), technical information, product licenses, financial services, and professional services (businesses and technical consulting, accounting, architectural design, legal advice, travel services, etc.) has grown rapidly in the past decade, now accounting for well over $40 billion of U.S. exports alone.[271]

In truth, U.S. surpluses of exported over imported computer services and of sales of computer services by affiliates of transnational corporations were already surging. The growth of these strategically vital "exports" testified eloquently that, as they migrated onto networks, proliferating business services, such as computer consulting, architecture, engineering, management advising, and advertising, were indeed becoming "tradable."[272] Capacious networks, able to support an unprecedented range of new applications by merging voices, images and data, were being deployed to expedite and enlarge these new markets. Capital's stewardship of the Net, taking the form of multilateral support for cyberspace as a stateless jurisdiction, works to ensure that the market development process will only deepen and broaden its incursions on national sovereignty.[273]

This process of market development via networks bears down on both existing services and, by way of an even more radical economic transformation, also on activities long sheltered from any direct profit-and-loss calculus. Unevenly and sometimes laboriously, that is, the frontiers of accumulation themselves are being steadfastly rolled back in a process that economist Edward S. Herman calls "the deepening of the market."[274]

In the remainder of this book we travel to some of these frontiers. In chapter 3 we examine the erection of a new consumer medium, in the form of the World Wide Web. Then in chapter 4, we turn to an equally charged social domain, education. Both chapters attempt to trace the profound social and institutional changes that are being forged as the outposts of digital capitalism advance.

3

Brought to You by . . .

Cyberspace comprises an enormous construction site on which a great variety of political-economic projects are underway. One of the most ambitious is the erection of a new consumer medium. Already, by using the World Wide Web, television viewers may add to their knowledge of favorite shows, sports enthusiasts may lay claim to the latest game statistics, readers of women's service magazines may find supplemental features, news hounds may follow breaking stories, and film buffs may gain access to movie reviews and celebrity interviews. The drive to tie the Internet to the existing media system is thus already far advanced.

Why is this convergence taking place? Who are its chief sponsors and beneficiaries? What does the Internet's growing interaction with the established media entail for the structure and function of cyberspace? How, finally, is the Internet's metamorphosis impinging on the greater mediascape? What distinctive features does the Web add to the panoply of existing media services? These are the issues with which we grapple in chapter 3.

Spinning the Web

The first task must be to inquire: How did a system that was created chiefly for use by universities, government agencies, and large corporations come to claim a place on the mediascape? What forces pushed or pulled the Internet in the direction of consumer media services? I engage this question first of all by situating the Internet's development within the cycles of wrenching change that have episodically gripped the computer industry.

The Computer Industry Converges on the Internet

Between around 1980 and the mid-1990s, the center of gravity of the computer industry shifted from large mainframe machines to desktop personal computers. This quantum jump testified to unrelenting price and performance improvement summarized and celebrated by Moore's Law. Moore's Law holds that, as a result of continuing improvements in the design and fabrication of semiconductors, the price of a given level of computer processing power will halve about every eighteen months.[1] A frenetically expansive PC market correspondingly tore through the economic fabric of the computer industry.

With its 65 percent market share, IBM had dominated the global market for mainframes. Seemingly moving from strength to strength, IBM proceeded during the early 1980s to grab 70 percent of the PC market. "Big Blue," as the company was often called, appeared poised to seize control of the industry's next evolutionary stage. But the giant computer company made what turned out to be a dire miscalculation. It farmed out to independent supplier companies two vital PC components—microprocessors and operating system software. Microprocessors comprise the critical hardware inside PCs and dictate the fundamental parameters of PC performance; they are closely aligned with the equally indispensable operating system software that tells PCs how to process streams of data. "Without control of the critical component technologies," explains one analyst, "IBM's high cost structure, slow time-to-market, and paralyzing bureaucratic in-fighting would soon make it extremely vulnerable to direct and open competition."[2] Within a few years, IBM lost pride of place to a pair of outsourcers—Intel and Microsoft—which had realized that they could leverage their hold over IBM-compatible chips and software to boost their own fortunes. The maker of the only significant rival operating system, Apple Computer, contributed significantly to this result. Convinced of the superiority of its own proprietary technology, Apple refused to license its system software to outside developers—and thereby rapidly ceded market share to IBM-format PCs. Intel became the supplier of some 85 percent of the microprocessors utilized in PCs. Written to be run on Intel chips, Microsoft's operating system software—Windows—told nine-tenths of the world's base of installed PCs how to go about their business.

The rise to dominance of these two PC-era giants, often referred to jointly as *Wintel,* rested on a loosely shared strategy. By inflaming demand for increasingly *bit-intensive* software applications, continual hardware upgrades also could be justified. PCs needed ever-growing capabilities—greater processing power, more memory, add-ons such as CD-ROM drives—to drive the market for ever more powerful microprocessors. Sales of the most profitable high-end chips, in turn, depended on ever-expanding software functionality: word processors, dictionaries, thesauruses. Packed anew each season with an expanded array of features, stand-alone PCs could be kept above a fixed price floor. "PC buyers kept paying $2,000 or so for systems despite rapid declines in the price of computing power, opting for machines with the latest processing and data-storage capability."[3] Relying on a barrage of brand advertising for a product that most consumers don't understand, Intel managed to lift the total semiconductor content per PC from $300 in 1991 to $610 in early 1997—with the lion's share of that premium coming to it.[4] Its top-of-the-line Pentium II 266 megahertz chip for portables was priced at $637 in May 1998.[5]

For over a decade, the Wintel alliance therefore held Moore's Law at bay. As its axis extended and as ever-more-powerful PCs broadened the range of desktop applications, the entire PC industry could be seen as little more than "a value-added reseller for Intel and Microsoft." And why not, when the two companies together took in about half of the personal-computer industry's total profits?[6] Wintel's earnings comprised the envy of modern industry and, with successive turns of the annual product cycle, Microsoft and Intel transformed themselves into global corporate powerhouses.

Yet it also became plain enough that, even in the wealthy U.S. market, computers priced at $2,000-plus could be absorbed only by a minority of households. The U.S. home PC market stalled out at around 37 percent of U.S. households during the mid-1990s, up a bare 2 percent in 1996 over 1995.[7] There was, to be sure, a brisk trade in portable or notebook models, replacement machines, and niche markets, such as PCs for three-to seven-year-olds. And while Asian PC sales cratered in the wake of the economic crisis there, European markets—fewer than one-quarter of European households possessed PCs by 1998—remained active.[8]

Nonetheless, it was difficult to avoid a stark realization: "the PC industry, having already stuck a computer in every office and in the easiest 40 percent of American homes, needs new customers." Technology analysts quickly clustered around a new consensus: "The PC has become a mature product."[9]

The prospective saturation of the market for $2,000 home PCs prompted a question that is faced, sooner or later, by all big businesses: What steps can be taken to renew the prospect of profitable growth? What strategic market openings exist?

This question assumed a jarring urgency for the PC industry. Over-capacity in the supply of at least some kinds of semiconductors (such as D-Ram chips) contributed, as did slackening Asian demand in the wake of the economic crisis there. But the shock was triggered by upstart manufacturers—Dell Computer, Gateway 2000, and Micron—that had devised means of paring PC production and distribution costs. Existing producers thus were placed under fierce price pressure.[10] Manufacturers such as AST Research and market leader Compaq responded with an alternative pricing strategy and deliberately crashed through the standard PC price floor. Unveiling cheap, low-profit systems that could handle most computing needs, they tapped a powerful demand for the new machines during 1997 and 1998.

These "sub-$1,000" PCs took between one-quarter and two-fifths of the overall U.S. home computer market in 1997 and 45 percent during the first quarter of 1998. Rather than merely cannibalizing sales of high-end systems, moreover, the sub-$1,000 models also drew many first-time buyers. Perhaps as many as a third of all sub-$1,000 sales were to people who had never purchased a PC.[11] PC penetration in turn began to climb again; at $27,000, the median income of people hoping to buy sub-$1,000 models, was nearly half that for those who already owned a PC ($50,000).[12] Portentously, world PC sales (estimated at 82 million in 1997) began to close in on sales of color TV sets (119.4 million).[13]

The dropoff in PC prices harbored significant ramifications for the industry. Market leader Compaq's average selling price in stores dropped from $1,722 in December 1996 to $1,227 in August 1997, and the company saw its U.S. retail market share jump substantially. (Overall, the average retail price of PCs dropped 30 percent over the space of a single year to an estimated $1,169 by January 1998.)[14] Slower to bring sub-$1,000s to market, in contrast, IBM lost hundreds of millions of dollars—as well as market share—before successfully reorganizing to supply the new market.[15] Nor was this the only change. As PC manufacturers scrambled to purchase low-cost microprocessors and other cheap components to embed in their new sub-$1,000 models, Intel's traditionally hard-pressed rivals found sudden room to expand. Chip producers National Semiconductor and Advanced Micro Devices aimed low-cost, high-performance microprocessors at the sub-$1,000 market—and took a 23 percent share of it by early 1998. The top four PC manufacturers—Compaq, IBM, Hewlett Packard, and Dell—emerged from the fray strengthened, claiming an enlarged share of worldwide PC shipments. However, smaller producers, notably Packard Bell–NEC, countered by redefining the low-end of the PC market as a mass-market, $500 machine.[16]

The average price of microprocessors was stagnating, while the cost of state-of-the-art chip manufacturing facilities continued to escalate. With its high profit margins based on an estimated average selling price per chip of around $200, industry leader Intel faced rivals like Advanced Micro Devices—which claimed it could make money with an average selling price of only $100 a chip.[17] Intel in turn cast about for means with which to sidestep market stagnation, on one side, and to intensify price competition, on the other.[18] Fellow titan Microsoft likewise recognized that the path to growth lay in market diversification. While belatedly pursuing the new low-cost PC market (then-CEO Andrew Grove boasted that he had 650 engineers working on sub-$1,000 model products early in 1998),[19] Intel—like Microsoft—did not alter its commitment to high-end, high-profit PC applications.[20] Instead, Intel tried to kickstart a series of new microprocessor applications to relieve its dependence on PCs—which took some three-fifths of the semiconductor industry's annual output. Microsoft, similarly, sought to identify additional sites at which its operating system software might find use. There was scant reason to think that these diversification efforts would necessarily require or, indeed, even allow, the sort of alliance that Wintel had built up around personal computers.

Efforts to embed chips and software in new places brought the prime movers of the computer industry into interaction with a great range of consumer markets, from automobiles and home appliances to children's toys.[21] Concurrently, both companies sought to cultivate widespread brand awareness, which could be brought to bear on whatever consumer market ventures seemed promising. Increased reliance on big-money television advertising followed predictably. Presiding over this strategic move in Microsoft's case was a talented executive, Robert Herbold. Herbold—who is discussed more below—had previously been head of advertising and information services at Procter & Gamble, a diversified consumer products manufacturer that was also the world's largest advertiser.

Intel's plunge into new ventures centered on stimulating emergent multimedia services and programming tools. An early initiative involved a summer 1996 partnership with General Electric's TV network, NBC, for example, to create a system that allowed computers equipped with Intel's high-end microchips to receive video and audio signals. Applications and software tools intended to help programmers create digital content for PCs and related home "information appliances" were also unfurled. Intel's diversification strategy was far-reaching. Over a five-year period, its market-development projects called forth three-quarters of a billion dollars worth of investments in no fewer than 100 companies.[22] Between 1995 and 1997, similarly, Microsoft invested several billion dollars in fifty-odd partnerships and acquisitions.[23]

At the epicenter of this diversification strategy lay a medium whose sudden arrival startled even Microsoft and Intel. After a quarter of a century of prior development, during 1994 and 1995 the Internet erupted into the daily lives of millions of people. The Net presented vast market opportunities but likewise posed multifaceted and unpredictable challenges to the PC industry.

The explosive arrival of the Internet is typically associated with the growth of the World Wide Web, which made a large and growing share of Internet resources easily accessible. The Web's ascendancy in turn is associated with what began as a fledgling company called Netscape. Netscape successfully commercialized a tool, called a *Web browser,* which organized, simplified, and helped to expand the functions of Web access.

Staking its prospects on future markets, Netscape offered its browser to most individual end-users for free. The company made money by licensing its browser, as well as other software, to corporations.

This romance of entrepreneurship is often overdrawn. Behind Netscape lay *venture capitalists* (VCs) who sought to use their resources to reconstitute the Net's frequently unruly technical imagination on behalf of investors. These VCs, who typically demand ownership of four-fifths of a company's equity before they will sell stock shares through an initial public offering, pumped a considerable $1.8 billion into U.S. information technology companies in 1992, but this figure ballooned to $7.1 billion by 1997.[24] A handful of firms dominated the business, including Montgomery Securities, Robertson Stephens, and Hambrecht & Quist—companies (two of which were being digested by diversified financial services companies Merrill Lynch and BankBoston) whose principals were the true movers and shakers, working behind the scenes to organize fledgling Internet markets.

Netscape comprised their most successful early vehicle and rapidly acquired a near-monopoly over the browser function that was needed to channel novices onto the Web. The prairie-fire spread of Netscape's Navigator browser gave the Internet a sudden competitive edge over established proprietary online services—which had dominated the use of computer networking by individuals. Although by 1995 there were twenty-three national online service providers in the United States, in one estimate, the big three—America Online, H&R Block's CompuServe, and the IBM/Sears joint-venture Prodigy—claimed the lion's share of the business, collectively serving millions of paying customers. Signing up thousands of content providers—CompuServe had amassed about 3,000, ranging from United Airlines to most of the major computer software and hardware companies—the proprietary online services comprised middlemen who imposed substantial markups and who were also in a position to turn back to cooperating information providers only a fraction of the money that they collected from subscribers.[25] CompuServe had the most ample international coverage, especially in Europe; but a push by America Online, in concert with the German companies Springer, Telekom, and Bertelsmann, granted it an expanded territorial reach.

By 1995, however, in no small part owing to Netscape's browser, substantially more people (in one estimate, 5.8 million U.S. adults) were connected directly to the Internet than to the commercial online services alone (3.9 million).[26] Some companies were even bundling basic Internet service as a giveaway with long-distance service or specialized software programs.[27] Microsoft chose this inauspicious moment to introduce a rival proprietary online service, the Microsoft Network (MSN)—which by mid-1998 still had not identified a successful growth strategy or moved into profitability (the unit was losing an estimated $200 million a year).[28] MSN's travails were symptomatic of how the propulsive shift toward Internet access momentarily broke the effectiveness of the "middleman" strategy of the commercial online service vendors.

These proprietary outfits, which had imposed substantial hourly interconnect charges and other fees, scrambled to reposition themselves. As millions of new users began to flock to the Web's more comprehensive information resources, the commercial online services were forced to offer themselves as easy gateways to the Internet. They also provided email services and introduced low, flat-rate monthly charges. MSN and America Online sought to reincarnate themselves as media companies, creating original content for delivery over the Web. By 1997, Microsoft had spent an estimated $200 million developing such programming, while America Online had invested in or created about fifty online properties.[29] America Online looked for subscribers wherever it could find them: both through acquisitions and via a nonstop marketing blitz that ensured that the free software needed to sign up for its service got into millions of households. By mid-1998, AOL was garnering $2.8 billion in revenue on an annualized basis, enjoyed a stock-market valuation in excess of $20 billion, and claimed 15 million subscribers (compared with MSN's 3 million). Of the erstwhile proprietary services, only AOL had indisputably prospered in the Internet environment; in addition to its proprietary content, it had come to comprise a central hub—or *portal*—for a wide range of Internet services. Its acquisition of Netscape for $4.3 billion only confirmed AOL's status as Microsoft's chief rival on the Internet.[30]

The competitive threat posed by the Internet was multifaceted, however, and effectively carried across the greater communication and computer industry.

The Communication Industry Converges on the Internet

Media history teaches that control over distribution often creates a vital avenue to market power. During the late nineteenth and early twentieth centuries, as networking channels were created and commandeered—through the Associated Press news agency hook-up with Western Union,[31] and the fledgling NBC and CBS radio networks' preferential access to AT&T's long-distance lines[32]—the power to exclude would-be competitors was enhanced. Conversely, during the last thirty years, as distribution pathways built around geostationary satellites, cable television systems, and even prosaic video rental outlets were successively thrown open, a global scramble for control of the newly proliferating pipelines got underway. As a result of its rapidly increasing *functionality* (as computer jocks call it), the Internet unexpectedly crosscut—and climaxed—this ongoing trend.

Formerly differentiated distribution systems—newspapers distributed at newsstands and by cars and trucks to homes, magazines sent through the mails, radio and television signals transmitted over the air (via electromagnetic radiation) to receiving sets—are being merged onto the Internet's common technical platform. Kodak and AOL have already teamed up to offer a network service for distributing digitized snapshots developed by 30,000 retail processors direct to home subscribers. Electronic video systems for distributed digitized films to thousands of cinemas are also in development.[33] Radio and recording industry executives met to discuss the Internet's growing threat to radio's status as the music industry's preeminent promotional vehicle.[34] By year-end 1997, Amazon.com—the largest online bookseller—claimed 2.26 million customer accounts.[35] Music retailers expected to sell $110 million worth of recordings worldwide during 1998.[36] During its first month of online selling, November 1996, Ticketmaster sold 5,000 tickets; in November 1997, it sold 120,000 (for $4.5 million).[37]

Although these numbers comprised a small fraction of overall book, recording, and ticket sales, they were portents of real change. Overall, online buying in the Web's virtual mall was expected to double from 1997 to 1998, hitting nearly $5 billion in the latter year.[38] As the Net's functionality as a distribution system was enhanced and enlarged, existing product pipelines were placed at risk, and the balance of power between manufacturers and distributors was destabilized.[39] Media companies had to vie for "shelf space" on the new medium, however, without crippling their existing distribution systems: were the Internet to comprise nothing more than a new channel for familiar media products such as the *New York Times* or *Seinfeld,* it would still critically disrupt established industry structures.

But, of course, it *will* be more—much more—as Web product development already makes plain. Once again, formerly discrete media products and program forms are converging on a single multipurpose platform. How, in this emerging common context, will formerly disparate media products retain their discrete revenue streams? A precursor of what is in store comes with the news that local television stations have adapted their Web sites to seize a portion of the $15 billion annual market for U.S. classified advertising that has long been claimed by newspapers. In New York, Boston, San Francisco, and seven other top urban markets, CBS will try to get viewers to log on to view real-estate ads, help-wanted listings, and other classifieds. The CBS vice president who is coordinating Internet efforts for company-owned affiliates declares, "Now we can compete toe-to-toe with the print world."[40] Granite Broadcasting, a station group, already lists classified advertisements at its stations' Web sites. The competition for classified advertising is actually already broader than this, as Microsoft's Sidewalk and other local-information and entertainment sites mushroom up. And newspapers also have responded with their own Internet services, such as CareerPath.com, which offers an online employment listing.

How, we may even ask, in the newly shared milieu of cyberspace, will familiar media retain their identities? Newspapers are ink on woodpulp-based paper; radio is sounds attached to electromagnetic radiation; movies are images and sound on celluloid: but these differences are created *outside* cyberspace and can only be *indexed* (or referred to) on and through the Web. On the Internet, in contrast, a lengthening series of once-discrete media businesses are being placed in head-on competition as Web designers cast new multimedia genres out of digitized images, print, audio, and video. While conventional media are hardly about to be supplanted en masse, the Internet will play host increasingly both to the migration of familiar programming and to the development of novel program forms. Today's "content creators," as David Moschella relates, "face heightened competition from other content providers that previously relied on different media; they will also face competition from entirely new providers of all shapes and sizes."[41]

The Web platform in this sense comprises a venue that is perfectly matched to the diversified entertainment conglomerates that have been assembled during the past fifteen years. In a cascade of huge mergers and acquisitions, multibillion dollar media properties—film studios, broadcast networks, program packagers, cable systems, satellite channels—changed hands like marbles. Such vertically integrated megamedia as Time-Warner, Disney, and News Corporation were created to fulfill the strategic goal of cross-promotion and cross-media program development. In their search for profit maximization, these powerhouse firms typically try to design and move program products across individual media boundaries.[42] Interleaving new Webcast forms into their established mix is thus second nature for them.

Engaging the Internet thus nevertheless poses a dual challenge to these vertically integrated giants. As content providers, they must be concerned to keep their program product in front of audiences that may be gravitating away from established venues but to avoid cannibalizing their existing operations. As owners of distribution pipelines, they have to defend against depredations by rivals to ensure that they, rather than a competitor, continue to dominate the available channels—including the Internet.

Big media companies thus have little choice but to spring into action. Newspaper chains, already sensitized for a generation to the threat posed to their classified local advertising by computerized automotive and other listings, therefore quickly staked out a place on the Web.[43] By 1998, more than 2,700 newspapers around the world had online businesses (over 60 percent were based in the United States). But newspapers were hardly unique. Forty-seven of the top fifty U.S. magazines (by paid circulation) had also created Web sites, alongside some 800 U.S. broadcast TV stations, at least 151 U.S. cable channels,[44] and hundreds of radio stations, offering live sports as well as music channels to upwards of ten million desktops. In May 1998, an estimated 30,000 Web pages were transmitting (*streaming*) video; ABCNews.com was often the first place where ABC video news footage was seen.[45] Fox News also transmitted video programs on the Web, as did C-Span, CNN, Bloomberg News, and Trinity Broadcasting, the leading "Christian network."[46] Disney/ABC purchased Starwave, a Web-design company, to integrate content across ten sites that drew 2 million visitors each day; CBS made an estimated $100 million investment in SportsLine, a popular Web site.[47] Already by mid-1998, noted one analyst, the Internet boasted more audio and video content than the biggest established broadcaster.[48] Apparent, in addition, were Webcasting spinoffs of well-known television programs and services that added complementary services to these established franchises. These *brand extensions* of existing properties aimed to enhance viewer loyalty for TV shows or to merchandise products that could be connected with them. Less familiar services, evolving forms of *original content* produced specifically for the Web, were likewise evident, including, most notably, free-standing Web media businesses like Yahoo! and GeoCities (of which more below).

Analogous challenges faced consumer electronics manufacturers. Even giants like Sony, Mitsubishi, Toshiba, and Philips were concerned that an incipient market for appliances with which to gain access to Internet services would have a dramatic impact on existing markets for standalone machines: television sets, VCRs, CD players, and video game consoles, as well as PCs. As we will see, the circuitry built into or atop TVs and PCs—TVs that could stand in as Internet terminals and PCs that could accept television signals—comprised the most fiercely sought of these prospective market extensions.

Great prizes also lay in defining and developing the software that would run successive generations of Internet services and appliances.[49] Functions previously performed in and by stand-alone PCs now might be embedded elsewhere on the Internet. Software needed to perform a particular application, for example, could be stored across the Net on a remote computer, to be sought and downloaded only when and as needed. Computer content and programming services, previously incarnated as proprietary online services and as CD-ROMs, were also up for grabs. Although the so-called *network computer,* a cheap desktop machine lacking disk drives and relying on remote host computers for software, became an apparent casualty of the sub-$1,000 trend,[50] a growing reliance on network-embedded software resources was indisputable. As

David C. Moschella explains, the entire information industry's center of gravity might

shift away from the PC and out toward the network. In this manner, technology development can still proceed freely but without constantly destabilizing the individual desktop environment. Perhaps more important, like the telephone and television, the PC itself will become increasingly subordinate to higher-value network services.[51]

On the other hand, of course, if the Net could be coopted for this purpose, the PC's privileged position—with three hundred million in use worldwide, it enjoyed unchallenged initial supremacy as a means of accessing the Net—instead might be reinforced. Whatever else it might be or become, the PC remained the primary window onto the Internet. Might opportunities on and around the Internet be exploited to bolster the PC industry's search for new applications?

Corporate telecommunications behemoths, which had been freed by Congress to enter new markets and which faced a supply glut of their own in the market for plain old telephone service, also stirred at the prospect of gaining high-growth data-service markets (as we saw in chapter 1). Likewise in contention were nascent brokering and transactional services, like banking and ticketing; home appliance markets, as refrigerators, stoves, security systems, washing machines and toasters were endowed with signaling capabilities; electronic media commerce, beginning with book and record retailing and spreading outward from there; and—again—the host of Net-friendly software and hardware products that would be needed to build out each of these new industries.

Competing market visions thus began to dance through Silicon Valley, Los Angeles, New York, Redmond, Houston, and other enclaves. In prospect was an epic contest, as both individual companies and whole industries commenced to jockey on what suddenly appeared to comprise shared turf. Through their strivings, on this sprawling and untidy landscape, an Internet consumer medium was born.

The Battle for Position

To stay in front of a rushing tidal wave of Internet market development, PC industry leaders had to make bold moves. Outgoing Intel CEO Andrew Grove declared that, no matter which vectors of development drove the information industry, "Our job is to make sure that whatever happens ends up on some version of the Pentium platform."[52] Intel continued to pursue its ongoing multimedia strategy, notably by aligning itself with sectors of the U.S. broadcast television industry.[53] The company, actively developing technologies for speedier Internet access to Web graphics and home computer networks, continued to place its strategic focus on how to convey multimedia digital content—data and video—to whatever kind of screen a user preferred: PC or television.[54]

Microsoft underwent a more convulsive conversion experience, in December 1995. The software giant's general endeavor, as we saw, already stressed expansion of the market for information appliances that would utilize its software. Now its management sharply refocused the company's endeavor on the Internet and, in particular, on the Web. Product development was reconfigured, and the company's strategic orientation shifted.

Microsoft's move onto the Net drew on some potent corporate assets. If it initially "infuriated . . . Microsoft that the Internet was free," as journalist Ken Auletta has observed,[55] then the software giant rapidly realized that it possessed useful means of coopting the Net so as to sustain the PC's traditional preeminence and, concurrently, Microsoft's own market dominance. When Microsoft brought out its own Web browser, dubbed Internet Explorer (IE), during the summer of 1995, the effort piggybacked atop its Windows 95 software—introduced at the same time and with the support of an unprecedented global promotion. Microsoft insisted, apparently by threatening to withdraw licenses for its blockbuster Windows 95 program, that PC manufacturers bundle IE rather than competing browsers (read Netscape's Navigator) into the software they shipped to run each of the tens of millions of PCs they sold each year.[56] As Microsoft secured agreements with major PC makers, including both IBM and Apple as well as market leader Compaq, it successfully leveraged its installed base of PC operating systems into a formidable Internet presence. Netscape's Navigator quickly lost market share, while Microsoft had captured upward of 40 percent of all commercial Web browsers in use as of mid-1998.[57] Protested by Netscape, Compaq (which apparently had sought to roll out its own rival browser), and other companies, by fall 1997 Microsoft's hardball tactics prompted a review by the U.S. Department of Justice. In May 1998 a full-scale antitrust proceeding was launched against the company.[58]

As the suit again demonstrated, activities performed on stand-alone PCs were indeed blurring into those that relied on network resources. Netscape and Microsoft vied with one another to roll out rival software with which users could integrate local and network functions. In fall 1997 and in summer 1998, for example, Microsoft released updates of its browser and operating system, respectively, which afforded users a comprehensive view of files stored on their hard drives, email, and preselected *channels* pushing Web content to individuals' desktops.[59]

The arrangements that gave rise to these channels constituted a sensitive area of negotiation in their own right. Seeking to enlarge its Internet audience, Microsoft struck deals with two dozen-odd major media partners, such as Disney, Time-Warner, and Dow Jones, to showcase their online offerings via packages of entertainment, business, news, sports, and lifestyle channels. Legislators and antitrust officials sought to learn whether Microsoft had used its market power over the PC operating system and the IE browser to extract exclusive or preferential concessions in these deals.[60] Thus the browser war comprised only one touchstone of the widening antitrust case against Microsoft, just as it also constituted but a single element in Microsoft's multifaceted response to the Internet.

Microsoft's own experiments with media content provision, however, met with indifferent success. Its Webzine, *Slate,* launched in June 1996, claimed 150,000 readers a month by early 1998—but that figure would plummet after the company began to charge $19.95 a year for the service (which hitherto had been offered for free). *Slate* was losing an estimated $4 million annually before the new fees were introduced.[61] An online travel magazine called *Mungo Park* was summarily shut down. No less chequered was Microsoft's experience in a joint venture with General Electric to provide news over the Web and, concurrently, via cable TV. By summer 1997, this MSNBC network, despite reaching a scant 100,000 households, was widely cited as a successful business. But what kind of business was it? Hyped as the first instance of a successful merger of television and the PC, which would meld cable and Web programming, MSNBC actually succeeded essentially as a cable-broadcast TV hybrid. The new service, cross-promoted effectively on GE's NBC broadcast network and absorbing an estimated $80 million in annual expenditures by its parent companies, claimed its viewers' average annual income exceeded $90,000—and advertising revenue ran ahead of forecasts. Although the companion Web site continued to be supported with $40 million in annual investment by GE and Microsoft, it took a back seat to the cable news channel, and MSNBC's ability to merge television with the PC remained in dispute.[62]

As its Interactive Media Group eliminated production of online "shows" and closed Web sites dedicated to music and movie reviews,[63] Microsoft pursued an ever-widening series of other—and likely more successful—Internet ventures. Again attempting to build up its customer base, it purchased the fourteenth most-visited Internet site, an electronic mail provider known as Hotmail—and integrated Hotmail's free email service, with its 9.5 million subscribers, into its MSN operation.[64] Only months later, Microsoft bought Firefly Network Inc., whose technology relies on individually personalized user profiles to scour the Web for targeted information about goods and services of prospective interest to a given subscriber.[65] In hopes of winning transaction fees, the software company unwrapped a travel ticketing service named Expedia, which claimed over 2 million bookings and $2 million in revenues a week by early 1998. Its popular automotive sales site, CarPoint, was expected to generate sales of $10 million a month within a couple of years as more shoppers bought automobiles over the Net. Sidewalk, an online guide to arts, entertainment, and shopping opportunities in the top fifty U.S. cities, was beating forecasts in usage and advertising revenue.[66] Overall, Microsoft was spending a colossal $2.5 billion a year on new-product development—more than the annual profits of the next ten largest software companies taken together.[67]

Particularly noteworthy was Microsoft's effort to establish entry points to the tens of millions of households that did not yet possess PCs equipped with modems—via hybrid offshoots of the ubiquitous television set. The company paid $425 million in April 1997 to acquire WebTV Networks, which sold a system for around $200 (plus keyboard costs and a monthly subscription charge of $25) that permitted TV sets to tap into the Web through ordinary telephone lines. Microsoft claimed 325,000 WebTV units in service by May 1998, chiefly among those who did not already possess a PC. WebTV promised to coordinate more closely in the future, both with traditional TV program producers and electronic home shopping and ticketing services.[68] The software giant also took stakes in a range of other pioneers of Web video services and standards: 5 percent ($5 million) in VDONet for videoconferencing; 10 percent (since relinquished) in RealNetworks to license its free "streaming" software, which permits registered users to receive real-time audio and video on the Web; and sole ownership ($75 million) of VXtreme, which further builds up Microsoft's video streaming capability.[69]

These investments, through which Microsoft acquired the ability to embed state-of-the-art video reception and transmission capabilities throughout different software packages, were only the most ambitious of current attempts to merge television with the Internet. Underway was a more general process of development, encompassing but also prospectively extending beyond a simple carryover of modernity's dominant medium. The multimedia program forms that were in such active ferment, however, required greater *network bandwidth* (as signal-carrying capacity is known) than was yet widely available.

Notwithstanding ingenious attempts to get more out of the prevailing technical infrastructure, Web programming that incorporated advanced televisual and interactive graphics—not to mention next-generation applications—was severely restricted by a dearth of broadband links. Even the costs for unsatisfactorily low-speed phone line connections were not trivial: up to $200 for a modem, plus perhaps $20 per month to tap into an Internet service provider.[70] Intensive effort therefore focused on creating both high-speed connections and software for *multicasting* Web transmissions. The primary bottleneck lay in the "final mile" (mainly just the last few yards) of circuitry that connects the nation's homes to telephone and cable networks. Absent a comprehensive upgrade, these local links would not support delivery of emerging multimedia program services.

Ceaselessly promoted as *interactive television* for an entire generation by the cable television and telecommunications industries, broadband channels to the home proved tantalizingly elusive. This was partly because what had to be reworked was, in a sense, the very relation of work and leisure: PCs were employed predominantly as business instruments, while television viewing was the quintessential leisure-time activity. By one estimate, in North America in 1997, 20.44 million home computers enjoyed connections to the Internet—compared with 25.8 million owned by businesses.[71] An executive at CBS SportsLine acknowledged that about half of his Web site's visitors used *company* networks to gain access—and, indeed, a whole industry sprouted up to create software filters to block employees at work from game and sports sites that are considered "unproductive." One small Internet company even created a "panic button" for employees to use when their boss lurked nearby, which suddenly switches the computer screen image to a nominating form for boss of the year, complete with a favorable write-up about the user's employer. Accessing the Internet, the *Wall Street Journal* observed in 1997, "is easier at work than at home, because access speed and bandwidth are frequently much better on company networks." The use of corporate networks for such purposes, however, was only a sign that the Internet indeed might be reconstituted as a full-fledged consumer medium.[72]

The obstacle to residential broadband access was not really technological; a variety of media to underwrite high-capacity services already existed. Nor did the critical blockage reside solely in the daunting expense of such modernization—a project that, if carried out on a systematic scale, might cost tens or even hundreds of billions of dollars nationwide. What then stood in the way?

The chief culprit was, ironically, the ascendance of neoliberal communications policies. As deregulation—a code name for this neoliberal impulse—swept through U.S. telecommunications, the industry was balkanized. Harmonized action on virtually any issue became difficult if not altogether impossible. Under the old regime that had governed the Bell System for decades before its 1984 breakup, technological modernization had proceeded concertedly, top-to-bottom and end-to-end.[73] Network modernization projects to underwrite broad shifts in telephone need and use (such as direct-dial calling) were conceived and realized on a nationwide scale. The events that culminated in the divestiture eliminated this option.

In 1984, the telecommunications industry was split by a federal consent decree into two segments—local and long distance. Barred from local wireline markets (and thus from developing broadband residential networks), AT&T threw itself into an ill-fated attempt to manufacture and market computers while MCI and Sprint focused on bulking up their networks for data applications. Local carriers, banned from providing "enhanced" services, explored a variety of other markets, from cellular telephony to international ventures.

Bemoaning this lack of market incentives, local-exchange carriers devoted themselves from the moment the divestiture came into force to lobbying Congress to relax the competitive restrictions the breakup had imposed. Only through liberalization of the rules keeping them out of long-distance markets and information services like video carriage, they were fond of repeating, could they afford the luxury of network modernization. However, when market barriers—alongside many traditional public-service obligations—were in fact dropped (especially through the Telecommunications Reform Act of 1996), local carriers still made only selective efforts to upgrade their networks. Even as they prepared to invade long-distance services and built up specialized offerings for business users, local carriers still shrank before the expense of residential network modernization. The telephone companies whose systems collectively lead into nearly 95 percent of U.S. homes thus put inclusive broadband access on hold.[74] Long-distance companies, on the other hand, had to contemplate either buying local network capacity from local-exchange or cable companies or swallowing the huge costs of creating their own parallel local networks in the face of these same already entrenched suppliers. Even after AT&T signaled its intention to purchase a route into local-service markets nationwide, through its planned acquisition of Tele-Communications Inc. in mid-1998, broadband residential service continued to face significant obstacles. As Bob Pittman, president of AOL, declared, it was "just not ready for prime time."[75]

Of course, there was, as this development suggests, a second wire, prospectively comprising an alternative route into some two-thirds of the nation's households. By the mid-1990s, however, cable television companies had likewise set aside earlier highly publicized plans to embark on the construction of broadband systems. Once more, this came about chiefly as the effect of a rampant neoliberalism. During the early 1980s, the cable industry had been freed of earlier regulations that had limited operators' pricing power and ability to sidestep municipal franchise commitments. The financial legerdemain that followed resulted in a series of massive mergers and acquisitions, dramatically increasing economic concentration in the cable industry and bequeathing staggering debt loads on most of the leading survivors.

Despite a whopping surge in cable fees,[76] there was little question that, by the mid-1990s, cable industry debt comprised a burdensome strategic factor, frightening investors and limiting management options. With $14.5 billion in debt, for example, the largest cable system operator, Tele-Communications Inc., paid out $1.053 billion in interest during the year ended 30 June 1996.[77] The company came under mounting pressure from investors to cut costs and laid off a significant fraction of its workforce. Likewise, TCI cut back on some high-tech upgrades to conserve capital.[78] Time-Warner, the second-largest cable system operator, was strapped with $17.5 billion in debt, much of it of subinvestment grade—again forcing it to spend billions in interest payments while watching its operating profits drop.[79] Though the high levels of short-term borrowing that brought Rupert Murdoch's News Corporation to the brink of insolvency in 1990 were avoided, the cable industry also had reached an impasse in building high-capacity circuits to the home.

The continuing lack of broadband residential access in turn jeopardized the larger goal of developing the Internet as a consumer medium.[80] As it turned out, however, the PC industry—in the form of Microsoft, with its immense cash reserves and its own strategic vision—possessed the resources needed to kickstart residential deployment of high-capacity systems.

By mid-1996, Microsoft had already allied with DirecTV—a subsidiary of Hughes Network Systems, itself a unit of General Motors, with minority participation by AT&T—to market DirecPC, utilizing a satellite-delivery system to furnish Internet service for a monthly subscription fee akin to that charged by cable television system operators.[81] Satellite dishes, available for a couple hundred dollars plus a monthly service charge of between $20 and $130, in 1998 provided very fast (400 kbps and up) download speed—but no comparable upstream capability. Intel developed a means of using a television signal's vertical blanking interval to carry Internet-type content; Microsoft later undertook a rival effort to deliver Internet news, financial information, and other content to PCs via TV signals.[82] In 1997, vastly upping the ante, Microsoft then invested $1 billion to acquire an 11.5 percent share of Comcast—about to become the nation's third-largest cable television system operator (after digesting Jones Intercable) and also a half-owner of QVC, the television-shopping network that claimed around $2 billion in annual revenues.[83] In a parallel billion-dollar bet, Microsoft co-founder Paul Allen then spent $2.8 billion to acquire Marcus Cable, a large multiple-system operator based in Dallas.[84]

Microsoft's support of the cable television industry sought an immediate strategic goal. Microsoft thought it saw prospectively vast markets in the digital set-top boxes that cable operators would need to transform TV sets into versatile interactive terminals. The software giant desired that the new appliance should employ its own Windows CE operating system. Thus, by seeking to use technical standards as a strategic weapon, Microsoft made yet another bid for a privileged place on the platform that would link PCs and TVs to consumer programming and information services. Content developers from game designers to home-shopping companies would then write programs for the new platform—and Microsoft, in addition to being well-placed to extend those of its own program services that managed to succeed, also would garner royalties and transaction fees from others.

Nor was Microsoft the only computer company to look with longing toward Internet TV. Sun Microsystems, hitherto a producer of high-end computer workstations and servers, created the new computer language known as Java and used it to allow programmers to create very small applications (*applets*) that could be sent over the Internet and run within Web pages—thereby opening up all kinds of program-design possibilities. Java applications running across the Internet were expected to generate growth in the market for information appliances that extend beyond PCs, as we saw, via television set-top boxes and hand-held browsers. Sun also acquired Diba Inc., giving it licensing ties to Samsung and Panasonic and furthering its goal of designing additional consumer Internet appliances.[85]

Corporate database vendor Oracle Corporation, another Microsoft rival, likewise made several investments in fledgling Internet TV ventures. One linked up Oracle with TV broadcasters in developing a new generation of decoder devices to integrate information from Web sites into television programs in progress. Hedging its bets, like its rival Microsoft, Oracle—with mixed success—also joined a cable-industry-led partnership to provide broadband Internet service.[86] Local television broadcasters themselves, meanwhile—most of whom were owned by networks and increasingly massive multistation groups—were given frequencies by the Federal Communications Commission to develop digital, *advanced,* or *high-definition* services.[87] How much use these emergent digital program forms would make of complementary Internet services was unclear, in part because relations between competing broadcasters and between broadcasters and cablecasters remained unsettled. The expected high price (upward of $5,000) of the first high-resolution television sets, and cable systems' projected difficulties in carrying high-resolution broadcast signals, also entered the competitive picture.[88]

Set-top boxes, as the intended "gatekeeper" for prospective interactive services via cable television systems, quickly became the object of fierce contention.[89] John Malone, the CEO of one of the largest cable operators, TCI, warned openly that Microsoft "would like to be the only technology supplier for this whole evolution." Declaring that "we would all be very foolish to allow that to happen," Malone found a means of offsetting Microsoft's bid for market power over the new interactive services industry. TCI and the cable industry basically divided the set-top box into a series of technology layers and insisted that products built for one layer work, or *interoperate,* with components built for other layers. In addition, rival suppliers were given orders for each hardware or software technology level. Microprocessors and other semiconductor components, for example, were to be provided by Motorola, QED, and perhaps other manufacturers. Systems manufacturing contracts were awarded to General Instrument, in which Sony acquired a small stake.[90] TCI likewise submitted orders for 5 million boxes equipped with the Microsoft's Windows CE operating system, but Malone contrived to embed in these boxes the Java programming language that was controlled by Microsoft arch-rival Sun Microsystems. In Britain, Cable & Wireless—the largest cable company there—picked software from NCI, a company owned by Microsoft competitors Oracle and Netscape, for its new digital set-top boxes.[91] *Open standards,* it was hoped, would check Microsoft's ambitions and ensure that the cable industry remained the master of its own destiny. As of early December 1998, a business writer commented that Microsoft's efforts to capture digital television markets indeed had been substantially "stymied."[92]

Microsoft's cable investments, nevertheless, were widely perceived as a strong vote of confidence in that industry, and North American cable stock prices shot skyward, registering a 90 percent gain during 1997.[93] Cash flows surged and debt loads declined to the point that ratings services like Moody's began to reclassify such debt as "investment grade."[94] During 1997, the nation's cable companies invested over $6 billion in infrastructure improvements. By the end of 1998, two-way systems were expected to pass almost 45 million U.S. homes.[95] Cable-modem-based broadband service was available, in these areas, at a cost of up to $300 for installation, plus a $40 to $50 monthly access charge. Although only 250,000 were in use by May 1998, cable operators such as Comcast were beginning to boast of installing thousands of cable modems a week in some markets.[96] So alluring had cable grown, indeed, that AT&T made a big strategic bet on it midway through 1998, when it sought to purchase TCI and through it access to 22 million cable-ready homes, in a mostly stock transaction valued at $44 billion including assumption of debt.[97]

Whether cable systems would preside over the introduction of broadband residential Internet service remained uncertain. Two factors contributed to that uncertainty. First, cable operators continued to feud with broadcasters over "must-carry" rules, which historically had obligated cable companies to pass along broadcast TV signals over their wires. Would this arrangement continue to prevail throughout the coming digital-TV era—or would cable operators successfully shrug it off?[98] Second, and more vital, the cable industry's move to address broadband markets now at last also spurred entry by local telephone carriers.

At a cost of up to $300 for installation and equipment, plus $30 to $200 a month for access, a rather cumbersome service known as ISDN—which doubled the speed offered by top-of-the-line (56.6 kbps) telephone modems—was actually already on offer from local carriers. In January 1998, however, Microsoft, partnering with Compaq and Intel, announced a venture with the nation's largest local telephone companies to standardize high-speed residential access to the Internet. This new service, called digital subscriber line (DSL), could nearly rival the speed of cable modems.[99] With this shift, the local carriers began to abandon the hesitation, discussed in chapter 1, with which they had regarded modernizing to supply broadband services. Pacific Bell announced that it would install DSL equipment for several hundred dollars, with an additional monthly service charge of between $90 and $340, depending on the package selected by a given household.[100] Bell Atlantic declared that the installation charge for its version of DSL would be held below $200; pricing for its sliding scale of monthly Internet access options started at $69.95 and went up to $189.95.[101] Microsoft also allied with one of the more aggressive telecommunications companies, WorldCom, whose Internet subsidiary UUNet had established a multicast service capable of reaching hundreds of thousands of users with a single transmitted stream of audio or video.[102] Through these means, Microsoft neatly answered the cable operators by playing them off against the telecommunications industry. An accelerating scramble to furnish broadband service was thereby ensured, as was the likelihood of additional strategic opportunities for Microsoft.

It would be mistaken to conclude, however, that market forces were on the verge of solving the problem—residential access to broadband services—that market-driven policies had created. This was because, concurrently, the obligation to roll out such services on a comprehensive social basis had been all but erased. Goaded and enticed by turns by the prospect of additional revenue streams, cable operators and telephone companies belatedly developed the market for broadband service *only* for favored customer segments. As a rough target, we might say that they aimed at the top half of the population and, above all, at the 10.5 million American homes possessing more than one computer in mid-1998 or, put differently, to the 12 percent of households with an income of more than $100,000 a year.[103] They made few promises to those who might not be able to afford the very substantial charges imposed for the new services. Only around two-thirds of American households subscribed to ordinary cable television service; what likelihood was there that even this many would be able to contract for broadband services, which would at least double their monthly bill?[104] Market-driven development thus gave scant prospect of unfolding toward univeral broadband access—a fact that, as we will see, proved troubling even to some industry participants.

During mid-1998, the jockeying over interactive services intensified. Week to week, new partnerships were announced, while existing consortia repositioned themselves. Microsoft and Compaq together took a 20 percent ($425 million) stake in RoadRunner, a high-speed Internet access provider serving 90,000 subscribers in a couple of dozen local markets; RoadRunner itself was owned by Time-Warner and MediaOne Group.[105] Microsoft's investment appeared to have short-circuited the cable industry's desultory effort to forge a united front against it: Time-Warner had been in talks with AT&T and with TCI's John Malone, to align RoadRunner with a rival Internet service called @Home.[106] In turn, @Home, a consortium of nine cable multiple-system operators led by TCI, boasted a market capitalization of no less than $5 billion by mid-1998. Minority backers included the Silicon Valley venture capital fund Kleiner Perkins Caulfield & Byers, as well as Netscape CEO James Barksdale, Sun Microsystems, Motorola, and Bay Networks. @Home's exclusive contracts with top cable systems promised to ease access to the 50 million homes they reached.[107] Rogers Cablesystems and Shaw Communications, which together controlled almost half of the Canadian cable market, were also partners.[108] @Home soon began to cut other international deals; a Netherlands service was inaugurated with two Dutch cable providers, and a United Kingdom–based service was also expected.[109] With 150,000 North American customers by mid-1998, @Home was among the properties that would come under AT&T control, were that long-distance carrier successfully to complete its planned acquisition of TCI—a point that appeared to rankle some of the cable operators backing the service.[110]

It was too soon to tell how this giant war of position would resolve. But the market momentum that had gathered behind the Internet as a nascent consumer medium was undeniable. In turn, the Web's most basic social function also was rapidly recast.

Market Power and Commercial Sponsorship

More than any other medium, television—in its different modes of delivery via cable, satellite, and local broadcasters—dominates the contemporary global mediascape. And, not surprisingly, of all the conventional media it is television that has also assumed the highest visibility as it attempts to transplant itself into cyberspace. Let us focus, therefore, specifically (though not exclusively) on the relationship of television to the emerging Internet media platform.

The Television Model

It is not *television,* of course, that is converging with the Internet, but a historically specific set of practices that we can more properly gloss as *commercial networked television.* These practices pertain not only to particular genres and formal styles but to an overarching institutional identity. Television's long-standing economic basis must be underlined if we are to comprehend even the most basic features of the established medium's figuration on the Web.

Each of the two adjectives—*commercial* and *networked*—hints at a crucial characteristic. First has been the concentration of television content, or *programming.* This concentration should be distinguished from the considerable geographical centralization in programming and related industries that it encouraged historically. Concentration of programming via networking meant that large producers and distributors, rather than local or nonprofit broadcasters, were enabled to gain market power sufficient to dominate the larger television industry. Thousands of U.S. musicians, and untold other performers, found themselves unemployed because, during earlier decades, networks and stations successfully pushed to utilize recordings in preference to more expensive and unreliable live performances.[111]

During the year leading up to summer 1997, Microsoft put an estimated $500 million into developing Web content, both on its own and, increasingly, with partners.[112] That's an order of magnitude above the annual investment that was required by Rupert Murdoch's Fox Broadcasting network (or, for that matter, by Gannett's newspaper, *USA Today*) before each began to pay off. This scale of expenditure makes it all but certain that one or another megamedia company (though, ironically, not yet Microsoft) will eventually figure out how to innovate profitable cyberspace program forms. Perhaps it will be America Online, which hired Robert Pittman, the *wunderkind* who launched MTV fifteen years ago, to manage its consumer online service. AOL's subscriber base of 15 million, and regular prime-time audience of 625,000, may not look like much when compared with 100 million-odd Net surfers or with 110 million U.S. television households, but they're formidable numbers when compared with the reach and ratings of many successful cable networks. *South Park,* the most popular show on basic cable, by comparison reached some 6.2 million viewers for some episodes.[113]

By 1997, efforts were already far advanced to link the two media and to identify means of migrating audiences from one to the other. Oprah Winfrey, whose talk show reached a daily audience of some 15 million viewers on television, successfully carried a portion of her audience to her AOL program service. Disney's popular ESPN *SportsZone* comprised another such crossover attempt. And NBC hoped to use set-top boxes to enable TV viewers to access supplementary digital information about its programs as they were aired.[114] During 1998, this carryover trend accelerated. NBC's *Seinfeld* finale looked to break Web advertising records from marketers seeking to tie in to the show through an ancillary Web site.[115] While Disney sought to coordinate and cross-promote its diverse Web properties under the umbrella of its expanding Internet Group and took a controlling interest in Infoseek, a starting-point search service for Web users, NBC purchased a stake in the online news company CNET and a controlling interest in its Snap! directory service.[116] Rupert Murdoch sold *TV Guide* for $2 billion to United Video Satellite Group (a venture affiliated with John Malone's Tele-Communications Inc.), hoping to migrate the program guide into an electronic format on the Web, concurrently with cable television and digital broadcast services.[117] It was, in short, a time of hothouse experimentation and market development. Again, however, it was still too soon to tell exactly which companies would successfully dominate the market for Web-based experiences.

The primary goal of the Webcasters who see the Internet as a nascent media platform is to concentrate and stabilize relations between program services and audiences. A succession of efforts have been made to realize this goal, therewith claiming additional market power: browser software, so-called push services, blockbuster programming investments, exclusive licensing agreements, content cobranding schemes, site aggregation into thematically coherent networks, and an emerging top-ten obsession with destination or gateway Web sites. There is little to suggest that this multifaceted attempt to stabilize the relation between programming and audience (further details of which are presented below) is fully formed. Many novel departures (intelligent agents, for example) no doubt will need to be accommodated. But neither must it be forgotten that this attempt is itself largely a function of the second abiding aspect of a commercial networked model—its reliance on advertiser sponsorship. The stampede to develop Internet TV itself is a sign that advertisers have become intent on bending the Web to their particular institutional purposes.

"TV," declares TCI's John Malone, "is the best sales mechanism we've ever had." Simplifying only somewhat, it was because of its ability to accommodate live-action demonstration, over and above identification and endorsement of products and product applications, that TV succeeded radio as the foremost advertising medium. Advertisers are not yet confident that Internet TV marketing tie-ins—what Malone dubs "impulse interactivity"[118]—portends an equally decisive new stage in the ongoing evolution of the sales effort. But they are certain that they cannot afford to overlook that possibility.

So much at least we may take from the celebrated address, in May of 1994, by Edwin Artzt, then CEO of Procter & Gamble. Before the American Association of Advertising Agencies, Artzt declared that the century-old advertising and marketing complex—the historical spearhead of consumer capitalism—should set itself the task of making new media dependent on commercial sponsorship.[119] Artzt neglected to take real note of the Internet, preferring instead to focus on interactive television, but his specific predictions were less significant than his broader call to action. At least, that is the view argued by Robert Herbold—the then–Procter & Gamble (now Microsoft) executive who actually wrote Artzt's pivotal speech.

In any given year, declared Artzt, P&G "has to sell 400 million boxes of Tide—and to do that, we have to reach our consumers over and over throughout the year":

Frequency and depth of sale in advertising are critical to preserving loyalty to frequently purchased brands like ours. For example, in any given month, P&G brands like Tide and Crest and Pantene will reach more than *90 percent* of their target audience *six or seven times.*

The only way you can achieve that kind of impact is with broad-reach television—which is why we spend almost 90 percent of our $3 billion advertising budget on TV.[120]

However, he continued, in the near future "there is a very real possibility that the majority of programs people watch will not be advertiser supported." Time shifting, channel surfing, video games, pay-per-view programming, and Internet access make it "harder than ever before just to reach consumers with our advertising, much less reach them with the frequency and regularity we need to build loyalty to our brands." Artzt took the long view in assessing the situation and in trying to craft a strategic response. Both his historical assessment of the role of advertising in media development and his reaction to the sheer possibility of proliferating commercial-free media are highly instructive:

Advertising started in print. When radio came along and we all had to buy time as well as space—and sell with words and music and no pictures—we, the advertising industry, took control of our environment.

We created programming. We molded the environment to fit our needs. We were no longer dealing just with newspapers and magazines that people bought and read every day. We had to create listener loyalty to programming we sponsored. We created soaps, comedy shows, variety shows, and mysteries. We made listening to radio every Sunday night a family institution.

Those were days when the advertising industry grabbed technology change in its teeth and made it the greatest selling tool ever conceived. . . .

Now, we're going to have to grab technology in our teeth again and make it work for us. But it isn't going to be as simple as it was to adapt to radio or TV, where everything favored the advertiser. Now, we've got competition, not just among traditional, ad-supported media but from unadvertised programming, as well—entertainment and information that will represent an entirely separate source of revenue for media suppliers and programmers alike.

This is the real threat. These new media suppliers will give consumers what they want, and potentially at a price they're willing to pay. If user fees replace advertising revenue, we're in serious trouble.

But I don't think that's going to happen. If this industry does what it's done before, you will turn this threat into an enormous opportunity.

Just think of some of the opportunities we've not had before:

• We can use interactive technology to engage consumers in our commercials.

• We can provide direct consumer response. If a consumer wants to know which Cover Girl nail polish matches the lipstick she saw in our commercial, we can tell her on the spot.

• We can target not just demographic segments but individual households. If a family has a newborn baby, we can make sure they get a Pampers commercial.

• We can use games, infomercials, video shopping malls. We'll have a whole bag of tools to engage and inform consumers, and if we do that right we can keep people in their seats when the commercials come on.[121]

Artzt underscored that this effort to safeguard communications technology for the only purposes deemed legitimate in a consumer capitalist economy depended on growing involvement "in programming to make certain that advertisers have access to the mass audience and to the best properties."[122] He also bestowed an intermittent—but unmistakable—gender identity on that audience, a point to which I return below.

Artzt's speech galvanized a commercial invasion of cyberspace. The Internet began to play host to major ad agencies, ready to assist corporate clients in creating campaigns and strategies. Within a short time, major agencies boasted of their newfound Web prowess and strove to build in an Internet advertising strategy when pitching services to clients. Redefined as what one executive called "a fundamentally new product opportunity," commercializing ventures began to draw "the brightest technical talent, the most ambitious entrepreneurs, the sharpest marketers, and the savviest managers."[123] As demand exploded for innovative Web sites, digital-talent agencies emerged to match up clients with cyberartists, including designers, programmers, producers, photographers, and consultants.[124] Over a mere span of months, as the likes of IBM, Ford, AT&T, and J. C. Penney began to test electronic waters, the Web morphed from a scientist's research tool into a corporate billboard. But the sponsor system would have to labor to claim the heart and soul of this emergent medium. A whole institutional infrastructure had to be brought into being in a concerted attempt to develop the Web's selling capabilities.

Safeguarding the Net for commerce became a virtual obsession. One correlative was a continuing effort to devise software standards for secure online payments using credit-card accounts. Following a period of frenetic competitive activity, the Secure Electronic Transaction consortium, consisting of VISA, MasterCard, GTE, IBM, Microsoft, Netscape, SAIC, and others, rolled out a standard protocol for credit-card transactions on the Web.[125] A related technical (and legal) initiative concerned encryption software, which was needed to scramble information to make the Internet safer for financial transactions, particularly those involving credit-card payments.[126] A third intertwined effort, spurred by recording companies and publishers set to plunge into electronic commerce, armed information vendors with a new software technology—digital watermarks—hoping to foil uncompensated distribution (*piracy*) of music and images.[127] To be sure, trustworthy, affordable, and simple-to-use payment systems continued to prove elusive, and the security of the open Net remained dubious. Although fears about credit-card transactions kept many users from participating in electronic commerce, nevertheless, during 1997 some 6.5 million individuals are estimated to have undertaken 23.4 million online credit-card transactions (the lion's share of which went to Visa).[128]

A research base for consumer marketing and promotion in cyberspace also had to be established. Protracted debates erupted over how best to track Web users' behavior and attention.[129] More than a dozen companies scrambled to provide profitable answers, including Nielsen Media Research (the originators of the dominant TV audience-tracking system, active in ninety countries by 1998), to measure Internet audiences and sell the data to Fortune 500 clients.[130] A trade association, the Internet Advertising Bureau, aimed to ensure that the sponsors who were, according to one writer, "trying to turn the once-eclectic Web into the ultimate twenty-four-hour marketing machine," did not lack for an institutional voice.[131] Data-mining of corporate Web sites directly by their own sponsors also became a focal point of software companies' design energies. By mid-1998, leading advertisers continued to express the view that, because Web measurement services still seemed inadequate, it was necessary to press on with the attempt.[132]

So-called *push* Web services commenced early in 1996 and directly engaged advertisers' need to gather and stabilize Internet audiences. Akin to functionally similar (but sometimes incompatible) offerings by other push companies, PointCast—the pioneer of push—delivered customized information directly to users' screens when their computers were idle. During 1998, PointCast aggregated news and information from some 600 different content sources, into fifty-odd channels delivered to around 1.2 million subscribers; the system was supported by 200 advertisers.[133]

It is the institutional intention behind push services that is important. "Advertisers like the early signs of push," declared one analyst late in 1997, because "it's more intrusive and it's more like TV."[134] Push services also were used to build bridges back to conventional media programmers and to a familiar litany of stock quotes, sports scores, and news headlines. Netscape employed push capabilities on its browser to pair with Walt Disney, News Corporation, Knight-Ridder, Federal Express, Excite,

Hearst Home Arts, and CBS. Several of these megamedia programmers struck push deals as well with Microsoft's IE—which also collared a series of apparently exclusive arrangements with megamedia companies including Warner Brothers, America Online, and CNN.[135] Microsoft also signed up some of the largest business-information providers, including Dun & Bradstreet, Forbes, Fortune, Dow Jones, and Reed Elsevier.[136] Although Microsoft's updated browser gave users a choice of more than 700 channels, the *Wall Street Journal* explained that "the two dozen or so major channels that come bundled with the software, and are prominently displayed, are expected to attract the bulk of Web traffic and advertising dollars."[137]

Nevertheless, it was soon apparent that push services would not offer comprehensive means of stabilizing audiences. Many users did not want to be relieved of the need to search the Internet's vast troves of data, in favor of automatically preselected information sources.[138] Push services responded to lackluster interest by trying to market themselves to corporate information system managers. The latter used them to feed varied kinds of content—updated computer programs, sales data, product specifications, benefits plan changes, marketing plans—as needed throughout dispersed enterprises. Toyota Vision, for instance, comprised an internal corporate channel that featured sales and leasing data by model and region, a demographic breakdown of the automobile manufacturers' customers, and even information on the Toyota Golf Association.[139]

Once more, however, the typifying feature of push services—the attempt, on behalf of advertisers, to stabilize the relationship between users and particular Web services—did not abate. It simply reasserted itself in other ways.

The ability to control the viewer's startup screen, for example, acquired a signal importance. Both Netscape and Microsoft sought to leverage their control over the desktop screen, and in mid-1998 there were signs that some PC manufacturers would also make efforts in this direction.[140] The *Wall Street Journal* viewed this initiative as "an important experiment in audience-building."[141] "Every time you fire up your browser software to explore the World Wide Web," wrote an irate columnist, "the first thing you see is an annoying promotional home page for the company that made the browser—Netscape or Microsoft—or for the company that is providing your Internet access."[142]

Such frequently visited *default start pages* soon joined other heavily trafficked sites as the most valuable commercial real estate on the Web. Search engines—the directory services that help users identify Web sites they wish to visit (with indifferent results)[143]—provided a leading example of the trend. The Internet's most trafficked site, in 1998, was a search engine—Yahoo!—that reached an estimated 25 million people a month in 1997 (and 65 million page views a day during that year's fourth quarter). More people searched at Yahoo!, commented one writer, than watched MTV, Nickelodeon, or Showtime in any given week or than read the typical issue of *Time* or *Newsweek*.[144] Yahoo! in turn set about extending its franchise by transforming itself into a major Internet hub or *portal*. Its strategy was to build its audience by striking deals to provide users with specialized content, free electronic mail, games, community offerings, and shopping services.[145] Users—who would have to stick around at its site for longer periods to use these new offerings—would thereby become more accessible to the advertisers that furnished the bulk of Yahoo!'s revenue stream.

An identical ambition fired other leading Web companies, and a veritable war of the portals got underway. To gather advertising revenues, rival search engine Excite bought eight companies to build additional features that would lure a larger regular audience.[146] The *online community* GeoCities, with its sixty distinct *neighborhoods* targeted to different users' ages and interests, provided access to the segmented audiences (of which more below) most desired by sponsors.[147] Industry leader America Online sought to augment its subscription revenues, as its subscriber base increased, by adding an advertising revenue stream. AOL's 9 million subscribers in mid-1997 accounted for an estimated 55 percent of all time spent online by households, and its proprietary content accounted for a claimed 80 percent of its users' total online time.[148] Why not reorganize operations to maximize advertiser interest, while continuing to build its audience—which, at peak periods, already exceeded the number of people who tuned in to watch cable's Comedy Central and The Learning Channel? AOL purchased NetChannel, an Internet-via-TV service, setting its sights prospectively on every U.S. household. AOL also took a 20 percent stake in FamilyEducation Co., an ad-supported Internet company that in turn has partnered with 330 school districts to engage with parents in cyberspace about a wide variety of school topics. In addition, AOL moved to enlarge its audience transnationally by renewing its assault on the European online service market.[149]

Microsoft likewise announced that it would unite its two chief Web properties—msn.com and Microsoft.com—and throw in free email, a search engine, and personalized push services, again in hopes of creating the kind of successful *destination site* that could be marketed to advertisers.[150] Netscape, lacking Microsoft's powerful clout, likewise shifted direction to stress the sale of advertising over the sale of software. By mid-1997, advertising sales and publishing partnership services accounted for 27 percent of Netscape's total revenue; bolstering its Web site, *Netcenter,* Netscape's strategic goal was to turn itself into a media network. When AOL purchased Netscape and thereby gained access to the nine million users of Netcenter, the goal of establishing a full-fledged Web media company remained fundamental: the combined company will have 50 percent more visitors than Yahoo!, its nearest competitor.[151]

All the while, Web program development costs continued to escalate—by an estimated 300 percent over the course of 1996 to 1997—to $3.1 million per average-content commercial site.[152]

As a shakeout in the market for Web advertising got underway, attention turned to how to make the pioneering forms of commercial representation—banner ads and corporate home pages—succeed more efficiently or give up pride of place to "new and improved" genres. Hunter Madsen, vice president for commercial strategy at *Hotwired,* made the case for unremitting experimentation, toward less standardized banners or *brand modules,* and toward ever-deepening interpenetration between commercial and editorial matter (sponsorships or *content cobranding*).[153] Advertisers, wrote Joan Voight, a reporter for *Ad Week,* "want to work hand in hand with publishers to coproduce the material that packs Web pages." ParentTime, a joint-venture between Procter & Gamble and Time-Warner, thus provided parents with interactive advice and promoted Time-Warner magazines such as *Parenting* and *Sports Illustrated for Kids.* Although its Web advertising outlays remained small, P&G registered domains for dozens of sites, including crisco.com, badbreath.com, and dentures.com; but ParentTime was a collaborative effort by the world's leading advertiser and a media industry goliath to experiment with interactive program forms.[154] David Wertheimer, chief of Paramount Digital Entertainment, underlined the importance of such collaboration, stressing that his company was "working with a small number of large sponsors to use our creative talent to create original entertainment for them . . . much like sponsored programming of the 1940s or '50s, whether it was the quiz show, the *Texaco Star Theatre,* or the *Hallmark Hall of Fame.*" Women's Link, developed by Paramount for Bristol-Myers Squibb, was one fruit of this partnership.[155] On the Web, the distinction between commercial and independent programming was often supplanted, as original content creators worked ever more closely with marketeers to shape generic form and content to sponsors' dictates.

The Effects of Advertising

Advertisers had proclaimed the necessity of colonizing cyberspace and of making it dependent on their ability to provide funding. Does anyone still truly think that they will realize the folly of this ambition and abandon the Net? If advertisers ever recognized that the culture of the Net was unreceptive, that time is long gone. "We have a vested interest in making the Web the most effective marketing medium in history," declared Procter & Gamble's top advertising executive in 1998—reiterating Artzt's theme, four years later, with unslackened fervor.[156]

The chief historical basis for advertising (whether or not the latter succeeds efficiently in any given instance) is the pan-corporate need to harness consumption to production.[157] Branding, marketing, and consumer product advertising have been historically indispensable adjuncts of an economy—a "perpetual-innovation economy," as it is termed in chapter 4—that has reached a certain general level of productivity and of social surplus (the amount of goods and services it can produce outstrips the concurrent socioeconomic ability to absorb this surplus). In the United States, the center of the perpetual innovation economy, no less than 17,571 consumer products were introduced in 1993 (in a *slowing* trend); and, as of 1996, Gillette decreed that 40 percent of its sales every five years must come from entirely new products. "That requires about

twenty new products a year."[158] But the same trend asserted itself globally. By 1987, for example, no less than 30 percent of all products sold
by the Japanese transnational corporation Toshiba had been developed
within the past three years, and executives predicted that this fraction
would rapidly increase.[159] These products need to be moved off the
shelves and, to make sure that they do, marketeers have grown ingenious
at reminding consumers to replace their razors, batteries, beer, and tooth-
brushes at increasingly frequent intervals.[160]

Through the decades, this compulsive sales effort has enfolded around
a continuing succession of media, from magazines and radio onward. As
many as one in every four U.S. workers is presently employed in advertising, marketing, or sales jobs.[161] Consumer advertisers have plunged into
cyberspace, accordingly, not because of some peripheral or momentary
whim to test unknown waters. They act, rather, as the representatives of
a generative social force.

There is, however, every reason to believe that the ongoing advertiser-
led establishment of an Internet media platform bears some unique—and
profoundly important—historical features. Before looking more directly
at these critical characteristics, let us turn to a general question: What
does advertiser sponsorship do to the media that become dependent on it?

There is plenty of evidence that advertising seizes and reorients the
social purpose of any media it can make dependent on it, substantially
affecting their organization, content, and relationships with audiences. It
is not so much a matter of poor ethics or lapsed standards as of a systematic overall orientation. When advertisers foot an appreciable proportion
of overall media costs, they come to dominate that medium's workaday
self-consciousness, one effect of which is also to place determining pressures and limits on its relationship with audiences.

After *The Dana Carvey Show* offered a sketch featuring Carvey as President Clinton breast-feeding a baby, one of the show's sponsors, Taco
Bell, removed its name from the program; soon after, ABC abruptly
dropped the show, citing weak ratings.[162] The example is emblematic of
the power exercised by corporate sponsors over the leading institutions
of cultural production. Recent documentation of advertisers' role in determining magazine content supplies additional evidence of the everyday,
and ever-more invasive, effects of the sponsor system.

"It has long been routine," writes a *New York Times* reporter, "to warn [advertisers] about potentially objectionable content and offer the option of moving an ad to another issue." Companies including Chrysler, Colgate-Palmolive, Ameritech, and IBM easily exert editorial pressure, yanking millions of dollars worth of advertising when articles they do not like appear. To the chagrin of some editors and many journalists, however, major magazine advertisers have now also begun to demand formal prior review of upcoming articles. After Ford pulled ads from the *New Yorker* when the journal failed to alert it about a 1995 article containing a swear word, the *New Yorker* established a formal system to warn about fifty companies about articles that might offend them. Chrysler's advertising agency, BBDO Worldwide, even sent a letter in 1996 to more than 100 magazines, which stated: "In an effort to avoid potential conflicts, it is required that Chrysler Corporation be alerted in advance of any and all editorial content that encompasses sexual, political, social issues, or any editorial that might be construed as provocative or offensive." It went on: "Each and every issue that carries Chrysler advertising requires a written summary outlining major theme/articles appearing in upcoming issues. These summaries are to be forwarded . . . in order to give Chrysler ample time to review and reschedule if desired."[163] Such glaring infractions prompted the American Society of Magazine Editors and the Magazine Publishers of America—concerned about salvaging editorial credibility—to declare that *detailed* information about coming articles should not be provided to sponsors.[164] But when, in response, Chrysler decided not to continue its policy of insisting on warnings or editorial previews, the company also said it would reduce the number of magazines in which it places ads and might even cut overall magazine ad spending (the nation's fourth-largest advertiser overall, Chrysler spent about $270 million in 350 periodicals in 1996). And the automaker reported that it would not drop its editorial code aimed at keeping its advertisements out of journals carrying controversial articles. Its strictures had already penetrated far enough into the publishing world for a company spokesman to suggest that publishers "know our guidelines. We're sure [they] will use good judgment."[165]

The sorry history of U.S. press dependence on tobacco company advertising offers further sober testimony to the routine, but usually invisible, effects of sponsor power. A 1992 University of Michigan study of ninety-nine American magazines found that those magazines without cigarette advertising were 40 percent more likely to run stories on smoking and health. For women's magazines, those not reliant on tobacco sponsorship were 230 percent more likely to run stories on this subject. Such is the power of the conglomerates that control the tobacco industry—and the pliancy of broadcasters who depend on other brands sold by these same diversified companies for advertising revenue—that, in what the *New York Times* characterized as "an extraordinary act of contrition," ABC News publicly apologized to Philip Morris and R. J. Reynolds for asserting in a news program that these giants add extra nicotine to their cigarettes.[166]

But it is not only the exclusion of particular kinds of content that advertising puts at issue; it is also the character of the content that *is* purveyed. For example, companies that put up $94,000 to $140,000 to buy at least two pages of advertising in *Vanity Fair* magazine, owned by the New-house family's Advance Publications, were recently offered profiles as promising investment outlets in a sister publication called *Businesses to Watch*.[167] Kimberly-Clark, the manufacturer of Huggies diapers, demands in writing that its ads in such journals as *Parenting, American Baby,* and *Child* be placed only "adjacent to black and white happy baby editorial." "Sometimes we have to create editorial that is satisfactory to them," concedes one editor.[168] Magazine marketing departments, which help advertisers create persuasive messages by researching and deploying editorial content in more singleminded pursuit of this goal, have also blossomed.[169]

Before a public outcry forced it to abandon the plan, the History Channel—a cable network—planned to sign up companies such as AT&T, DuPont, and Anheuser-Busch as both advertisers in and coproducers of its new Spirit of Enterprise series. Each company would have editorial power over an hour-long profile of itself, helping to fund the show and committing to buy ads during the series.[170] Mark H. Willes, earlier an executive at General Mills and today the CEO of Times Mirror and the publisher of its flagship paper, the *Los Angeles Times,* has undertaken to permit that journal's editors and reporters "to consult regularly with advertising and marketing executives, breaching a wall that has long separated the two at most major newspapers." The business side of the paper is being restructured around discrete editorial sections—sports, business, and so forth—whose executives and editors, akin to brand managers, will develop individual profit goals.[171] Similiar initiatives are being undertaken at other papers and throughout other media.[172] NBC, like the other broadcast networks historically a purveyor of advertising on behalf of outside clients, has now also become a direct marketer of its own video products.[173]

The sponsor system is also undergoing a vigorous secular expansion. More and more film directors, for example, are finding work making television advertisements.[174] Attempting to "experiment[] with edgy, unique sounds as a way to appeal to hip young consumers," moreover, advertisers moved to sign up alternative bands—musicians who in the past often disdained such partnerships as exercises in cooptation.[175] Procter & Gamble helped bankroll TV shows such as *Sabrina, the Teenage Witch* and *Clueless;* Virginia Slims, owned by Philip Morris, even started its own recording label, Woman Thing Music, to bundle CDs in a variety of genres with packs of cigarettes aimed at women in supermarket promotions; Bob Dylan and the Rolling Stones joined scores of bands performing at private shows for corporate audiences.[176] And, in an era of proliferating product placement in films, it is at least suggestive that a survey of the five top-grossing films each year found that only one lead character smoked in 1990, while 80 percent of Hollywood's male leads did so in 1991 to 1996.[177] Marketers have lately extended their reach to include airport baggage carousels, automatic cash machines, gas pumps— even Mir cosmonauts, hawking items live from outer space for QVC.[178]

The Web, whose ten most-visited sites garnered two-thirds of total Web advertising revenue,[179] offers prime real estate for this more comprehensive enlargement of sponsorship. As we have already seen, moreover, in cyberspace the line between advertising and editorial matter is being further eroded through a sprawling series of joint ventures and cross-promotions that link advertisers directly with content creators. As one publisher contends, "editorial is in many ways for sale today on the Web in ways that would be unequivocably objectionable in print."[180]

Thus the importance to media of advertiser sponsorship goes far beyond the question of censorship of content in deference to whatever idiosyncracies may be brought to bear by particular sponsors. It's also, and more substantively, a question of emphasis on particular program forms and the priorities that they express—particular creative practices rather than others. The practices that saturate our culture and that are being transferred wholesale to the Net are market-driven in intent and in effect. That doesn't mean they cannot sometimes eventuate in true artistry but rather that art itself is generally placed in harness to a narrow and exclusionary social purpose: selling.[181]

Of course, the trail is already littered with the effects of poor strategic judgments and corporate missteps, and there will be many widely heralded failures to come. Nobody can be certain that any particular venture will succeed, let alone that it will transform the Net. But that doesn't mean the whole thing is simply an open question. Most significant, it seems to me, is that the outcome itself is being left essentially to "market forces." If the present trend is not comprehensively interrupted, the extent to which cyberspace becomes a commercial consumer medium will be very largely determined by profit-seeking companies themselves. Non-profit prospectors of alternative visions of cyberspace will either be marginalized or else incorporated—and exploited—by sponsors seeking access to their services and perhaps a patina of legitimacy. Just as sponsors have already done with museums, orchestras, college alumni associations, public broadcasting stations, and just about anything else that draws the right kind of crowd, innovative Web masters are enrolling *non*commercial sites in the sales effort. By early 1997, the bookseller Amazon.com had established links with 8,000 formerly unrelated Web sites, and this parasitic program expanded dramatically over the next eighteen months.[182]

The debate over the propriety of advertiser-supported radio broadcasting (the so-called American system) unfolded through years of public discussion[183] and drew outbursts of anticommercial concern from highly placed political and church leaders, business executives, educators, and philanthropists. In the United States, the introduction of commercial television also occasioned at least some mainstream criticism, albeit of a more diffuse kind. In contrast, the debate over commercialism in cyberspace has been a nonstarter. Some outcries have been heard over *spam*, as the rising flood of junk email is called.[184] Privacy infringement issues also episodically erupt into public view and for good reason. Yet scant substantive attention has been accorded by established media to the grave questions that commercialization raises in regard to the overall control and direction of cyberspace. Can this be accidental?

The Specificity of Cyberspace

All new media must borrow off the shelf of prevailing practice. So, too, the Internet evinces obvious carryovers from established print and electronic media. However, absent some unique or qualitatively intensified ability to cater to the needs of the reigning sponsor system, a medium must be content to claim a marginal presence in the wider culture. The ongoing metamorphosis of cyberspace into an advertiser-dominated consumer medium betrays just such specific, vital functions. A good entry point for examining them is provided by the spring 1997 upset of world chess champion Garry Kasparov by IBM's supercomputer-powered chess system, Deep Blue.

Columnists and broadcasters speculated effusively on what they took to be the issue at hand: the fate of human intelligence under putative challenge from computational machinery. We may assume, however, that IBM's own zest to sponsor the match was not motivated by a sudden taste for philosophy.

IBM's ongoing attempt to endow computers with commercializable functionality sought, rather, to utilize the contest as a means of showcasing the corporation's ability to handle a complicated, high-volume event on the Internet. "IBM blanketed the Web with what may have been the biggest single-event ad campaign ever conducted on the Internet," by one account; "clickable" banner ads were placed at fifty Web sites. The Web site set up by IBM itself utilized a graphical chessboard whose pieces moved in synch with the progress of the contestants' competition and that—in preparation for expected heavy traffic—required a supercomputer of the same kind that also powered Deep Blue. Over the entire course of the six-game match IBM's site registered more than 4 million visits by individual computer users hailing from 106 countries. During the final game, the site garnered about 420,000 individual user visits: enough, as the *Los Angeles Times* reported, to "compare . . . favorably with the viewership of some cable television programs."[185] IBM had succeeded, in short, in demonstrating that Internet-based events can rival television in targeting "most-needed" audiences—and on a global stage.

Demonstrated for whom? IBM's display of media programming prowess intended, of course, to impress the advertising industry. For the Internet to be developed as a consumer medium, wrote *Business Week* matter-of-factly, "there has to be something to draw millions of consumers—and advertisers hoping to reach them—to a particular corner of cyberspace."[186]

Interactivity and Relationship Marketing

For this purpose, the advertising community had already begun to fix on one of a handful of "old-standby" program genres with a demonstrated global popularity: sports and games, in a plethora of formats and business models. Games in turn engaged the potential implicit in the first of cyberspace's critical typifying features: its interactivity or, as Malone put it, in a hint of its incipient commercial harness, "impulse interactivity."[187]

As commercial media distribution channels were thrown open internationally, world sport sponsorship expenditures soared between 1989 and 1996 from around $3 billion to nearly $11 billion annually.[188] With one eye on building audiences, and the other on drawing advertising dollars, online developers were therefore quick to seek out sports and game properties.[189] By the time of IBM's demonstration, Microsoft's Internet Gaming Zone was attracting 275,000 users (Microsoft claimed 1.5 million registered members for the Zone by mid-1998).[190] Major forays into online games were also being made by America Online, Mpath Interactive, SegaSoft Heat, and Total Entertainment Network. (Computer games overall comprised a $1.2 billion market.)[191] Megamedia developers of sports Web sites included CBS, Disney, News Corporation, and Time-Warner.[192] The National Football League Web site (itself linked to Disney's) also drew big crowds—360,000 users on each of the two days of the league's college draft early in 1998.[193] AudioNet presented the 1997 Super Bowl, with play-by-play coverage in three languages to 500,000 listeners—impressive enough figures for IBM to want to host the official Web site for Super Bowl XXXII in 1998 (with chequered success).[194] Marketeers plunged into intensive analysis of how best to integrate sports and games into advertiser-supported Internet services.

For more than a year, nevertheless, the attempt to recreate the Internet as an advertiser-supported medium appeared to some to be ill-starred. Concern floated through a solicitous press that the fortunes of Web-based advertising, and of the Web publishers who sought to make it a staple, had not mirrored the earlier unprecedented stampede into Internet stocks. Spending for brokered online ads grew steadily during 1996, to around $265 million to $300 million, while online shopping revenues also increased—but not on the exponential slope hoped for by boosters. "Advertisers Still Trying to Get a Line on Net Users," suggested the *Los Angeles Times;* "Payoff Still Elusive In Internet Gold Rush," declared the *New York Times.* What, the press wondered, were the sources of the malaise?[195]

Was it that Internet advertising was too narrowly based, being confined mainly to computer-related companies? Or that systems of audience measurement were still in development so that proof was lacking that Internet promotions actually work? Or that "click-through" rates remained low—testifying to viewers' sluggishly indifferent movement from banner ads to sponsors' sites? Or was it that trying to generate business on the Internet was intrinsically like "dropping your business cards on a Manhattan sidewalk during rush hour[:] Almost no one knows you exist, and the few who stumble upon your card are unlikely to be the kind of business prospects you were looking for"?[196]

The questions posed were suggestive—but *not* of the collapse of advertiser support as a leading Web business model. Far from it: by the second quarter of 1997, Web ad spending had picked up by an estimated 25 percent over the first quarter to some $162 million. Internet advertising, though still accounting for less than the total advertising expenditures garnered by outdoor media, continued to grow. Moving through eight successive quarters of growth, in 1998 it became a billion-dollar business.[197] As the number of Netizens grew larger, high-tech companies like IBM and Microsoft (which suggested that its Web ad expenditures might soon exceed its TV budget)[198] were (somewhat unevenly) joined by major consumer manufacturers like Toyota, Kellogg, and Ford.[199] Exclusive marketing tie-ins were springing up throughout cyberspace, as retailers hungry to develop their brands paid top dollar to gain preferred links to the Web's most popular entry points, the portal sites described earlier.[200]

At these destination sites, advertising revenues were driving overall growth (at America Online by mid-1997 they were outpacing subscriber fees), and thus there was every reason to agree with Intel CEO Andrew Grove that "Net advertising is becoming a big deal."[201]

But Web advertising trends hinted at a second key typifying feature of the new consumer medium. It is important to stress here that brokered space actually comprised only the tip of the Internet's commercial advertising iceberg: thousands of corporations had already ponied up *billions* of dollars to furnish themselves with serviceable Web sites.[202] The rationale for these expenditures is that marketers, as one writer suggests, "cannot ultimately succeed on the Web by planting themselves between another site's content and its audience. A brand must rather seek to 'create itself as a destination' in its own right."[203] Corporate sites *themselves* thus must be counted a critical category of Web advertising. The proper balance of expenditures on corporate home pages and brokered Web ads thus began to preoccupy learned disputants within the advertising community.[204]

Less than explosive early corporate interest in paying for brokered Internet ads was, in part, a consequence less of advertisers' indifference than of a newfound ability to mediate Web experience for users independently. During 1997, for example, no fewer than 7 million users visited Toyota Motors' Web site, which overtook the company's 800 number as its best source of sales leads.[205] A survey revealed that during 1997 an estimated 72 percent of online users claimed to have visited a company's home page, up from 53 percent a year earlier; the vast majority of users (90 percent) said they visited corporate Web sites to find product information.[206] Small wonder that the leading form of branding on the Web among fifty major advertisers—each spending more than $100 million on advertising over a two-year period—was not interstitials or push ads, or even sponsorships or banners, but corporate Web sites.[207]

Not all consumer manufacturers, to be sure, were making commitments at this level. Procter & Gamble, still purchasing only around $12 million worth of Web advertisements on an annualized basis in mid-1998, worried explicitly that the Internet remained too inaccessible. With at least one of its brands in the pantries of 98 percent of U.S. households, P&G hoped to gain more inclusive reach than the Web provided.[208] However, consumer product companies became the second-largest category of Web advertisers during the fourth quarter of 1997.[209] Procter & Gamble joined wholeheartedly with other advertisers, moreover, in seeking to use the Internet as an extension of direct marketing, by which sponsors interact with individual customers via records of product purchases and media preferences.

Originating in direct mail and freephone (or 800) numbers, direct marketing quickly also made its way onto the Internet media platform. Transnational consumer products manufacturers, as Joseph Turow has aptly emphasized, searched out means of implementing "an ongoing conversation with every desirable customer."[210] "The whole purpose of a Brand," declared the chairman of Unilever in almost identical language, "is to create a long-term relationship with the Consumer, and advertising is simply one way—the most efficient way we've yet devised—to conduct a dialogue with that consumer."[211] By taking advantage of the Net's unparalleled abilities to target well-heeled consumers' interests and tastes, to provide "depth" to brand-related interactions, to offer transactional services, and to audit audience behavior, companies were hopeful of utilizing the Internet media platform to attain an altogether new level of involvement with their most-needed customers—worldwide.[212]

Carrying over into cyberspace as sponsors flexed their muscles, in turn, are practices that have long since become customary throughout conventional media. Who said advertisers have an obligation to support all the publishers that may choose to throw in with them? Advertisers clustered around the most heavily trafficked Web portals, where they could reach the largest needed audiences; by one account, these leading sites raked in nearly three-fifths of Internet ad dollars by 1998.[213] The effect was, predictably, to put financial pressure on less popular sites,[214] much as advertisers' preference for the cost efficiency of a municipality's leading newspaper once helped to transform newspapers into local monopolies. Indeed, after an equivalent and related proliferation, general-interest print magazines about the Internet began to face their own shakeout during summer 1997. "There's not enough consumer interest nor is there enough ad revenue to support all these magazines," declared a media director for the J. Walter Thompson advertising agency. A contributing factor was the shift away from consumer magazines, in favor of weekly

trade journals aimed at business subscribers, by Internet company advertisers.[215] "You're not going to have 400 Web sites selling advertising,"
one Internet company executive brusquely summarized—let alone ten
thousand.[216]

Similarly, as we have seen, sponsors were not imprudent enough to
commit large sums to the Web without reliable audience measurement
systems. A company called DoubleClick promised significant innovation
on this score and thereby pointed up a third critical feature of the new
medium. DoubleClick sold space on behalf of Travelocity, AltaVista,
USA Today, and about sixty other Internet sites—just four of which provide 60 percent of its revenue—and displayed 900 million ads to 20 million users in November 1997 alone.[217] DoubleClick links together
thematically congruent Web sites into relatively coherent networks and,
by monitoring their usage, builds user profiles on the basis of which it
can instantaneously deliver customized ads. During 1996, DoubleClick
identified the preferences of some 10 million Web surfers, with a reported
100,000 more profiles flowing in each day since. The firm advertised
its Web "branding tools" and claimed "a dedicated team of Sponsorship Specialists who develop integrated promotions and build Web
communities."[218]

Sponsors seek stable access to specific, most-needed audiences. This
translated into a growing fashion for "Internet communities," virtual
neighborhoods populated by steady Netizens rather than cybertran-
sients—Web surfers—whose unfocused forays are less easily exploited.[219]
(Nabisco, PepsiCo, and Kellogg were among the corporations that incorporated—what else?—games "to get Web surfers to stick with their
sites.")[220] The horizon of the Internet consumer medium in turn re-
ceded toward experiences that give Web users incentive to interact
under the sign of one or another brand. Sponsored chatrooms, for example, encouraged users to exchange personal messages that context-
ualize their use of particular commodities—detergent say, or malt
liquor, or jeans—within the span of everyday social interaction.[221] Interactive genres of different kinds, from drama to news to games, seemed
certain as well to evolve under the watchful eye of sponsors who
can lard them in all sorts of creative ways with product mentions and
demonstrations.

These ongoing reformulations of Web experience often put a premium on audience engagement. But the sponsor system mandated that use of the Net be subordinated to its straitened terms of attention and priority. "Lately," expounded Robert Herbold, in an advertisement aimed at business executives,

there's been a lot of debate about who really owns a brand. Is it the company or the consumer. I think consumers own the products, and if you listen carefully, they can help you shape them very, very well. But the brand belongs to you. And if you're going to be successful over time, you can never abdicate that ownership. That might not sound politically correct, but it's true.[222]

Microsoft's own brand, declared Herbold, constituted "a sacred statement": "what Microsoft is working to stand for."[223] Thus was a cultural practice on the Web consecrated, on advanced capitalism's most hallowed ground.

All told, the typifying features of the Web—its interactivity, its use in building more direct relations between sponsors and consumers, and its unparalleled capacity for auditing and surveillance—carried profound implications for "relationship marketing." To what structuring impulses did these new practices lend themselves?

The Changing Mediascape

The assumption is insistently promulgated that the Internet comprises a prospectively universal mass medium in which "everyone" will soon participate. Nothing could be more unlikely. Instead, there is reason to believe that the Internet is bound up in a profound threefold shift of the greater media system, from "mass" to "class" marketing, from national to transnational marketing, and from what we might call probabilistic to individualized marketing. Advertisers have been pivotal to this triple reorientation.

Rapid deployment of the Internet as a transnational consumer medium is the next step in a multifaceted, and currently very aggressive, expansion of this same kind.[224] Web-originated programming, from the Mars Pathfinder probe to ordinary radio shows, has demonstrated an arresting potential to reach global audiences. Advertisers have not been slow to post their wares on this transnational venue. Always looking for prospective "premium" readers, for example, the *New York Times* boasts to advertisers that its brand name "deliver[s] a high-quality audience" of Web subscribers around the world.[225] Yahoo!'s search engine, with 900 advertisers in the United States, had attracted a not inconsiderable seventy European advertisers by mid-1997; some 30 percent of visitors to Yahoo!'s Web site were from outside the United States.[226] AltaVista, said to be Europe's most popular search engine, sought to outflank home-grown rivals by offering service—and advertising—in seventeen languages, while another rival, Lycos (a corporate spinoff of Carnegie-Mellon University) teamed up with the German media giant Bertelsmann to furnish access to its directory in thirty-seven local languages.[227] In a sophisticated multilingual attempt to sell both advertising and computer products, meanwhile, International Data Group consolidated its cyberspace operations to establish a more heavily trafficked gateway to 140 ad-supported Web sites in forty-five countries.[228]

Concurrent with this transnational extension, however, the Internet is also paradoxically implicated in a calculated social *contraction* of the mediascape. The point may be made by turning to the ongoing metamorphosis in the United States from the near universal coverage achieved by unbilled (that is, "free") network television broadcasters a generation ago to what is now termed *broadreach television.* Four network broadcasters in 1998 commanded less than 60 percent of the prime-time TV audience, while cable channels and other new media continued to augment their collective audience share. This was not simply the result of some kind of ineffable audience preference for fee-based cable channels, VCRs, and the Internet.

Rather, once more, viewers' desires were mediated and channeled by sponsorship. Sales by direct marketers in the United States rose an average of 7.8 percent a year between 1991 and 1996 to $1.2 trillion compared with a growth rate of 5.4 percent a year for all consumer and business-to-business sales. Even manufacturers of the most everyday commodities, such as soaps and over-the-counter medicines, in turn unevenly endorsed altered product development and media marketing strategies. Brylane, a catalog company that sells clothes for large people, had 21 million customers on its database, who can be segmented in no less than seventy-five different ways. The company's catalogs were targeted to reflect this segmentation strategy as *The Economist* reports: pink dresses on one cover, blue trousers on another.[229] Harrah's Entertainment, with its casinos on riverboats and in Reno, sought to compile the gambling industry's most extensive customer database, with personal details about 6 million people amassed from banking reports, credit-card records, and the casinos' own systems. "We can target customers based on . . . how valuable to me as a customer you are," explains a Harrah's marketing executive.[230]

Across the mediascape, advertisers want audiences delivered to them in predictable quantities and at standard and comparably efficient costs. However, leading consumer products companies have long since abandoned one-size-fits-all pitches to an undifferentiated mass market. The sweep of advertiser practice over the past two decades instead has been toward increasingly disaggregated market segments. Access to the relatively large broadcast audience that remains still commands a premium, which helped over-the-air network television ad spending to grow by a healthy 12.8 percent (to $13.08 billion) between 1995 and 1996. Yet during 1997 network ad volume experienced an absolute—though slight—decline. Disney's ESPN cable channel became more profitable than its ABC broadcast network; equally portentous, over 1995 to 1996, ad spending on audience-segmenting cable TV networks increased by more than twice the network broadcasters' rate (26.5 percent to $4.47 billion); during 1997, cable network ads shot up a further 22 percent to $5.45 billion.[231] Other direct marketing media have likewise enjoyed raging growth.[232] Future media development—the Internet included—is being hostaged to this trend.

There will be no turning back to an era offering only basic, undifferentiated channels to a heterogeneous audience. Even providing access to a guaranteed number of women ages eighteen to forty-nine, as Turow comments, is often no longer sufficient; in contrast, the preference today is for, say, owners of four-year-old and newer Japanese automobiles who subscribe to *Time, Sports Illustrated, Money,* or *Life.*[233] Kraft Foods, a maker of cheese and hot dogs, is testing a system with cable system operator TCI to target different commercials to specific viewers, isolated according to ZIP codes, ethnicity, and income. Long-term, Kraft thinks it may connect interactive Web sites to TV commercials, so that as an ad for macaroni and cheese materializes, viewers can click onto a Kraft icon on the screen and connect to a Web site featuring a recipe.[234]

We have already seen that efforts by media and marketing companies to compile precise profiles of individual behavior comprise an organic aspect of this proliferating attempt at segmentation. The Web in turn makes possible a qualitative advance over previous, probability sample-based techniques for gaining knowledge of audience preferences. The *New York Times* relies on a registration system to gather data on its 1.7 million Web-site users; its market-segmenting technology obtains data on individuals' age, gender, income, and ZIP code, and ties these to identifiable email addresses.[235] Database marketing programs built up around Web-site registration information, as well as inadvertent data trails, turned personal privacy into a commercial as well as a more traditional political ("Big Brother") issue. "Privacy is always at risk as you surf," noted one newspaper headline. In a study of 1,400 Web sites in March 1998, the Federal Trade Commission found that 85 percent collected personal information but only 14 percent provided any notice about what they do with the data.[236]

Targeted Web programs comprised the other half of this same effort. This brings us back to the most-needed audience singled out by consumer products manufacturers such as Procter & Gamble: women. Until recently, such marketers aimed messages at women mainly in product categories considered feminine: fashion, frozen foods, women's hygiene. By the mid-1990s, sometimes gingerly, advertisers also began to market traditionally male categories—automobiles, home repair, and, most salient, technology—to women.[237] Ed Meyer, then CEO of Grey Advertising, was asked in March of 1995 what "key issues" had to be explored with regard to new media. He responded: "One of the biggest issues is how we get women to use new-media applications and embrace these new technologies. With 70 percent of traditional advertising directed to women, it's vital to the success of new-media opportunities to appeal to and be used by women."[238]

There is an outstanding doctoral dissertation to be written detailing the intensive efforts made throughout the last several years to lure women onto the Web. Barbie dominated the list of top-selling kids' computer games during 1997;[239] the most prominent female TV industry executive, Geraldine B. Laybourne, resigned from Walt Disney to form a company devoted to creating programming for women and children using television and the Internet.[240] Women's use of the Internet has duly increased since 1995, at least in the United States; women accounted for less than 10 percent of Internet users a few years ago but, according to two tallies, totaled nearly one-third by summer 1996 and almost 40 percent a year later.[241] By mid-1998, Denis F. Beausejour, Procter & Gamble's vice president for worldwide advertising, could boast that "more than 40 percent" of 42 million U.S. Internet users were women, "the vast majority of whom represent the target audience for most of our brands."[242]

A lengthening series of startup Web sites, some backed by name-brand media, targeted women. Hearst New Media's HomeArts, for instance, billed itself as "the online home of *Bob Vila's American Home, Cosmopolitan, Country Living, Country Living Gardener, Good Housekeeping, House Beautiful, Marie Claire, Mr. Food's Easy Cooking, Popular Mechanics, Redbook, Town & Country* and *Victoria*."[243] A magazine for women called *UnderWire*[244] was one of Microsoft's six introductory (since failed) TV-like channels. The Women's Forum collected a not-insubstantial 15 million monthly impressions during 1997 by aggregating twelve different sites, ranging from Super Model to USA Bride to Garden Escape; the network delivered this audience to sponsors aiming to reach females eight to forty.[245] THRIVE, a Time, Inc. service, boasted that "Every month, over 1,200,000 of the most active and affluent people on the planet use THRIVE. And 65 percent of THRIVE users are women."[246]

Major advertisers flocked to try out at least some of these services. Levi Strauss sponsored a fashion and trend content area presented by a site that targeted six- to twelve-year-old girls, using games built around celebrities such as Justin Cooper and franchise characters like Hercules, Xena, and Woody Woodpecker.[247] Procter & Gamble launched PHYS, a site focusing on women's health, in partnership with CondeNet.[248] P&G also helped launch ParentTime at Work, an attempt to reach women who work outside the home that signed on 90,000 viewers in its first two months.[249] And, on the other hand, high-tech companies moved into traditional media to target women. For example, in a $3 to $4 million campaign—its first major effort to target women—Intel used a fashion-show theme in a magazine ad running in such titles as *Martha Stewart Living, Glamour,* and *House Beautiful*.[250]

The term *demographics* is often used to denote the sponsor system's dual embrace of media targeting and market segmentation. But *demographics* can harbor a profoundly misleading implication. Current marketing practice portends no carryover into the consumer domain of the principle of equality of representation. Just as the market does not cater to every background and personal taste, so the practice of demographic marketing is not truly pluralistic: by no means is every member of society equally sought.

On one side, advertisers select and lavish attention on media content that they hope will gain them disproportionate access to favored audiences. On the other hand, as Turow underlines, the greater the income possessed by a given social grouping, the more extensive the segmentation to which it will be subjected. Dayton Hudson, a department store chain, found that a small fraction of its customers—some 2.5 percent—purchases 75 percent of its goods. Its Great Rewards marketing program—typical of other frequent-buyer campaigns to ensure customer loyalty—accords special perks to this select fraternity.[251] Indeed, as Oscar Gandy has shown,[252] even the prices commanded by different types of mailing lists are scarred by social inequality: frequent fliers who own Range Rovers will reliably command a higher cost-per-thousand names than, say, microwave oven owners who are also buyers of canned baked beans.

Thus the uneven distribution of wealth is massively ratified across the mediascape, through the practice of sponsorship. Even apparently disparate axes of market segmentation—gender, race and ethnicity, age—often lead back circuitously to the uneven capacity for discretionary expenditure. In an age of increasing *class* inequality, companies from AT&T to Disney to General Motors have even openly embraced *two-tier marketing* plans, whereby products and sales pitches are deliberately polarized so as to reach "two different Americas"—rich and poor.[253]

Actually, there are no guarantees that the poor will even achieve such a second-class kind of inclusion. Radio stations that aim programming at African American and Hispanic audiences are a tough sell to advertisers; even when they enjoy strong audience ratings, they must charge lower rates than Anglo-oriented rivals.[254] A similar plight afflicts a magazine called *City Family,* which is aimed at low- and middle-income immigrants in New York City. *City Family* can claim a respectable circulation— 210,000 after four years—and offers English and Spanish editions with practical information on such subjects as handling debt, guarding against fires at home, and becoming a citizen. (Often the periodical doubles as a textbook tool for adults learnings English or high school students learning Spanish.) Most of its readers earn less than $20,000 a year, and it is written at a fifth-grade level. *City Family* is distributed free in places like health clinics and community centers. Its expenses are paid out of foundation grants and a few well-meaning individual backers. But its editor, Arthur Schiff, recounts how advertisers have yet to respond, despite recurrent appeals. "The resistance among advertiser stems, Mr. Schiff suggests, from classism," writes a *New York Times* reporter: " 'Ad people don't have a category called 'immigrant,' Mr. Schiff said. 'Advertisers say, "If my client wants to reach women eighteen to thirty-four, I'll get the women in the highest income level who buy the most. You have something unusual, but we don't want it." ' "[255]

In this context, the Internet itself helps to animate what some writers have called "a digital divide"—between wealthy, educated Internet users and poor, disproportionately nonwhite nonusers.[256] This is not simply a matter of basic access. The Internet's social exclusivity comprises an alluring enticement to many market-segmenting advertisers. Perversely, however, even a steady extension of household Internet access cannot be expected to alter the picture, except by affording sponsors a larger canvas: audience segmentation and targeting, backed by the Internet's vastly enhanced apparatus for surveying and tracking audience behavior, will be generalized across the length and breadth of the Internet consumer medium, whatever the latter's ultimate scope.

· · · ·

By 1998, the prospect of an open Net, with carefree mores and informal codes of organizational conduct, had been laid to rest. This is not to say that alternative and oppositional uses of cyberspace did not remain widespread, sometimes securing significant political or sociocultural achievements. But the overall process of commercialization drove these contrary uses to the margins; they occurred despite, rather than because of, cyberspace's institutional reorganization.

Audience members turn to the media for recreation, for relaxation, for news and entertainment, and as I have tried to show, media companies are eager to provide these as a consumer marketing service. Viewed from a different angle, however, the media marketing complex actually furnishes a *business* service: that of assembling and delivering audiences to sponsors. In turn, the Web's marketing makeover is merely a specific instance of a more encompassing change. An analogous shift is apparent in efforts to harness the Internet for delivering a second leading business service, which is not usually even associated with the commercial, for-profit economy: education.

4

Networking the Higher-Learning Industry

New profitmaking institutions are emerging to provide education. To compete in this growing and increasingly segmented market, many traditional educational institutions may have to curtail some of the services that they provide, retaining only those that have the greatest economic and political return. Changes such as these are, in fact, already occurring in almost all sectors of the educational system.[1]

What peoples, what cultures, what languages will take control of these new education industries and impose them on the world? Those who do not succeed will disappear from the historical map.[2]

The vision of untrammeled information access has long accorded a special role to communications media. In 1972, for example, an influential commission on higher education and instructional technology gave voice to what it called the "ultimate dream": "national interconnection of independent information, communication, and instructional resources, with the combined capacity of making available to any student, anywhere in the country, at any time, learning from the total range of accumulated human knowledge."[3] As it expanded beyond its secretive military origins, cyberspace practically invited this prophecy to its table. Via the Internet, the dream of an informational cornucopia seemed to be nearing actualization.

Through the 1980s, the fledgling Internet—anchored increasingly firmly within the university community—sustained new kinds of information sharing among dispersed groups of researchers. Particularly noteworthy was its impact on the scale and range of international scientific collaboration. Researchers tapping in from remote locations gained routine access to the Net's growing trove of interconnected information resources; ideas and data began to be shared across continents on an hourly basis.[4] The vision of information abundance gained widespread credibility.

During the mid-1990s, however, the sweeping process of commercialization described earlier in this book (in chapter 3) impinged dramatically on the Internet's scientific and educational function. In 1995, the total number of commercial Internet sites exceeded the number of educational and governmental sites for the first time; the percentage of Web sites running from the *.com* domain in the United States shot up from 1.5 percent in June 1993 to 50 percent in January 1996.[5] The demise of NSFNET and of its system of subsidies threatened the nonprofit regional networks that had emerged to grant universities preferred access to cyberspace. As these regional systems were acquired by private Internet access providers, universities had to reckon with the implications of their newfound reliance on for-profit vendors.[6] The massive growth of commercial Web applications, meanwhile, clotted traffic to the point of crippling scientists' access to research resources on the Net.[7]

However, an even more forbidding cloud cast the vision of cyberspace as an abundant tree of knowledge into deep shadow. The Internet had been overlaid on a domain—education—that was itself already awash in change. Indeed, it was becoming apparent that the entire established system of skill formation and knowledge creation was heading for a makeover. Where once had existed nonprofit institutions, increasingly, there were now commercial vendors. Where once had existed relatively autonomous instructional and learning processes, increasingly, there were now attempts to cater more directly to labor markets. The system of educational provision was being reoriented toward familiar corporate practices that were foreign to the bulk of earlier educational endeavor: growing utilization of casualized labor, productivity enhancement measures, and product development based on profit and loss potentials. A concurrent and related reform, toward school-to-work programs, lifelong learning, and "new partnerships," symptomatized an intensifying vocationalization of the educational process.

Far from portending a radical breakthrough into information plenitude, the Internet's effect was to broaden and deepen these main channels of change: Cyberspace lent itself both to an unparalleled market takeover of the learning process and to a relentless vocationalism. Indeed the Internet actually catalyzed the late stages of this complex reaction; or, if you like, the Net kicked the ongoing metamorphosis of education into overdrive.

The Shadow System

To gain our bearings, let us begin with a backward, contextualizing look. Between 1875 and 1913, the number of North American colleges and universities increased from around 360 to around 500, at which time Europe boasted only about 150 such institutions.[8] U.S. colleges also were extensively restructured to accommodate new corporate demands for scientific research and for access to greater numbers of educated white-collar workers. Individual capitalists endowed entire universities, such as Stanford, Vanderbilt, and the University of Chicago, and structured them so as to emphasize these new priorities. Philanthropic organizations—notably, Carnegie and Rockefeller—deployed their considerable resources and deftly effected disproportionately far-reaching changes in the organization of higher education.[9] Aggravated rivalry among resource-poor colleges permitted these well-endowed philanthropies to reorganize a system that had limited higher education to a narrow stratum. Juxtaposed on several decades of less coordinated initiative, and on the unprecedented coordinative mechanisms created during World War I, their efforts helped to place the system of American higher education on its modern footing.

The elective system of courses had already long since begun to encourage specialization and graduate instruction and to hasten coalescence of individual departments. Generally standardized instructional criteria were under cultivation; administrative bureuacracies had been effectively introduced. The intellectual division of labor was rapidly and dramatically extended and enlarged. About fifty top universities collectively came to comprise the nation's premier institution for basic scientific research. The expanding number of high school graduates fed into a growing stream of college enrollments.[10]

Incomplete Corporate Domination

Higher education had been brought into communion with business, and educational practice was made subject thereby to a loose corporate hegemony. Thick with enterprisers, the governing boards that set university policy insisted that the functions performed by their faculty cater broadly to business demands. Curricula were adjusted in light of labor-market needs; scientific research of long-range import for business growth became a fixture. Corporate employers garnered access to legions of skilled technical and white-collar workers, whose training was subsidized by the state, and to basic research, also heavily subsidized. A new institution—the community college—was created to widen the distribution of needed vocational training skills.

Higher education, however, had not been entirely dominated. Market forces and vocational objectives had intruded, and corporate influence had been widely regularized and legitimated. But the nation's colleges remained relatively free of *direct* labor-market functions and profitmaking imperatives. Economic, physical, and temporal factors permitted this loose separation of the two interdependent spheres. The university remained a noncommercial institution rather than a for-profit enterprise, housing its inhabitants at some distance from the workplace and preparing a cohort of young adults for a worklife to follow. Arguments were mounted over how and to what extent education and business should mesh their functions, but debaters had to take into account that the two zones of practice remained essentially discrete.

The higher-education system continued to expand mightily. During the early Cold War decades, state and federal support for higher education swelled from year to year, as universities built up faculties, libraries, plant, student enrollments, and budgets. Social movements for equal opportunity at work and in education itself expanded as women, minorities, and blue-collar workers transformed the demographics of higher-education attendance. Community and junior college enrollments mushroomed; total attendance in public community colleges increased tenfold between 1960 and 1980 from 400,000 to 4 million.[11] In contrast to the experiences of other nations and previous decades, by the 1970s higher education in the United States had become broadly accessible. Working-class students, moreover, tended to reverse the priorities set for them by vocationally oriented institutions and utilized community colleges as a springboard into comprehensive four-year institutions.[12]

During the 1970s, however, the long-standing distinction between education and business began to erode. A trio of linked changes was responsible. Inhouse corporate education began to subvert the structural position of postsecondary education as a quasi-state function. Adult learning and recurrent education shattered the notion that schooling serves to prepare the young for a subsequent worklife. New information technologies, among which the Internet ultimately loomed preeminent, eradicated the physical and social barriers between college and workplace. Building on these changes, a vocationally driven *learning industry* began to coalesce. And education as a whole began to transform, unevenly but unmistakably, into a leading edge of digital capitalism.[13] Let us look more closely at these parallel shifts, beginning with the trend toward inhouse corporate education.

Inhouse Corporate Education

Throughout the twentieth century, most prospective workers pursued training within the state-subsidized system in four-year and, increasingly, in two-year colleges. A few companies, however, early on created their own pedagogical programs, forming inhouse schools and institutes. Hoe and Company's factory school, established in 1872, permitted that New York City manufacturer of printing presses to train machinists, the better to accommodate its expanding volume of business. Similar schools were created at Westinghouse in 1888, at General Electric and at the Baldwin Locomotive Works in 1901, and at International Harvester in 1907. Technologically progressive firms, such as Western Electric, Goodyear, Ford, and National Cash Register, were at the forefront of this initiative. Often supplanted thereby were systems of apprenticeship that had sustained a greater measure of worker control of recruitment and shop-floor labor processes. By 1913, there had been sufficient growth in corporate provision of entry-level training that sixty representatives from thirty-four different companies formed a National Association of Corporation Schools.

Over the last century, then, beside that portion of postsecondary education provided by colleges and universities, a second or "shadow" system of education and training also took form. Only recently did notice begin to be taken, however, of the enormous range of pedagogical activity that had come to be housed outside the academy.[14]

To be sure, the gap between these corporate training programs and the system of formal higher education was still wide. Thoroughly vocational in orientation, corporate classrooms were hardly given to the heady abstractions of the liberal arts. For their part, the colleges remained residually influenced by genteel nineteenth-century traditions. Though vocational curricula entered numerous universities via business and professional schools, and though a new educational institution, the community college, was created largely to instill vocational skills among nonelite youths, a multifaceted liberal arts education remained hegemonic. *Training* and *education* in turn remained largely disparate.

But significant subterranean change was underway. Some companies began to extend the sweep of their training activities; the National Association of Corporation Schools became the American Management Association in 1923, signifying that the field now encompassed both blue- and white-collar segments of the division of labor. Encouraged by growing federal appropriations for vocational education after 1917, the nascent shadow system began to grow.

A variety of historical exigencies contributed to its expansion. The Emergency Fleet Corporation of the U.S. Shipping Board, established during World War I, trained several hundred thousand workers to build ships in support of the war effort, pioneering industrial skills training techniques as it did so.[15] In the Great Depression of the 1930s, with millions of workers unemployed, prevailing processes of skill formation were massively disrupted; innumerable apprenticeships were sacrificed, while much formal training by industry was abandoned. With little work to be found, skill acquisition through on-the-job experience declined. World War II, on the other hand, created a huge civilian labor pool harboring unprecedented numbers of women and older persons lacking training in required wartime production fields, as well as a huge, likewise untrained, military force. To meet these needs, government-sponsored education and training were introduced on a national scale.[16] During World War II, the Training Within Industry section of the War Production Board taught training methods to no less than 2 million plant supervisors and foremen.

Training was identified as "an integral part of the supervisory function," and training directors emerged to coordinate the effort.[17] Corporate leadership came from Standard Oil of New Jersey, Western Electric, and U.S. Steel, in some cases from the same individuals who had supervised the World War I initiative. Wartime production was also expedited by a new Engineering, Science, and Management War Training program. Conducted under college and university sponsorship, both on and off campus, the latter aimed to upgrade employees in newly crucial management and technology subjects.[18]

As in so many other ways, World War II laid the groundwork for a transformed civilian reality. To add to the craft of sales, which business leaders hoped might play a role in persuading people to abandon the "habits of restraint" fixed by the Depression, the National Society of Sales Training Executives was created in 1940 in Cleveland.[19] And, guided by representatives of the petroleum industry, whose training directors had been meeting since 1939, a national organization—the American Society of Training Directors (now the American Society for Training and Development)—was established in 1945. The process of secular enlargement continued thereafter, as the objects of training, originally manufacturing and marketing personnel, came to include government, utility, and bank employees.[20]

During the early 1970s, the turf occupied by corporate training and education expanded decisively. "We are seeing an almost explosive growth of the field," observed Robert L. Craig, vice president of the American Society for Training and Development, in 1976: "Education and training in the world of work has become a major part of the real education system. *Employers* are increasingly recognizing the pragmatic need for the continual development of the knowledge and skills of the workforce as essential to organizational success."[21]

IBM had created its first education center back in 1933. By 1969, the computer manufacturer engaged a full-time and part-time faculty of 3,417, offering 18.5 million student contact hours of instruction—equivalent to nearly 40,000 full-time students and comprising a significant percentage of the firm's entire U.S. workforce of 150,000.[22] By 1981 IBM's Systems Research Institute had supplied intensive education to 6,600 engineering alumni. Training was furnished at numerous locations, although in 1979 a full-fledged campus was also established near corporate headquarters at Armonk, New York. On average, each IBM employee received ten days of education per year, ranging from special lectures to bonafide courses, both inside and outside company facilities.[23]

Before its mammoth corporate divestiture, to choose another example, AT&T annually spent $1.7 billion on employee education, offering 12,000 courses at 1,300 locations in 1980. By 1982, just before its court-ordered breakup, AT&T's total education and training staff numbered about 10,000. Indeed, as deregulation began to shift AT&T's aims and strategies, the company offered training to encourage workers to acclimatize to the liberalizing environment.[24] Around that same time, Xerox was spending $125 million on educational programs to train roughly 40 percent of its 120,000 employees each year.[25] Although training programs had proliferated to the point that companies with just a few hundred employees had involved themselves, between 200 and 300 of the largest corporations accounted for half of the overall formal training paid for by business and industry.[26]

This burgeoning corporate system of training and education was beginning to impinge directly on higher education. By 1987, some twenty-six "major educational facilities" on corporate grounds "offer[ed] baccalaureates through Ph.D.s."[27] General Electric, for example, maintained an in-house university, the Crotonville, New York, Management Training Center, run by a former Harvard professor. In 1981 the Center serviced 5,000 new employees and high-potential middle managers; 25,000 others attended courses elsewhere within GE.[28] More often, bonafide higher-educational institutions were integrated as partners. GE, for example, expanded its advanced engineering program during the early 1980s to operate at eleven locations throughout the United States via cooperative relationships with fifteen universities. The program required three and one-half years of study, alternating company-taught courses with periods of on-campus academic work. It was intended to supply General Electric with engineers of sufficient depth and breadth in their technical understanding "to make basic contributions in the development of new or improved products."[29]

By the 1990s, inhouse corporate education had progressed yet again, in part as a result of tax laws that allowed large corporate writeoffs of education and training costs. First, the range of automated applications had widened. Computerized simulations for airline pilot training had been used for years; now simulations likewise began to be used to train cashiers, by Dayton Hudson's Target stores, by Motorola for teaching workers how to operate robotic machinery, and by the KFC division of Pepsico for meal packers. The cost of computerized multimedia CD-ROMs, seen throughout corporate training divisions "as a substitute for live instructors," ran as high as $25,000 to $250,000 per instructional hour, depending on the complexity of the material and the media used. However, once the initial capital investment was made, the resulting product could be reused indefinitely, for any number of trainees. Any organization whose training needs involved more than 200 people was urged to consider this cost-efficient technology.[30] New forms of computer-aided instruction proliferated to teach subjects—such as word processing or geometry, foreign languages or computer programming—that can be learned, after a fashion, through a hierarchically organized sequence of lessons. *Expert systems* proffered additional means of on-the-job training by teaching employees cost-efficient techniques by which to perform complex tasks; by 1988, some 8,500 corporate expert systems were said to be in development.[31]

Even more impressive was the proliferation of corporate education programs. In 1983, around 400 business sites in the United States included a building labeled *college, university, institute,* or *education center.*[32] But there existed no fewer than 1,200 so-called *corporate universities* by 1998.[33] Still mostly small outfits, to be sure, corporate universities were also operated by a roster of blue-chip companies, including Arthur D. Little, AT&T, Bell Atlantic, Anheuser-Busch, Dell, Disney, Ford, GE, GM, Intel, MasterCard, McDonnell Douglas, Oracle, SBC, Sears Roebuck, Sprint, Sun Microsystems, and Xerox. Making increasing use of partnerships with traditional accredited universities, the 100 top corporate universities handled a combined volume of over 4 million students.[34] The largest such operation, Motorola University, boasted more than 400 full-time faculty, with another 800 part-time contract teachers. Hoping ultimately to grant accredited degrees, Motorola University taught some 100,000 students annually, 22 percent of whom came to it from outside the company.[35]

As this example suggests, corporate training programs had burst beyond inhouse applications. Companies that had originated training programs for internal use often went on to assemble catalogs of instructional materials and services for vending outside their own organizations.[36] Nell Eurich hailed the change, as "corporations and companies . . . are opening their classrooms to each other and selling educational services to other companies."[37] Northrup University, a global center of aeronautical training, supplied contract educational programs to foreign companies such as Saudi Arabian Airlines.[38] Walt Disney University ran an M.B.A. program for other firms hoping to master the Disney technique.[39] Arthur Andersen, a big accounting and consulting firm, tailored computer-embedded training programs to client needs worldwide; its rival Peat Marwick boasted teaching facilities in sixty countries.[40]

The same trends were evident, albeit in a somewhat less developed way, among transnational corporations based outside the United States. "Large Japanese employers expect to provide virtually all the vocational education that new recruits need after they are hired," wrote two authorities in 1992: "Toyota plans to put every new high-school graduate it hires for the front line through a two-year full-time course in digital electronics and mechatronics before they ever see the assembly line."[41] NEC, with overseas operations in twenty-eight countries by the early 1990s and 25,000 overseas staff, developed an extensive and multifaceted inhouse education program to support its transnationalized activities.[42] Having dedicated significant resources to inhouse education for several years, in 1989 Fuji Xerox spun off its staff training division into a separate company to sell its training programs—based on Xerox's own Learning International subsidiary—to others.[43] British Aerospace undertook to develop a university sporting a business school, a faculty of engineering and manufacturing technology, and a faculty of learning.[44] Although European companies generally lagged in creating such subsidiaries, one report suggested that they were edging toward acceptance of corporate universities by the mid-1990s.[45]

The annual dollar volume of this shadow education system was uncertain but unquestionably great. During the 1980s, the most reliable estimates placed it in the $30 billion to $60 billion range (in the United States only) for formal courses and training programs, with far more than this amount expended by companies for on-the-job skills.[46] No less than 250,000 full-time and an additional 500,000 part-time trainers were estimated in 1984 to be teaching at postsecondary organizations *outside* the U.S. formal higher education complex. The American Society for Training and Development claimed that around 14 million workers were served by company-sponsored training in 1987, when there were 12.3 million students attending two- and four-year colleges.[47] Such figures showed that the shadow system had become roughly comparable in size to the higher-education system itself, where the professoriate numbered about 700,000, including instructors and part-timers and where total revenues were then in the $80 billion to $110 billion range.[48] For adult students, however—which as we will see comprise a particularly important market segment—corporations provided substantially more education than higher-education institutions.

Less easily measured was the accelerating organizational momentum behind vocational training initiatives. The American Society for Training and Development's Public Policy Council was chaired in 1997 by the president of Motorola University and included twenty additional members, representing corporations such as Ford, AT&T, IBM, Corning, and Andersen Consulting, as well as "other leading institutions with recognized and successful learning systems."[49] Not only had the range of instruction offered in the shadow system now grown "as wide as in colleges and universities—from maintenance of photocopiers to basic research and theory in polymer chemistry"—but, critically, there was little evidence that any given form of instruction or course content could be privileged for the formal higher-education component. Unhappily, perhaps, no less than 18 percent of U.S. companies nevertheless offered remedial training in basic math and reading skills in 1998—up from 4 percent in the late 1980s.[50] Corporate education, in short, was radically uncontained and was encroaching on its twin as it continued to grow. As corporations expanded their reliance on networks, moreover, the border they shared with not-for-profit educational institutions lengthened. It became "progressively more difficult to decide where the university ends, where the corporate world begins and where they both fit within the larger education and training system."[51] Proliferating corporate classrooms had dramatically narrowed both the institutional distance and the programmatic distance between the workplace and the school.

Changes in accreditation comprised a revealing index to the larger shift in favor of vocationalism. (*Accreditation* is the process whereby decisions are rendered as to which institutions and programs are permitted to grant degrees and degree- or college-equivalent credit.) The New York State Board of Regents began in 1974 to evaluate and accredit *noncollegiate-sponsored instruction*. This action by a leading accrediting agency responded not to corporate demands to enter education markets but to efforts to democratize the educational franchise—to open up academe to nontraditional, *experiential* learning among working-class students. Still, it was not long before New York evaluators went on to approve courses offered by AT&T, Corning Glass, Kodak, Equitable Life Insurance, Grumman Aerospace, Manufacturers Hanover Trust, McGraw-Hill, Merrill Lynch, Mobil, Pepsi Cola, Sperry, Union Carbide, and others. At Xerox, fifty courses were approved for academic credit; General Motors, GE, and AT&T each also offered several dozen.[52] The American Council on Education by 1983 recommended college course credit for 2,250 courses offered by more than 140 business and industrial companies and other nontraditional providers.[53] In 1990, ACE had a waiting list of companies desiring evalution,[54] and accreditation continued to comprise a charged field on which adherents struggled to enlarge corporate educational prerogatives as they incorporated networked educational applications.[55]

Accrediting bodies concluded that they could not follow two sets of criteria for *traditional* and *nontraditional* institutions. The way to evaluate the growing range of educational forms and structures was, rather, to emphasize the results, or *outcomes*, of the educational process. An unaccustomed accent on monitorable *performance* was thereby introduced. Complaisant researchers began to extoll academic "productivity" and "performance-based education," dependent on apparently rigorous "statements of intended outputs in terms of skills and knowledge," along with "measures" to determine "the degree to which outputs have been achieved."[56]

Apparently intended to furnish a meaningful, fair-minded point of comparison between courses offered at liberal arts colleges and at, say, automotive manufacturing companies, this emphasis harbored implications that were actually far from neutral. Who would establish the requisite performance criteria? The measured-outcomes movement introduced a point of ostensibly valid comparison between socially disparate entities: for-profit and not-for-profit institutions. Its growth portended the subjection of formerly more autonomous educational programs and practices to a familiar management calculus.

The measured-outcomes initiative, however, comprised just one aspect of the overarching movement toward for-profit provision and vocationalism. In turn, these larger trends accelerated not, as critics repeatedly charged, owing to the failures and inefficiencies of the nation's educational system[57] but for wholly different reasons.

The Perpetual-Innovation Economy and the New Partnership

Fear and anger at the explosion of campus unrest during the 1960s doubtless boosted many employers' willingness to contemplate a more direct and expansive role in employee education. On the other hand, the heightened fear of joblessness during and after the recession of 1974 to 1975 contributed to a widespread popular acquiescence to vocationalized curricular objectives. Over the generation to follow, this anxiety was transmuted into what passed for common sense. Mainstream politicos of every shade admonished that, because "no job is truly permanent anymore . . . people will have to learn new skills and renew old ones even when their jobs are seemingly safe and stable."[58]

The movement toward for-profit vocational education was unquestionably triggered by a secular shift in the strategic orientation of the giant corporation itself. As Craig and Evers suggest, within modern science-based industry employees need to be continually trained and retrained in the state of the art as other employees continually reinvent it.[59] This compulsion is, moreover, generalized. Companies develop education programs for the engineers and scientists who devise new production processes and new products, for the production workers who build them, for the salespersons who market them, and for the service and support personnel who maintain them. Corporate training efforts are also directed (indeed, disproportionately so) at the managers and executives who try to guide these waves of technical and organizational change.[60]

Science-Based Industry

This powerful surge in demand for vocational training was virtually intrinsic to the postwar surge of science-based industry. Between 1953 and 1969, total expenditures on research and development in the United States—the center of high-tech development—climbed from $5.2 billion to $26.2 billion; by 1997, U.S. R&D spending had powered up to $206 billion.[61] Until around 1980, the federal government was the largest source of funding for such research, but since then its share of the total has steadily declined—to just under 30 percent by 1997; corporations, on the other hand, have reciprocally increased their contributions to R&D and now foot two-thirds of the overall bill.[62]

Major pharmaceutical companies were one contributor to these vast research budgets; Merck, the largest drugmaker, plowed back 19 percent of sales revenues, or around a billion and a half dollars, into R&D in 1997.[63] But information technology companies led the trend. Xerox owned around 7,000 active patents in 1998; IBM, with its $5 billion annual R&D budget, amassed an unsurpassed patent portfolio, from which it derived annual revenues of around $1 billion by 1997—up threefold since 1993.[64]

Significantly increased corporate reliance on R&D was not solely a hallmark of U.S.-based companies. The top 300 corporations worldwide spent $216 billion on R&D during 1997 (up 13 percent over 1996). The United States chipped in 133 firms to this list, and these companies contributed proportionately (45 percent) to the overall outlay. Foreign corporate pursuit of high-tech R&D, once again, was noteworthy among electronics and telecommunications companies, such as Ericsson (Sweden); Siemens (Germany); Hitachi, Matsushita, NEC, Toshiba, and Sony (Japan); Philips (The Netherlands); Northern Telecom and Bell Canada (Canada); and Alcatel Alsthom (France). Strikingly, however, U.S. networking companies such as Microsoft and Cisco powered the largest individual corporate increases in research spending, while expenditures by U.S. electronics and information technology firms more generally helped to raise total research outlays by the top U.S. companies by 17 percent—far above the increases claimed by their German, French, or Japanese counterparts.[65]

Nor, however, was R&D confined to exotic fields like software development or human genome studies. Procter & Gamble is a consumer products company that is not usually identified with high-tech innovation. Nonetheless, P&G began to mass-market throw-away diapers as a substitute for cloth ones in 1961, ushering in a market that reached nearly $4 billion in annual revenues by 1997. The legendary chemical engineer who led the diaper effort also had a hand in creating or improving products ranging from Ivory soap to stacked potato chips.[66] A record 25,261 different new packaged goods of every kind were marketed for the first time by companies in 1997, and this cascade could not have occurred absent the flow of corporate R&D.[67]

This generalized corporate compulsion to innovate intensified alongside increasing competition between transnational businesses after 1970. As the brief American Century drew to a close, monopolistic controls over technological change, like those practiced by the Big Three automakers in Detroit or by AT&T in the telephone industry, were eroded by competitors utilizing new products and production processes. Procter & Gamble applied for 16,000 patents worldwide in 1995, more than double the number three years earlier.[68] More generally, the average engineer's knowledge was said to have lost its edge (by the National Academy of Engineering) only three to seven years after formal education had been completed.[69] Firms from every sector became ever more reliant on high-technology development: to create novel commodities, to erect strategic barriers to market entry, to extend operations overseas, and to improve their ability to extract more from each unit of labor. Those that could not keep up would fall by the wayside. The mergers, acquisitions, downsizings, and corporate restructurings that characterized the 1980s and 1990s, meanwhile, placed an additional premium on management education.[70]

What economic historian Tessa Morris-Suzuki calls the "perpetual-innovation economy" thus redoubled the giant corporation's need for incoming streams of scientific and technical knowledge with which to reconfigure products and production processes.[71] And that perpetual-innovation economy was, in turn, increasingly focused around information technology—on networks.

The process of computerization placed a special premium on vocational training, and, as corporate investment in networks accelerated, vendors of software and hardware technologies came to constitute the leaders in selling training and support services to their customers. Control Data's Institute for Advanced Technology was an early foray in this direction, while AT&T's Institute for Communications and Information Management subsequently utilized direct mail advertising and toll-free registration to market courses to prospective students.[72] During the 1990s, Microsoft created an entire OnLine Institute, which standardized courseware provided by authorized third-party vendors to Microsoft's platforms, linked these vendors with an emerging group of authorized online classroom providers, and connected them to students. Microsoft also produced more than 2,000 seminars around the world to promote the outside companies that furnished specialized software and services using its products.[73] As software packages multiplied and incessant updates were released, not merely training but retraining became a corporate fixation. In the European market alone, by the mid-1990s computer vendors' technical certification courses and training materials generated annual revenues approaching $1 billion.[74] Overall, in one estimate, ten times as many vendors were selling training services in 1990 than had done so a decade before.[75] Information technology training comprised the largest portion of this burgeoning market.

But why supply such training inhouse or through contracts with vendors? Why not turn, instead, to established higher-education institutions? In truth, as we will see, the choice was not so stark: both components of the system of skills formation were called on. But one historically important reason to enlarge inhouse training programs merits particular mention: to permit major corporations selectively "to bypass the search for new employees."[76] This response was not merely a reflex of tight labor markets or of a fickle supply of required skills and competencies. There were real benefits to be derived by companies that could train their employees continually, moving them from job to job with increments of training as needed. These strategic advantages included a heightened ability to cultivate familiarity with the company's "corporate culture"; an increased flexibility in devising products and production processes; and—not least—an enhanced proprietary control of "corporate" knowledge.

The trend to inhouse education also initially harbored an important paternalistic element—in the United States through the 1970s and in Japan all the way until the 1990s' economic downturn put at risk large corporations' widespread (though far from universal) practice of lifetime employment. At high-tech companies like IBM or Hewlett-Packard, particular employee skills could be made obsolete because of something as simple as a change in a product mix or the overhaul of a production line.[77] Two top IBM executives stated in 1975—before the full-scale attack on the welfare state and the commitment to neoliberalism that marked the Reagan administration—that "the easy solution of generous early retirement to remove those whose skills are out of date from competition in the workforce may be appropriate in individual circumstances, but it is philosophically unacceptable. We cannot discard intelligent and useful human beings at an ever earlier age when in fact their life span and requirements for useful activity in the retirement years are growing."[78] IBM instead advocated promotion from within. Such a policy virtually mandated reliance on systematic and massive job retraining programs such as those the company pioneered.[79]

That was then. As neoliberal policies consolidated and growing numbers of jobs became casualized, however, the idea of a lifelong career based on a particular skill came under fire. Akin to dozens of other giant companies, IBM shed a considerable proportion of its workforce—100,000 employees—during the downsizing craze that commenced during the 1980s and continued into the 1990s. Henceforward, politicians and executives almost unanimously declaimed, workers would no longer be able to acquire a single set of skills that would serve them over the full course of their work lives. Recurrent education—*lifelong learning*, its proponents termed it, as if human beings were capable of anything else—instead became the watchword.[80] What Newt Gingrich called "the responsibility of the learner"[81] indeed would be paramount; individuals would have to master whatever skills they might come to need—or take the consequences. Thus a program that had been initially introduced as a paternalistic measure was transmuted into a neoliberal justification for increased insecurity.

Higher-education institutions were far from aloof to the imperatives of the perpetual-innovation economy. University administrators, in particular, were quick to sense the turf-threat posed by inhouse corporate education. Perhaps danger could be turned into opportunity, if the nettle could but be grasped. The prospect of an enlarged role for colleges and universities prompted efforts not only to adapt to but also to activate a transformed matrix of provision.

Reorganizing the University: "What Business Are We Really In?"

Higher education took in and spent roughly $250 billion a year by the mid-1990s through more than 11,000 campuses run by around 3,600 institutions, attended by 14 million students.[82] For twenty-five years, however, times had been hard. Federal and state support for higher education had been cut back; from 1980 to 1994, for example, states reduced real per-student funding to public universities by no less than 22 percent.[83] (During the mid-1990s, appropriations experienced an uneven rebound.)[84] Higher education's economic malaise was deepened by a changing national demography. As the cohort of baby-boomers completed its education during the early 1970s, traditional student enrollments had begun to stagnate.

Competition accordingly ramped up among colleges and universities for research funding, general revenues, and student enrollments. And disproportionate costs were passed along. College tuition, according to a government study, increased by 234 percent over the fifteen years before 1996, while income rose only 82 percent and inflation 74 percent; college costs had increased to over 20 percent of median household income by 1997, from 14 percent in 1975.[85] Although student aid funding likewise increased, a growing share of total costs took the form of unsubsidized loans. Family indebtedness and, alongside it, popular dissatisfaction, thus increased.[86] Uncertain job prospects combined with personal sacrifices, nevertheless, triggered rising college attendance among those not too hardpressed or unfavored—the high-school dropouts disproportionately found in nonwhite neighborhoods. Increases in the college continuation rate (the proportion of students graduating from high school each spring who go on to enroll in college the following fall) had helped to offset the prospective decline in attendance: in 1960 the continuation rate was 45 percent, but by 1996 it had risen to an unprecedented 65 percent. More than 60 percent of all high school graduates thus continued their education at some sort of postsecondary institution.[87] As we will see, however, college was no longer only for eighteen- to twenty-two-year-olds; by 1993, nearly two-fifths of all college students were at least twenty-five years old, three-fifths were working, and over 42 percent were attending part-time.[88]

In this rapidly changing and consistently difficult context, administrators bruited a standard set of institutional survival strategies. One was a much-vaunted New Partnership with industry. By 1986, in an unprecedented "cooperative boom," the number of joint ventures between industry and academe reached "all-time highs" and embraced "large and small businesses, public and private colleges, major research universities and local community colleges in every state."[89] The creation in the 1980s of the Business–Higher Education Forum, a high-level group comprised of ninety corporate and university executives, led during the following decade to ever more intimate ties.[90] The New Partnership sought two superordinate goals: more expeditious commercialization of university research and a closer matchup between what was being taught to students and labor-market needs.

The bulk of basic research (research that adds to general scientific knowledge rather than commercial products and processes), perhaps four-fifths, was carried out by universities rather than by corporations. Most of the funding for this research had long been provided by the federal government, principally through military agencies. MIT's president, Charles Vest, stated flatly, indeed, that "the whole development of federal R&D support was driven by national-security concerns."[91] The demise of the Cold War undercut some of the rationale for federal support (although federal money continued to furnish nearly 60 percent of university research funds in 1997).[92] Universities in turn had to seek new patrons— and a new institutional role—if they were to keep their laboratories functioning.

The New Partnership aimed to construct such a changed foundation. On one side, it helped corporations gain attractively subsidized access to cutting-edge basic research at universities and to the pricy research equipment (such as supercomputers) that was often based on campus. In

1980, there were twenty-odd research parks set on U.S. university land and drawing on an adjacent university's research base as a lure to attract high-tech companies; by 1997 there were 136 (and rapid proliferation overseas as well).[93] After antitrust laws were loosened, hundreds of business-university research consortia were created—at Stanford in semiconductor design and fabrication, at Rochester University in optics, at Rutgers in ceramics, at Carnegie Mellon in robotics, at Indiana in educational technology. "Probably no single Fortune 500 company is not a member of at least one such research alliance with a university," noted one analysis. Campus-based research centers funded by and servicing big corporations and industry groups increased rapidly and numbered more than 1,000 by 1990 in the area of science and technology.[94] Research, another observer found, increasingly was "conducted in a network of peri-university institutions—research institutes, think-tanks, consultancies, and campus-based companies—organized loosely around the campus and making opportunistic connections with one another."[95] Netscape, Sun Microsystems, and Cisco comprise three leading Internet companies that were each direct spinoffs from academe.

Universities, it must be stressed, were active parties to the growth of these *knowledge factories*. Academic and business enterprises had enjoyed long and often mutually profitable associations. They shared board directors who helped to determine policies for both institutions. And they shared professional personnel, who intermingled through scientific, scholarly, and trade associations. In some of the sciences it was not uncommon for publication standards and practices at journals to be decided by editorial boards drawn alike from businesses and universities. Universities in turn saw little reason to allow companies alone to reap whatever economic advantage stood to be derived from the New Partnership. The prospect of software licensing royalties and patent revenues comprised a significant inducement, rather, for university administrators and favored faculty to extend business practices directly into academe. It became unobjectionable, even praiseworthy, to assert that "anything we can do to encourage new avenues of communication and collaboration between the university . . . and the marketplace is a good idea."[96]

Early in the 1980s, accordingly, legislation was passed authorizing universities to gain title to federally funded research. By 1994, U.S. universities and colleges were earning about $360 million annually from patent royalties and license fees. For the top institutions, the amounts generated were indeed alluring. The University of California's nine campuses, for example, brought in $55.9 million from hundreds of inventions during 1994 to 1995—a fivefold increase in income over recent years and an 18 percent increase over the previous year. In 1997, licenses for 832 technologies developed by UC researchers generated $74.7 million—still just a small fraction of total university revenues but growing rapidly. Stanford's royalties and fees—generating $600,000 annually during the mid-1980s—in 1995 came to $28.6 million.[97] Growth hormones, antismoking remedies, medical tests, skin creams, and new varieties of plants and animals all became significant income sources for research universities. Commercial exploitation of university-based intellectual property of course required assiduous oversight and policing. With substantial pots of gold at stake, hardball legal fights over patent rights predictably followed.[98]

Perhaps more significant was the internal reorganization of the university that accompanied its programmatic enlargement of profit-oriented ventures. True, only a small fraction of university research projects would end up generating significant commercial revenues—perhaps one in four hundred—but the scramble to increase royalty revenue and, indeed, the New Partnership overall, vitally influenced the evolving shape and character of the university.

Profound changes, for a start, were evident in the research ethos. Academic independence and open scholarly interchange were called into grave question. In some fields (biotechnology surely provided the premier example), the tentacles of industry extended to the point that virtually every senior university researcher of note had some tie to a financially interested company.[99] University conflict-of-interest policies, despite being reinvigorated in 1995, did little to stem such structural changes.

Corporations often imposed onerous legal conditions on scientists' use of research tools and materials on which they held claims—to preview discoveries, for example, to require the surrender of ownership in them, or even to restrict publication results.[100] Entire subfields of inquiry emerged virtually as products of corporate sponsorship; *contestability theory*, for example, comprised an area of economics that attained visibility through the good offices of AT&T. Where an ethic of open scientific interchange had prevailed, now proprietary secrecy was insinuated through agreements that many scientists signed with drug and biotechnology companies.[101] Where, more generally, scientific research had once claimed at least a comparative disinterestedness, now it became unexceptionable for it to function as blatant propaganda; the University of Maine's Lobster Institute, for example, substantially supported by the seafood industry, offered a study "purporting to show that lobsters don't suffer when boiled alive."[102]

Profound changes thus began to be worked in the internal structure of higher education. A frequently quoted theorist of change summed up the new management wisdom in 1983: "Each institution needs to see itself as if for the first time and ask, What business are we really in? Of the 3,100 colleges, universities, technical institutes, seminaries, and two-year community colleges, what special role do we play in America's higher-education network? What attractive and important set of services does our institution provide that people cannot obtain elsewhere better, faster, or cheaper?"[103] Cost reduction therefore became the watchword. "The pressures on education to improve its productivity may be intensified," announced a government panel.[104]

Administrators often sought to portray the reorganization that ensued as an effort at *cost efficiency*. Yet the term actually portended a radical overhaul of governing priorities, as higher education's cost structure, program goals, and educational practices began to be continually reviewed and altered. "If universities were to operate as firms which seek to maximise their profits and which are subject to market prices," wrote a thoughtful analyst in the early 1970s, "significant reorganisation within universities would have to be made so that internal decisions could be evaluated in accordance with their effects on profits."[105]

Later observers were less plain-spoken; a high-gloss public relations sheen was characteristically applied to the ongoing process of change. Prominent members of the educational policy establishment thus asserted in the 1990s that only by "revitalizing" the educational process could the American economy be readied for the challenges of the twenty-first century. Redoubled economic rivalry, they claimed, could be effectively addressed by improving the productivity of U.S. workers—and educational reform alone would facilitate such productivity enhancement. "The key to both productivity and competitiveness," went the argument, "is the skills of our people and our capacity to use highly educated and trained people to maximum advantage in the workplace."[106]

But there was no doubt that education *itself* constituted a preferred site for productivity-enhancing measures. And it was not only through recourse to high technology that administrators sought to cut costs and improve efficiency. Rather, university decisionmakers committed their institutions to a comprehensive sea-change in structure and purpose. When the University of California decided to fund research in part through patent income, therefore, it virtually ensured that program priorities would be set more directly by the search for profit.[107]

One leading symptom of this general transformation comprised a rapid extension and hardening of class divisions within academe. At elite research universities and in favored fields (not least including administration itself) a tiny elite of executives and tenured professors enjoyed incomes once reserved for high-level corporate personnel. Professors of medicine commonly took in half a million dollars a year, while business schools regularly offered $300,000 salaries to entice Wall Street economists. Although the tendency to spend lavishly to recruit top professors was certainly far from novel, the perquisites of academic office seemed unusually bountiful—for this privileged minority. Robert Barro, a prominent Harvard economist, refused an offer of a $300,000 base salary, as well as unusually generous benefits such as a tony Manhattan apartment, to move to Columbia.[108]

More important, on the other hand, real salaries for professors were lower in 1997 than in 1972,[109] while colleges continued to expand their use of casualized academic labor in all its forms. A 1993 survey by the National Center for Education Statistics found that the proportion of part-time professors had doubled over twenty-five years to more than 40 percent.[110] In Washington, home to Microsoft, half of the instruction proffered by the state's thirty-two community and technical colleges was performed by part-timers; part-timers who taught a full-time course load made just 39 percent of a full-time salary; and part-timers outnumbered full-timers by a factor of at least three.[111] While the number of full-time, tenure-track professors fell over the course of the twenty years after

1975, nontenured contract appointments were on the upswing—from 19 percent of the full-time professoriate in 1975 to 28 percent in 1995.[112]

In the sciences, postdoctoral appointees transformed into yet another category of second-rank employees, providing needed high-tech labor services at low cost. The duration of these supposedly limited-term appointments lengthened, while compensation, benefits, and job-placement opportunities languished. Though the character of postdoctoral education remained opportunistic and ad hoc, the number of such appointments in science, engineering, and health fields doubled between 1975 and 1995. Graduate students more generally found themselves serving not, as tradition would have it, as faculty apprentices but as performers of low-wage labor services for institutions whose main concern was to increase capacity utilization.[113] Prodded by state governors, many of whom sharply questioned the very need for tenure,[114] a two- or even three-tier labor force (tenure track, off-track full-timers, and part-timers and adjuncts), increasingly reliant on contingent workers, became a full-fledged academic phenomenon.[115]

Analogous disparities were deepening at the level of student access to education. I have already mentioned the growing use of debt to finance schooling, which created yet another obstacle for poor students. But deliberate policies also contributed to tying erstwhile educational choices more directly to market forces. The trustees of the State University of New York in 1995 proposed to institute a sliding scale for tuition by campus or type of campus.[116] The SUNY system soon afterward also began to offer off-peak pricing discounts to students taking courses at night, on weekends, or at underused sites off campus; lower per-credit tuition was also commonplace among summer-school programs.[117] Skirting the question of whether academic majors and course schedules should be tied to income, such efforts at *cost-based educational pricing* seemed all but certain to expand.

Attempting to compensate for the growing scarcity of students between eighteen and twenty-two years old, meanwhile, during the 1970s administrators also began to respond to reformers' democratizing efforts to make them accord increased emphasis to adult learners. As already noted, a large minority of degree-seeking students were at least twenty-five years

old, and part-time students, the majority of them women, began to account for similar proportion of total college enrollments.[118] By 1998, an
estimated eight out of ten students worked while pursuing an undergraduate degree.[119] Provision of advanced education and training to a
well-defined cohort of full-time students coming directly from high
school—a long-time hallmark of higher education—was no longer the
sole, or often even the main, priority.

Instead higher education again allied with corporate America to induce
adult learners to accept the prospect of *recurrent education* throughout
the lifespan. The economic incentive to do so was clearly paramount.
Colleges and universities entered the educational-contracting business,
one analyst noted, "primarily to make money" by viewing millions of
American workers as "potential replacements for declining numbers of
traditional college students."[120] Targeting adult learners was also predicated, however, on administrators' recognition that corporations provided key "institutional connecting points for access" to the new group
of learners.[121] In addition to this bottleneck, businesses also controlled
employees' schedules, wages, benefits, and career development plans, as
well as needed facilities and technologies.[122] Employers, in short, were in
a position to demand additional leverage over the nature of education
programs offered to them by colleges that hungered to reach their
employees.

Community colleges, especially, responded by contracting with particular companies and industries to supply courses made to order. They
began not only to seek company business but also to study company
needs, to modify curriculum content, and to adjust course schedules.
As many as half the nation's two- and four-year institutions were estimated by 1984 to have some kind of contractual relationship with employers, however modest; by the mid-1990s, over nine-tenths of
community colleges had embarked on such a pairing. Usually, the college
provided the instruction, tailored as needed to specific corporate objectives. The company in turn recruited and selected employees and provided
classroom facilities and some administrative assistance. Intermediaries,
known as *education brokers*, emerged to match businesses harboring un-
filled training needs with community colleges willing to establish flexible
retraining programs.

Companies sometimes found, in addition, that a community college partnership could qualify for state government subsidies, in the name of economic development, via matching grants of public funds. General Motors ran more than thirty training centers of its own but found it could not keep up with its own need for dealers with electronics skills. An Automotive Services Education Program was created for GM by Delta College in Michigan in 1979 to prepare entry-level technicians for GM dealerships. By 1987 the program operated a network of thirty-seven institutions in thirty states.[123]

But adult education also proceeded in other venues, under more direct guidance by colleges and universities themselves. The latter thus typically instituted or expanded noncredit and university extension programs to market to adult learners as individuals. Initiated on the margins of the university, again initially in response to demands to democratize access to higher education, continuing education divisions hawking nondegree curricula enjoyed remunerative growth beginning in the late 1970s. At UC Berkeley Extension, for example, enrollment rose 40 percent and course offerings 50 percent over the five years through 1997.[124] Professional training on campus also enjoyed an uneven resurgence. Existing professional schools strived to forge programmatic links with professional associations and sought out technical and institutional innovations with which to upgrade practitioners' skills—and, not coincidentally, to draw revenues into the coffers of host universities.[125]

Baldly vocational initiatives in turn produced unfamiliar areas of pedagogy on campus. At the University of Wisconsin at Stout, a Burger King Fast Food Laboratory doubled as a "research facility" and a school for hotel and restaurant management students. Supervised, as reality outdid fiction, by a Professor Buergermeister, the "lab" boasted a full complement of advanced equipment, including "computerized deep-fat fryers, conveyor-driven burger-broilers, and a calibrated beverage-service system"; its products—hamburgers and fries—came in Burger King wrappers and students not surprisingly "don't always remember we're a class."[126]

I had better clarify the objection to such endeavors. The higher-learning institutions have historically disdained vernacular knowledge as a means of buttressing their own privilege, and a thinly cloaked antidemocratic impulse continues to flourish here. The problem is not, however, that supposedly lesser forms of knowledge are being countenanced. By studying hamburgers one may learn something of biology, of contemporary industrial organization, or of consumer culture. But how is such pedagogy in fact arranged? Does it open the learning process to imagination, serendipity, and disciplined study? Or is pedagogy simply treated as an expedient appendage to the corporate labor market?

On one side, this is a pragmatic concern: As the distance diminishes between workplace and school, are students being prepared for real jobs?[127] Businesses themselves, after all, evinced no uniform view of what sort of labor force they want.[128] Some declared in favor of general skills and "flexible" workers equipped with literacy, basic science, and mathematics. Others insisted on technology-specific vocational training. Uncertainty about emerging skill requirements reflected both the diversity of U.S. industry and the inherent difficulty of planning in a private economy, where quarterly dividends take precedence over new capital investment, research and development, and other long-range needs. But, on the other side, a deeper problem is also manifest. Are the jobs for which vocational training serves as preparation good jobs—even adequate jobs? Does vocationalism expand the realm of freedom—or of necessity?

The result of the market drive in and around higher-educational instruction was, in any case, that an increasing fraction of courses taken by adults were provided outside the purview of academic senates and traditional degree programs. Adult education, meanwhile, became the fastest-growing educational sector. Vying for student dollars were community colleges, four-year colleges, professional associations, and corporate vendors. Higher education had evolved, in short, into *postsecondary education*: an expanded array of institutions, programs, and delivery systems under manifold sponsors surrounded the traditional degree-granting college serving full-time students coming from high school.

It was private industry that represented the dynamic element in this emerging matrix. Businesses spent $11.8 billion for tuition payments to colleges, universities, and other outside providers of education during 1985, and, of this, just over half ($6.1 billion) went to the formal higher-education sector—enough to underwrite 14.8 million of the 40.8 million courses taken by adults in 1984.[129] For, as we saw, corporations were becoming substantial vendors of education and training in their own right.

The trends just described augured general change throughout the system of educational provision. Recalling the late-nineteenth-century crisis that had ushered in the modern university system in the United States, the time was again ripe for a systemic transformation of the mission, structure, and product of the educational process. All that was lacking, one might say, was the opportunity to bring the emerging matrix of postsecondary providers online. With the arrival of the Internet, this deficit stood to be comprehensively overcome.

Digital Capitalism in Education

By the time of the Carnegie Commission Report on instructional technology in 1972, educational media—radio, film, television, and others—had been heralded so loudly and so often, *without* effecting especially momentous alterations, that skepticism about the educational impacts of emerging electronic information technologies could easily have been forgiven. Educators faced with harsh quotidian realities—lean equipment, programming, and support budgets, student boredom in mass TV classes, and lack of any comprehensive vision or plan—could hardly be blamed for cynicism. Instead, years before the Internet became popular, the Commission vigorously insisted that a "revolution" was underway.[130]

Except for their quaint domestic focus, these seers proved correct. Less than a decade passed, and the Congressional Office of Technology Assessment reported that information technology was "profoundly affecting" American education. It was "changing the nature of what needs to be learned, who needs to learn it, who will provide it, and how it will be provided and paid for."[131] "The chief impact of 'the second information revolution' will be . . . on education," wrote management guru Peter Drucker in 1997: "In thirty to forty years, education will look wholly different, not only in delivery but in content."[132] The issue, therefore, was not simply the installation of bundles of inert wiring and computer equipment. It was, rather, adaption to the ensemble of changed socioeconomic relationships that was energized by emerging network applications.

Even before the Internet resoundingly confirmed the point, it was apparent that networked educational provision contained a prospectively decisive for-profit potential. By the mid-1970s, for example, two top IBMers could observe that "the use of computers and computer networks in industrial education and training has just begun. All indications are that the use will expand significantly under cost pressures. . . . Now that more advanced educational technologies are beginning to be applied on a large scale, and with prospects of further substantial reduction in both communications and data processing costs, will institutional inhibitions against the introduction of these techniques into public education prevent their use even if they should prove cost effective in that environment? If so, the stage may be set for the emergence of a major profitable learning industry oriented to skills training."[133] Network systems offered means of delivering standardized instruction cost-efficiently to multiple sites, thereby enhancing the productivity of the educational enterprise. Top educational administrators in turn became determined to jump on this bandwagon before it left them and their institutions behind.

Preparation for an expected new deluge of students comprised a particularly critical additional factor in their thinking, for when baby-boomers' children began to swell college enrollments during the mid-1990s, the higher-education system was left essentially unprepared. How could institutions that had been worn down by stagnation and a consistent lack of maintenance meet the challenge of educating millions of additional students?[134] Could they not harness networks to reach out to the millions of new students they were imminently to face?

With the growing importance of education and training for modern industry, the fiscal crisis afflicting universities, and the proliferation of information technology throughout the home, the school, the factory, and the office, the stage was set for networked educational markets to burgeon. At every level, from preschool and remedial to doctoral and crafts-based education, and in an endless variety of genres and formats, both old and new, networked educational provision furnished alluring prospective entry points for profit-making companies.

Three overlapping market segments could be identified, each with its own relatively separate strategic focus. In the market for corporate (and governmental, chiefly military) training, both vendor-supplied contract services and inhouse programs proliferated, often via alliances between universities and companies. In the market for self-schooling, diverse for-profit suppliers grew into diversified education conglomerates, forging links both with primary and secondary schools and, in addition, directly with individual customers. Finally, in the market for degree programs and continuing education, proprietary schools and other established companies again alternately partnered and competed with colleges and universities. Each of these markets had been thrown open to growing participation by for-profit educational providers. And, in each of them, networking technologies—including, preeminently, Internet technology—played a growing role.

Corporate Training and Retraining for Engineers

Before becoming a paragon of the New Partnership, engineering education had already molded itself for a century to the demands of science-based businesses.[135] During the postwar period, the need to keep practicing engineers abreast of rapid technical change had grown urgent.[136] "The rate of introduction of new science and technology is such," one analyst observed in 1973, "that updating the education of professional or chartered engineers is under perpetual discussion."[137] Louis Ross, Ford Motor's chief technical officer, underlined two decades later that "the shelf life of a degree in engineering is about three years."[138]

Throughout the entire postwar era, colleges and science-based companies joined up with professional societies and federal agencies to create new institutional and technical arrangements for training engineers.[139] Continuing education programs constituted the centerpiece of this effort. By the 1960s—when over half of all engineers employed by American industry had already participated in some kind of continuing education program—some proposed that an engineer should typically spend between one-fifth and one-third of his productive time continuing his education.[140] A decade later, continuing education reached one out of every seven engineers in any given year.[141]

In truth, it was not engineers alone who turned to continuing education programs. An increasing fraction of the states required continuing education for practitioners in fields from accounting to veterinary medicine.[142] In concert with universities and corporations, professional associations—

in chemistry, law, medicine, and other fields—quickly became prominent in organizing educational services for members. But engineers *were* at the forefront in trying to harness *networks* to answer this more general need.

Networking began modestly enough, with conventional over-the-air television broadcasts on special *instructional frequencies*. Already by 1983, 70,000 engineers were enrolled in 2,000 such courses; and, over the two decades starting in the middle 1960s, a score of major universities awarded over 3,000 master of science degrees to engineers who completed *all* requirements as part-time instructional television (ITV) students.[143] ITV systems, operated by colleges, initially attained only local reach. For example, Stanford's system, in place since 1969, provided four video channels from the campus to 120 classrooms in plants within a thirty-five-mile radius, circumscribing much of Silicon Valley.

Hewlett-Packard, a major semiconductor manufacturer, played a pivotal part both in instituting this service and in extending it outward to dozens of more distant plants.[144] The advantages of such extension had grown obvious. Recognized leaders in any subfield could be asked to convey their expertise to dispersed audiences. An individual instructor, moreover, could handle as many as eight to twelve groups numbering half a dozen students or so each. Unparalleled cost economies thus could be achieved, both in pedagogical productivity and in commuting time. The cost of producing courses, finally, could be spread over a large client base, and thus, production values often could be raised. Demonstrations, elaborate graphics, even animation could be justified.[145]

Utilization of networks continued—indeed, increased. Southern Methodist University commenced ITV service to job sites in the Dallas–Fort Worth region in 1967, through the Association for Graduate Education and Research (TAGER). The system connected several university campuses with local firms such as Texas Instruments, Collins Radio, and General Dynamics. TAGER courses in engineering, computer science, and management, either with or without college credit, could be chosen from a catalog—or designed to employers' specifications.[146] The University of Southern California serviced Los Angeles area clients such as McDonnell Douglas, Rockwell, and Hughes. The Illinois Institute of Technology broadcast to Bell Laboratories, Motorola, Northrup, and others on seven channels out of Chicago. The University of Maryland at College Park transmitted engineering courses after 1981 to IBM, the National Bureau of Standards, the National Security Agency, and Westinghouse Electric, as well as other organizations in the Baltimore-Washington conurbation.[147]

The Association for Media-Based Continuing Education for Engineers—a university-professional group established during the 1970s—became a particularly noteworthy locus of innovation around networks. By 1984, AMCEE sported twenty-four engineering school members and had created the first full-fledged university (granting only M.S. degrees) organized "exclusively" for the purpose of offering graduate degree programs by television.[148] Participants in its National Technological University prepared courses, which NTU distributed to clients: industrial firms, research centers, government agencies. Daily programs were delivered, beginning in 1985, by satellite; experiments with electronic mail also got underway. By 1988, NTU was broadcasting accredited master's degree courses in seven engineering disciplines to over 3,000 students at 245 receiving sites, mostly large corporations. Course-originating schools included Colorado State, Northeastern, and a half dozen other state colleges. Additional instructional programs originated, however, directly from corporate facilities at high-technology firms.[149] Financial support for the system, initially arranged by the Department of Defense, came from a roster of corporate titans, while industry executives also comprised the majority of the board of trustees governing the institution.[150]

By the mid-1990s, AMCEE's forty-seven participating universities offered 1,200 academic courses and 400 noncredit courses—about 25,000 hours annually—via fourteen compressed digital video satellite channels to more than 100,000 adult employee-students located both in the United States and other countries.[151] Email had been incorporated, and the group boasted an increasing presence on the Web. Regular service had been extended to the Asia-Pacific region. NTU proffered directly vocational programs to "customers," including AT&T, Kodak, Hewlett-Packard, Honeywell, IBM, Lockheed-Martin, Motorola, and Texas Instruments. In 1998, finally, NTU created a for-profit subsidiary to market its courses more widely.[152]

Forays into networked provision of engineering education proved to be harbingers of a more comprehensive transnational effort. In the future, declared a 1997 article coauthored by the CEO of Boeing and the president of Rensselaer Polytechnic Institute, "Americans will comprise a smaller percentage of the global engineering workforce." What "new model" of engineering education could be formulated "that will better meet the current and future needs of multinational companies and the global engineer"? Branch campuses set up by "global universities," to serve "either a single large corporate-customer installation or a cluster of companies," were deemed desirable as "a conduit for industrial practitioners to participate in education as instructors, curriculum developers, and mentors."[153]

In truth, as we have seen, "corporate classrooms" already operated on a global scale. "A single corporation," wrote Nell Eurich in the mid-1980s, "may be educating in New York, Rio de Janeiro, Tokyo, and Rome."[154] Already by 1988 there were over forty corporate-owned satellite networks delivering a variety of services to nearly 12,000 inhouse sites—with dozens of other such systems in the planning stage. "With the networks in place," writes Eurich, "companies soon realize their value for training."[155] At IBM, a "global classroom" approach attempted to keep the firm's 103,000 "technology professionals" up to date via a worldwide "Field Training System."[156] At another large computer company, Digital Equipment Corp., a training curriculum offered 300 courses in seventeen languages to 18,000 support personnel in thirty-nine countries.[157] NCR, General Motors Institute, and other business organizations furnished courses to employees throughout dozens of nations. Chase Manhattan Bank used videoconferencing to link 2,500 employees in eight countries for live discussions of bank strategy.[158] Even McDonald's got into the act. The company trained employees in sixty-five countries; its Hamburger University sported instant translation facilities for eighteen languages at an Oak Brook, Illinois, campus facility.[159] Transnational corporations deployed their network systems in part to gain access to foreign nationals, whose cost-effectiveness increased as they now could be brought within effective reach of training.

Business schools were quickly integrated into this emerging system of corporate-centered distance education. By 1995, Westcott Communications

Inc.'s Executive Education Network—with cooperation from eight business schools, including the University of Pennsylvania's prestigious Wharton—boasted nearly 100 corporate classrooms at Kodak, Disney, Texas Instruments, and other sites.[160] Business schools offering executive education programs by satellite to corporate classrooms included Aspen Institute, Carnegie Mellon, USC, Wharton, and others.[161] Other professional school disciplines were equally avid. Baylor College of Medicine, for instance, teamed with Williams Learning Network Inc. to launch a satellite television offering called The Health Channel for forty-two hours monthly of continuing medical education (already a $3 billion enterprise in the United States) to doctors and other health-care providers. The school "may seek advertising from pharmaceutical and medical equipment companies" but assured an analyst that "Baylor will control the content of the courses." Williams Learning Network added that the venture might become a template for education programs aimed at financial analysts or real-estate salespersons.[162]

Incessant experimentation, meanwhile, accelerated development of cost-efficient media for "delivering" education and training. When they arrived, therefore, the Internet and corporate intranets comprised only the latest in a succession of technologies for distributing learning services within and between corporations and universities. The American Society for Training and Development claimed, however, that Internet-based educational applications boasted an especially marked rate of increase; in 1994, 12 percent of its member companies utilized Internet-based electronic distance learning, whereas by 1996, 53 percent did so.[163] According to another analyst of trends in educational technology, the Internet was fast becoming the *primary* agent of distance learning, both for corporations—many of which already had access to inhouse broadband networks—and for individuals, most of whom still did not.[164]

Corporate Education Conglomerates

Private investment in education entailed growing corporate and commercial penetration of a practice—schooling—traditionally provided as a local, tax-funded public service. *Market creation*, rather than simple *market entry*, thus comprised the best name for the process underway throughout virtually all segments of educational provision.

By the mid-1990s, for example, for-profit companies took in $30 billion of the $340 billion that the United States spent each year on preschool through high school education. "Education today, like health care twenty years ago, is a vast, highly localized industry ripe for change," declared Mary C. Tanner, a managing director at the investment bank, Lehman Brothers, which—following its rival, Smith Barney—held its first education-industry conference in 1997.[165] Investment analysts, some of whom expected education stocks to explode during the decade to come, were quick to search out attractive price-per-earnings ratios among a growing field of education-related companies. Among twenty-five publicly traded education companies in the United States were Advantage Schools Inc., Apollo Group, CBT Group, Sabis Educational Systems, Education Alternatives Inc., DeVry Inc., and the notorious Edison Project.[166] School privatization came in vogue, meaning that companies took over the schooling function from local governments. By late 1997, two dozen businesses operated about one in ten of the 781 charter schools that had been opened, out of a complex tangle of motives, in twenty-three states—up from just one in 1991.[167] The Edison Project, while subject to considerable buffeting by the market, nonetheless held sufficient investor confidence in 1996 to raise $100 million in investment capital. A year later, the company hoped to double in size over the 1997 to 1998 year, to twenty-five schools in eight states, while bringing in about $70 million in projected annual revenue.[168] Business entry involved not only direct takeovers of selected schools, however, but also sales to consumers of *courseware* and *edutainment* commodities.

Already by the early 1980s, explicitly educational software (*courseware*) constituted a notable component of the market for home PC software.[169] There existed no fewer than 620 U.S. manufacturers of computer courseware.[170] Plans to develop this market already hinted at novel fusions of entertainment and informational content.[171] Not least, this was because some of the multimedia conglomerates that were assembling themselves, especially through existing or prospective publishing subsidiaries, were sniffing out the market for educational commodities. CBS (now owned by the company that used to call itself Westinghouse) and Gulf + Western (now Viacom), for example, were among these early market testers.[172]

A leading publisher thus reported in 1985 that "the growing interdependence between academia and industry has important implications for our business, and we believe it offers new opportunities for us."[173] Major book publishers commenced to integrate forward into education markets. John Wiley's acquisition of Wilson Learning Corporation in 1982 vaulted that company into worldwide provision of industrial training products and services. Wilson had formed a "research alliance" with the University of Minnesota to explore technology applications for different areas of learning, with a focus on adults, and became a cosponsor of the National Technological University, which—as we have seen—offered continuing education for engineers via satellites direct to industry worksites. Wilson itself operated in dozens of cities, supplied courses in ten languages, and—following the lead of many major publishers at the time—enlarged its product line and transnational distribution network to embrace subsidiaries in Australia, Canada, England, Japan, West Germany, and France.[174]

Macmillan, another power in school and college publishing, moved to integrate forward into industrial and vocational textbook publishing. Computerized software, in specialized scientific, technical, and professional fields, became an additional corporate priority. Home learning, reference materials, and information services gave Macmillan an increasingly diversified entree into the learning business. Macmillan also ran proprietary schools; its Katherine Gibbs schools, for example, offered training in office skills, secretarial, wordprocessing, and business subjects in suburban markets on the east coast. Macmillan's 218 Berlitz Schools of Languages, meanwhile, operated worldwide. Macmillan also owned the United Electronics Institute in Tampa, which provided a two-year program in technology to high school graduates and qualifying adults. Over 1,000 students annually embarked on a 1,500-hour curriculum of lectures, workshops, and laboratories in specialities such as communications, computers, and robotics; according to a report to stockholders "this acquisition represents Macmillan's initial thrust into the broad-based electronics skills training field." "Instruction" markets in 1985 already accounted for sales of $116 million out of a total of $677 million.[175]

In addition to proprietary schools and conventional book publishing, publishers' emerging markets embraced computer courseware, audiocassettes, testing materials, video, training systems, school and curriculum management software (computer-managed instruction), interactive videodisks and CD-ROMs, online databases, and educational information services. Computer-managed instruction became an especially portentous application as it involved commercial publishers in organizing curricula and monitoring student performance, evaluating and prescribing learning outcomes, and providing planning information for instructors. Major publishers, among them Macmillan, Science Research Associates (acquired by McGraw-Hill), SFN (a Time-Warner subsidiary), Addison-Wesley (now owned by Pearson), and Scholastic Corp. entered CMI, putting them just a few short steps away from managing schools.[176] Scholastic, long zealous in developing new markets "linking school and home," identified a ballooning market for what it termed "fun/learning software of the kind we produce."[177] Scholastic's further diversification from children's books into "the grade-school curriculum market" placed it in a risk-laden fiefdom worth $2 billion annually by 1997.[178]

By this time, the prospects for the education market had begun to make would-be participants salivate. When Viacom put the educational and reference divisions of its Simon & Schuster subsidiary on the block in 1998, bidders leaped forward with multibillion dollar offers. The market leader in U.S. higher-education publishing, Simon & Schuster, had become adept at "repurposing" its traditional properties to fit electronic formats; it also operated an in-school satellite television network that sends educational programming to 2 million children in 4,600 schools each day.[179] The roster of claimants seeking to acquire Simon & Schuster was indicative of the breadth of interest in education markets. Rivals included two leveraged-buyout firms (Hicks, Muse, Tate & Furst; Kohlberg Kravis Roberts); Knowledge Universe, a billion-dollar education conglomerate formed by one-time junk-bond impresario (now convicted felon), Michael Milken, with Oracle CEO Larry Ellison; and two more traditional book publishers, Harcourt General and Pearson, Britain's largest publisher.[180] The CEO of Pearson, which already owned Scott Foresman and Addison-Wesley, declared after gaining victory (at a cost of $4.6 billion) that "education is one of the great growth industries of our time."[181]

This view was still shared even by Viacom, which had sold off Simon & Schuster largely to pare its debt. Nickelodeon, its successful advertiser-supported children's cable TV network, concurrently teamed up with the Children's Television Workshop, the leading producer of educational programming (including *Sesame Street* and other popular shows), to create the first "all educational cable channel for children." This venture portended the increasing privatization of control and operation of erstwhile not-for-profit educational services, such as those hitherto supplied by the Public Broadcasting Service.[182]

There remained, to be sure, obstructions and blind alleys. Prior to 1995 and 1996, for example, consumer education markets looked likely to be dominated by CD-ROMs. Madison Avenue selling techniques were easily transferred; trade journals began regularly listing the top-selling educational software programs, while a newsweekly sought to confer its "Editor's Choice Award" on "exemplary" CDs for "creativity," "learning," "problem solving," "reading," and "reference."[183] Acquisitions and mergers in the educational software market were accelerating, as new entrants and established companies alike sought to achieve economies of scale and access to major distribution and retail channels. In 1995, the Learning Company was acquired by SoftKey (the merged operation took the Learning Co. name). Other significant mergers included CUC International's purchase of Davidson & Associates the next year. Taking what one writer called "its first big step toward becoming a major seller of educational software to schools and homes," IBM acquired the languishing Edmark (whose titles it already bundled into its Aptiva PCs) for $110 million.[184] In 1998, finally, Learning Co. (maker of the Reader Rabbit, Oregon Trail, and Sesame Street series) sought to make its fourteenth acquisition since 1994 by purchasing Broderbund (producer of the Carmen Sandiego series, as well as the game Myst) for over $400 million. If successfully concluded, the deal would vault Learning Co. to first place among educational software vendors, giving it nearly 40 percent of that market and putting it slightly ahead of rival Cendant Corp.[185]

But following earlier double-digit growth, retail sales of educational software slumped, growing at a lackluster 3.8 percent during 1997 to $461.5 million. One cause was the onset of intensified competition, not least from Disney, which began to leverage its best-selling children's movies with CD-ROM "animated storybooks" such as the *Lion King*. (In December 1995, Disney claimed leadership over the market, based on unit sales.)[186] A more significant contributor to slackening demand was the growth of the Internet. The Net diverted customers from buying software programs, in favor of surfing the World Wide Web. Its escalating multimedia capabilities and its global reach also portended a more basic strategic threat to educational software markets based on stand-alone media, such as CD-ROMs. To be sure, publishers did not foreswear entry into digital publishing but rather intensified their explorations of online information dissemination. Wiley, to follow up on an earlier example, deployed its Web site to support its education and textbook offerings with online companion sites, links to Internet resources, suggested curriculums, discussion forums, "and other features helpful to instructors, librarians, and students."[187]

Expedited development of a residential education market segment, however, was contingent on two factors: an agreed legal regime for the commercial deployment of intellectual property over networks and a wider roll-out of broadband Internet service to U.S. households. The Net's sudden interposition made publishers nervous about their intellectual property. They turned, accordingly, as we saw in earlier parts of this book, to the federal government for help; they also stepped up development of digital watermarks and other protective technologies. As also was discussed previously, widespread access to multimedia services was assuredly on the way. Perhaps first in high-income districts, *Sunrise Semester* was nonetheless all but certain to give way to overtly commercial forms of learning.

A second, and interlinked, market segment was comprised of the nation's elementary and secondary schools themselves. These institutions spent more than $4 billion on technology in 1995—twice their outlays on textbooks and an 11 percent increase over 1994; by 1996, the figure had increased to an estimated $5.2 billion, and funding of an estimated $7.8 billion was slated for 1997. Of 591 schools in San Diego county, to take a proximate example, 208 (or 35 percent) boasted their own Web sites by fall 1997.[188] Widespread Internet access for schools—which in 1998 became a contested policy at the federal level as it became intertwined with continuing liberalization of telecommunications—bid fair to establish a vital new channel through which corporations might gain access to students.

Computer companies were characteristically in the lead in understanding this. Referring to the number of students in U.S. schools, thus, the manager of Microsoft's education subsidiary conceded that "we are interested in the business proposition of having 50 million people able to create and produce using technology."[189] Apple Computer's 1997 strategic repositioning, according to CEO Steve Jobs, would turn on recognizing that the personal computer manufacturer was "the biggest education company in the world."[190] (Actually, during the second quarter of 1997, Gateway 2000 overtook Apple as the top provider of desktop and portable computers in the U.S. education market, according to one market researcher: Gateway had 22.4 percent, Apple 11.6 percent, and IBM 7.7 percent.[191]) A conference on school networking was sponsored by such companies as 3Com, Advanced Network Services, America Online, Bay Networks, Bell Atlantic, Compaq, Cisco, IBM, and Microsoft.[192]

The shift toward digital capitalism in education was also already obvious as well in an unprecedented generic reformulation of learning materials. In part, this was a matter of educational products and services being brought into position beside established lines of business by conglomerates harboring multiple media subsidiaries. *Crossovers*, as these formal blendings are sometimes called, were a regular reflex of the ongoing process of vertical integration in media industries. Also playing a role, however, were increasingly insistent efforts by corporate sponsors to target and address "youth" markets. Rarely rigid in a commercial culture that routinely turned to novelty as a selling point, and where advertisers aggressively exploited successive new media, distinctions between education, promotion, and entertainment were therefore deliberately blurred.

By the early 1980s, public relations practitioners already could advise that there existed opportunities "to reach a far greater and more selective audience" by "using a new communications vehicle—corporate-sponsored educational computer software." A company that marketed systems "to improve business-education partnerships . . . and corporate training through sponsorship" hired one-time educators to develop courseware "by blending the best practices of entertainment software with the basic elements of instructional design." It supplied First Interstate Bank of California with a tutorial on money and banking, for example, that was distributed free to 1,800 California high schools. The bank gained a new venue for its corporate logo, mention within the program, and identification on the software packaging and also underwrote a student workbook and a teacher lesson guide. In sharp contrast to an otherwise ubiquitous corporate concern to protect intellectual property rights, students were *encouraged* to duplicate and take home copies of programs—to increase the audience for sponsored messages.[193]

A decade later, the process of commercial penetration of schooling had been institutionalized. One recent report declared: "Book covers, billboards in school corridors, calendars, and broadcasts—these are some of the places corporate America places ads for kids to see in school. Commercial messages also reach kids in the classroom through ad-bearing and corporate sponsored educational materials. If we tracked [a] school kid through the . . . day, we might find her learning about solid waste from worksheets provided free by Procter & Gamble, the makers of Tide detergent, Pampers, Luvs, and other products. The worksheets would guide her through a 'product life cycle analysis' and a discussion of how disposable diapers can actually be more 'green' than cloth ones. Later she might see other materials on solid waste from Browning-Ferris and the Polystyrene Packaging Council."[194] An ad-supported television "news" program beamed into thousands of U.S. schools—Channel One—went on to recruit school principals to hand out discount coupons for a sponsor's (J. C. Penney) blue jeans.[195] And the American School Food Service Association estimated that 13 percent of the nation's 86,000 public schools, up from just 2 percent in 1991, sold brand-name fast foods by 1997.[196]

An invasive commercialization process had taken hold. Four million children in forty states received color lunch menus, featuring multipage ads for News Corporation's film *Anastasia*—to coincide with that movie's fall, 1997 opening. The film was also promoted in schools with an *Anastasia* study guide that "teaches kids the importance of searching for their roots, as the movie's heroine does."[197] The film industry quickly institutionalized its exploitation of this new promotional venue. A specialized marketing company, School Marketing Partners, circulated "free"—that is, advertiser-supported—teaching and marketing materials to 8,000 schools on behalf of films released by Time-Warner, Paramount, Disney, and Fox.[198] An earth science course, furnished to schools by Exxon, asserted that its objective was "[to examine] nature's powerful ability to recover from an oil spill." From the video, *Scientists and the Alaskan Oil Spill,* students learned that "it's difficult to know exactly how many [animals] died, but scientists know that the area contains large populations able to overcome these losses. . . . Once you have gotten rid of the oil, the natural environment will bounce back in a very short time, a matter of a few years."[199]

Network companies were at the forefront of this commercialization campaign. Pacific Bell gave pagers away to high school kids who agreed to obligate themselves to call designated numbers at regular intervals to listen to sponsored messages. An American history course brought to high school viewers by NYNEX, the local telephone company since swallowed by Bell Atlantic, declared that its course objective was "to learn how new technology could have helped during three famous points in history." From the video *Kids in Touch: Paul Revere's Ride and the Nynex Shuttle* came this revealing passage: "On April 18, 1775, Paul Revere had to deliver the message 'The British are Coming!' to John Hancock and Sam Adams. . . . If Paul Revere [lived] today, he would probably use something like the NYNEX Shuttle—he could have had hundreds of people around the world joining in on a video call."[200] Davidson & Associates released a netcasting product, called *Educast,* targeted at the teachers and school administrators whose goodwill helps Davidson sell courseware like its Math Blaster and Grammar Games direct to children. Educast pushed lesson plans, news, and customized professional information direct to educators' desktops. Sponsored by AT&T's WorldNet Internet service and PC manufacturer Compaq, the free service contained advertising and was pretested with 2,000 teachers before being rolled out on the Internet in October 1997.[201] Courseware familiar to children—and their parents—from school enjoys a marketing advantage over courseware that must sell itself without a known name.[202] College advertising networks linked up with Web site publishers and marketers to reach students via online student newspapers.[203]

Let us turn now to the third, again overlapping, segment of the new learning industry.

For-Profit Provision Enters the Academic Heartland

Already by the early 1980s, acute analysts wondered whether for-profit vendors had "invaded the campuses so far that they are not willing to pull back and let the colleges do the work?"[204] A decade later, marketization processes had notably broadened and deepened. A dual dynamic was at work: encircled by would-be rivals from without, education as a quasi-public service was also eroded from within by entrepreneurially minded administrators and professors.

Proprietary schools are profit-seeking institutions closely geared to preparing students to enter specific occupations and totally dependent on student tuition income. Organized in the 1880s, they evolved gradually toward corporate ownership; a century later there were about 8,000 licensed proprietary schools, enrolling hundreds of thousands of students. Let us look briefly at this impinging outside vector of change.

A wholly owned subsidiary of the publisher McGraw-Hill—the National Radio Institute—became the largest technical correspondence school in the United States, garnering annual enrollments of 60,000 by the 1980s. It went on to incorporate a computer-managed instruction system that permitted student examinations to be graded, annotated with comments by the teacher, and mailed back to the student within a twenty-four-hour period.[205] McGraw-Hill's ambition hardly slackened in the age of the Internet; rather, it established the McGraw-Hill World University on the Web.

Similarly, the DeVry Institute of Technology, founded in 1931, boasted in 1997 that it had come to comprise one of the largest private, accredited degree-granting "higher-education systems" in North America.[206] Stressing electronics, telecommunications, accounting, business administration, and computer science, DeVry claimed revenues of $117 million in 1983; by 1997, the company ran fourteen campuses in the United States and Canada, serviced 31,000 students, and garnered $260 million in annual revenues. Key to DeVry's success, it claimed, was "a highly structured curriculum with no electives, two student 'shifts' per day for maximum building use, and close ties to industry."[207] (These ties were particularly valuable for DeVry in allowing it to boast about its ability to place graduates in jobs following program completion.) The company employed 630 full-time and—significantly—550 part-time visiting and adjunct faculty. DeVry, too, was in the process of integrating the Internet into its operations.[208]

Yet another proprietary training powerhouse was the National Education Corporation, which originated in California in 1954 and which owned forty-seven technical schools by the early 1980s. NEC training programs were centered on vocational fields: PC repair, medical and dental assistance, law enforcement, telecommunications management, diesel mechanics, dress making, and design. Headed by David C. Jones, previously chairman of the Joint Chiefs of Staff, NEC awarded accredited master's, bachelor's, and associate degrees. Through specialized training programs for employers and professional associations, as well as correspondence courses aimed at individuals, NEC supplied training to hundreds of thousands of students annually.[209] In 1997, tuition for courses offered through its distance education subsidiary ranged from $400 to $1,000.[210]

NEC comprised a dense complex of interrelated subsidiaries serving corporate, professional, vocational, and school markets. Its ICS Learning Systems unit furnished distance learning to consumers and companies worldwide. During the late 1990s, ICS Learning Systems was actively increasing its "product offerings," not least by acquiring other businesses—including the California College for Health Sciences and a Dutch distance-education provider, Educatief. Its Steck-Vaughn Publishing unit produced supplemental learning materials, including CD-ROMs for adult markets and software for elementary and high schools. Its National Education Training Group "offer[ed] interactive multimedia products to train information technology professionals and end-users of technology," among other things in the use of software sold by Microsoft, Novell, Oracle, and others.[211]

Hard times and heightened job insecurity during the 1980s and early 1990s supplied a powerful impulse to consumer demand for vocational training. Like other vendors, NEC could boast of high job-placement rates—courtesy of the intimate ties that proprietary schools forged with other in-region businesses. The company also raced to expand overseas; more than one out of every three distance-education students (111,000 as opposed to 256,000) was categorized as "international" rather than "domestic" during 1996, and a similar proportion of net revenues (total-

ing $289 million in 1996) came from overseas sales.[212] International con-
tract training, in truth, had been booming for some years. U.S. firms,
noted the U.S. Department of Commerce, were searching "aggressively"
for overseas training markets early in the 1980s. Contracts could sometimes be very large, as in a $200 million contract to provide training in
Jubail, an industrial city in Saudi Arabia, built by Bechtel (which NEC
lost).[213]

By 1997, NEC made growing use of the Internet, as well as corporate
intranets, to deliver products and services to students. Characterizing
itself as "a global provider of interactive multimedia products and services for the education and training marketplace," NEC then allowed
itself to be acquired by yet another proprietary vendor, Sylvan Learning
Systems.[214]

Sylvan, spun off by KinderCare Learning Centers in 1993, designated
itself "a leading international provider of educational and testing services." Systemwide revenues were close to NEC's, around $286 million
in 1996—when the company had some 2,850 employees, of whom 1,600
were classified as part-time.[215] Sylvan's co-CEO, R. Christopher Hoehn-
Saric, was entirely candid about wanting to make his company "the
source of all types of educational content throughout people's school and
professional careers." In 1997, a partnership with *National Geographic*
to offer educational and entertainment after-school programs comprised
one contemplated market extension.[216]

Sylvan's existing operations were formidable in their own right. By
1998, its Contract Educational Services unit marketed education to 100
public schools nationwide.[217] During 1996, Sylvan had contracts to provide remedial education to public schools in states from Texas to Maryland, despite strong opposition by unionized teachers.[218] Individual
school districts in turn selectively outsourced the provision of instructional services to proprietary outfits; in 1998, the Los Angeles Unified
School District gave $10 million to five private firms, including Sylvan,
to offer teacher training and tutoring on eighty-three campuses.[219]

The company also catered to large corporations. Sylvan-at-Work provided programs onsite for Motorola and for Texas Instruments in Texas
and for Martin Marietta in Tennessee. Sylvan had expanded its corporate
training activities by acquiring the PACE group (in 1995)—which

supplied educational and training services to large U.S. corporations. Services offered by PACE included "racial and gender workplace diversity training and skills improvement programs such as writing, advanced reading, listening and public speaking." Program customers included Ford, IBM, BankOne, General Motors, and AT&T.[220] Sylvan also acquired Wall Street Institute International, which taught English in Europe and Latin America through its network of 170 franchised and company-owned centers.

International expansion constituted a long-term strategic priority. Sylvan thus began building a global network for the delivery of computer-based testing services through an alliance with Educational Testing Service (ETS), the developer of the Graduate Record Exam, the National Teachers Exam, the Advanced Placement Program, and the Scholastic Achievement Test.[221] Sylvan's own testing services subsidiary, Prometric, administered computer-based tests for corporations, professional associations, and government agencies, again through a worldwide network of certification centers. Principal customers included Novell and Microsoft.

Aiming directly at individual customers, Sylvan also designed and delivered tutorial services, typically costing around $1,500, to school-age children and adults—via a network of 700-odd franchised and company-owned learning centers, in forty-nine states, five Canadian provinces, Hong Kong, South Korea, and Guam.[222] (Franchise rights have also been sold in China and Israel.) Franchisees in foreign countries offered the English-language version of the Sylvan program and were not allowed to provide a foreign-language version without paying additional fees to the company. Instruction was proffered at U-shaped tables, designed, said the company, "to ensure that teachers work with no more than three students at a time." Material incentives supplied an integral dimension of Sylvan pedagogy—and, presumably, an opportunity for additional commercialization. One-hour lessons, for example, relied on "tokens redeemable for novelties and toys, to motivate the student to achieve the program's objectives and to strengthen the student's enthusiasm for learning."[223]

Learning Centers cost between $79,000 and $145,000 to open (exclusive of real estate and building costs); of this total a franchise licensing fee comprised around one-third. Franchisees, granted initial ten-year licenses to operate within specified territories, were obligated to purchase diagnostic and instructional materials, record forms, parental information booklets, and other brochures from Sylvan, which also specified requirements for computers, furniture, and additional instructional materials. Royalties of 8 to 9 percent of gross revenues—depending on "the demographics of the territory"—were due to Sylvan, while franchisees were required to spend between $1,000 and $3,500 on advertising each month. "Most Learning Centers are located in suburban areas," the company asserted, "and have approximately ten employees, two of whom are typically full-time employees and eight of whom are part-time instructors."[224]

Through a generation-long buildup, diversified education conglomerates have also thronged toward formal higher-education services. One precocious corporate foray was made by the Control Data Corporation, which by the 1980s held cooperative arrangements for specialized software development in engineering and computer science with over 200 colleges and universities.[225] The company's maverick chairman, William Norris, projected—in 1983, two years before bankers pressured him to retire in the wake of staggering corporate losses—that "fifteen years from now, education is going to be the largest source of [our] revenues and profits."[226]

While Control Data fell by the wayside, other corporations took up the challenge. Also ultimately unsuccessful, TeleLearning Systems, which inaugurated a for-profit Electronic University in 1983, nevertheless innovated some influential institutional arrangements. First, it looked to patronage from federal officials. The then–Secretary of Education, Terrel H. Bell, spoke at the press conference that launched the new company, announcing that the "advantage" of its approach was that it would help solve "one of the big problems in education—that it is labor intensive."[227] Second, it tied in with established educational providers. Not only courses but college credit, as well, came from its partners—Ohio University, the University of Nebraska, and De Anza College. Aimed at the exploding market for personal computers (there were 10 million in use in the U.S. by 1984), Telelearning Systems furnished its own software to broker an inventory of 170 courses provided by colleges, technical schools, and trade associations across the nation. Students received and sent all course work electronically, and—for an additional fee—conversed with instructors at predetermined times.[228] (Course fees ranged initially from $35 to $150 per hour, depending on course length and instructor credentials.)

Third, its labor policies presaged subsequent fashions; instructors were paid, piece-work fashion, by lessons completed. Fourth, TeleLearning was marketing-driven. Chosen, as one analyst noted, "for their entertainment value, their educational content, and the ease with which they can be put on a computer," courses of study included accounting, real estate, wine appreciation, mathematics, science, law, and foreign languages.[229] TeleLearning, fifth and finally, also sought to tap the corporate market by furnishing custom-tailored courses for "teaching employees about corporate procedures and management techniques or informing customers about new products and services."[230]

Through the 1980s and 1990s, PCs popped up all over campuses, libraries automated circulation and cataloguing systems, and universities installed private telecoms systems integrating voice, data, and video—both on campus and, often, beyond. The National Science Foundation, of course, seeded the process by subsidizing a high-speed computer network linking universities and other institutions—the system that evolved into the Internet. Leading information technology vendors targeted higher-education markets, both donating and selling computers, telecommunications systems, and software. By 1995, in consequence, an estimated 24 percent of college classes were held in computer-equipped classrooms, and one-fifth of courses were using email.[231] Proliferating network systems permitted direct linkages beween outside institutions and campus-based knowledge-producing resources and facilities—faculty, researchers, expensive equipment, libraries. Colleges and universities were now equipped to move into the mainstream of networked service delivery.

Their incentive to do so was largely a function of the emergent market complex. "If traditional colleges and universities do not exploit the new technologies, other nontraditional providers of education will be quick to do so," asserted one influential paper.[232] University administrators, warned the accounting and consulting firm Coopers & Lybrand, should begin preparing for corporations to move into academic territory.[233] Institutions that choose to retain their accustomed "labor-intensive" methods, in this context, stood to lose out to for-profit competitors.

And, suddenly, the landscape indeed was different. By 1997, with an appreciable fraction of all higher education already occurring in the form of distance learning, U.S. colleges and universities were being assigned public rankings on how well they used the Internet—meaning online homework, courses with home pages, courses in Internet use, computers and network connections available to students and faculty members, and the like.[234] The Benjamin Franklin Institute of Global Education arranged an around-the-world virtual tour to showcase thousands of online courses sponsored by colleges and universities worldwide. Some 5 million people annually were said to take electronic courses offered by more than 2,000 accredited colleges with online graduate or undergraduate degrees. Peterson's, the college guide company, produced a 500-page book devoted to schools offering online degrees.[235] Email, now utilized in almost a third of college courses, was heralded by erstwhile FCC Chairman Reed Hundt as portending "a giant step away from mass education, toward mass individualization." Some 14 percent of courses at all institutions were estimated to put class materials such as course outlines on Web pages, and nearly one-fourth used other Web-site-based resources.[236] The National Center for Education Statistics projected that nine-tenths of all institutions having more than 10,000 students were expected to be offering at least some distance-education courses within a year.[237]

It was still too soon to tell which institutions would succeed at purveying educational services via networks and which would fail. But it was incontrovertible that the race into networked provision had commenced in earnest within the core of the university. Typifying and, indeed, guiding the migration of courses onto networks, in turn, was a seamlessly merged group of hitherto not-for-profit programs and for-profit enterprises.

The New School could boast of a noble history. Established in 1919 as a nontraditional college for discussing economic and political issues by academics unhappy with World War I militarism, the New School later acted as a home away from home for refugee scholars fleeing Nazi Germany. During the mid-1990s, however, the New School pursued a less heterodox course. It now sought to bolster flagging enrollments by mounting online courses, backed by aggressive marketing and taught by low-paid, casualized instructors.[238] There was nothing marginal or deviant about such a strategic decision. Some of the nation's most elite private universities—Stanford, Cornell, Columbia, Chicago, Yale—were likewise testing the waters for electronic courseware.[239] Distance education courses were on offer from a growing proportion of all colleges and universities, which targeted them above all at current undergraduate populations.[240]

Internet initiatives fueled the movement of networked provision from the periphery—continuing education and professional school programs—into the core of the university. UCLA's College of Letters and Science tried to mandate that every course offered—some 3,000 during the 1997 to 1998 academic year—should produce a Web page. The previous year, just 6 percent of the university's humanities courses and 20 percent of science courses had Web sites; thus, the directive must be seen as an extraordinary policy intervention, whose repercussions went far beyond a $100-a-year increase in student fees. Where professors preferred, a standard template could be used to produce Web pages with basic information for each course, including meeting time, course description, and syllabus. Professors were encouraged "to step up to the plate" by adding reading, slides, audio and video clips, and links to related Web sites; each page also had a discussion area to facilitate *chatting* among students and between students and professor. A year into the venture, administrators hedged that this Instructional Enhancement Initiative was not actually mandatory; at least some professors had refused to participate—on grounds that the university might try to claim ownership of any course materials they posted on the network.[241]

Well might they worry. In an effort to gain clear legal title to prospectively valuable instructional materials, some universities asserted that course contents comprised works made for hire by faculty. Universities as corporate entities, rather than individual faculty, accordingly should be the rightful "authors"—and, thus, also the legal owners—of electronic courseware produced at their institutions.[242] At the University of Colorado at Denver, professors who teach online are made to hand over to the school title to their electronic courses; provisions even "bar instructors from using the online version of the course in class lectures, consulting work or at other institutions without permission."[243] As professors belatedly began to realize that administrators were staging a prospectively colossal turf-grab, their legal position, as both creators and users of intellectual property, remained in flux.[244] Property ownership of rights to online courses comprised a tinderbox of prospectively conflictful legal issues.

A fledgling industry comprised of software development companies, academic technologists, instructors, and, not least, students, sprang up to support online course production. The "central selling point of most of the[se] software packages" was that faculty members can "simply fill in the blanks, and the program produces a Web site."[245] Packages were priced according to how many courses a given institution wanted to put online, course enrollments, and whether the institution preferred to purchase the software or to pay for a predetermined period of use. When colleges turned to professional site designers, of course, they potentially ceded significant control over the character of what was being purveyed.[246] Microsoft cofounder Paul Allen's online education venture, APEX, paid for course development and took free and clear title to the property; teachers who help develop the courses did not necessarily teach them.[247]

Colleges, however, continued to comprise a ready market for vendors. At a cost of millions of dollars, Academic Systems Corporation—a company backed by Microsoft, Tele-Communications Inc., Softbank, and Jostens Learning Corporation—developed three algebra courses and a writing course in CD-ROM format. Academic Systems sold the algebra courses to dozens of colleges, including eight in the California State University System and several in the CUNY system. In at least one case, the university passed along the company's $80-per-student licensing charge to students as a course fee.[248] In a different example, Lexis-Nexis, an online company owned by the giant publishing conglomerate Reed-Elsevier, which offered access to legal documents and journal articles, pursued a strategy of forward integration by developing electronic materials for law-school students. The firm commissioned a board of seven Harvard University law professors to create an electronic first-year law-school curriculum. Kaplan, a subsidiary of Washington Post Co., likewise rolled out a for-profit online law degree program.[249] On a larger scale, in 1996 IBM announced the arrival of its IBM Global Campus, through which it hoped to sell technology and expertise to help colleges put courses online and assist with student registration and course counseling. Colleges in twelve countries, including the United States, Brazil, Canada, Mexico, Venezuela, and Australia, enrolled in the initiative.[250]

Vendors, however, also moved with alacrity toward more comprehensive rivalry with existing institutions. Founded in 1995, Virtual Online University Services International boasted that its nonprofit Athena University would deliver "cost-effective and accessible" liberal arts education.[251] International University, founded to act as an online complement of Jones Intercable, a megamedia company, offered a B.A. completion program and an M.A. in business communications and was seemingly on the path to accreditation by the North Central Association of Colleges and Schools.[252] Perhaps the best-known for-profit supplier, the University of Phoenix—a subsidiary of the Apollo Group—served up college courses to 43,000 students at locations in ten states; 6,000 of its students were online by mid-1998. Granting no tenure to instructors, Phoenix employed 454 full-time faculty members and an army of 4,500 part-time adjuncts paid around $1,000 for each five-week course they offer.[253] Students met in leased office spaces and motels and at military bases. The University offered accredited bachelor's degree programs for business, nursing, and education, as well as an M.B.A.— but it was, as James Traub observed, actually "a para-university. It has the operational core of higher education—students, teachers, classrooms, exams, degree-granting programs—without a campus life, or even an intellectual life."[254]

"Want to Give Students from All Over the World the Opportunity to Take Your Classes on the Web?" asked IBM's Lotus subsidiary in an ad targeted directly at educators.[255] "Join the Leader in OnLine Education over the Internet," boasted Real Education, an outsourcer that by mid-1998 ran online instructional services for twenty-nine schools.[256] But digital capitalism in education, alas, was not simply the result of exterior corporate pressure. Entrepreneurial professors, not to mention administrators, were sometimes positively eager to put university-based intellectual property to profitable use. USC profs, for example, teamed up with Interactive Multimedia Learning Technologies Inc. (IMLearn) to develop a cinema course for the Internet. After spending more than a year and nearly a million dollars planning the course, The Language of Cinema, the partners saw two perceived benefits. The first was cost efficiency. Students—who were slated to be sent videotapes and CD-ROMs of course materials, complete with copyright-cleared clips from Hollywood movies—could be sought worldwide. (A graded version of the course, limited to 400 students and offering both college credit and greater interaction with a teaching assistant, would cost $650; an ungraded version, costing $500, would have unlimited enrollment.) Administrators believed that small universities might be particularly eager to offer the course as a means of adding an enticing and flashy offering without investing much money. "The advantage of this progam from the university perspective," stated Jerry Isenberg, IMLearn's president—and, not coincidentally, also a professor of cinema and television at SC—was "that it enables the university to broaden its curriculum without investing in bricks and mortar and tenured faculty." Second, its cost efficiency came in another guise: the development effort was expected to pay off by decreasing the costs of production of future online courses.[257]

In the mid-1980s, Nell Eurich had observed that

the potential for faculty contribution to software instruction is great; it could be most beneficial to the quality of goods at the learning store.

The imperative is for the best teachers to create instruction of highest quality; they dare not leave the medium only to entrepreneurs and industry with skilled marketing to introduce educational courses onto the campus, schools, and homes of America and the world. That prospect offers an alarming vision of what people may be learning about history, art, social sciences, literature, or any other subject.[258]

Academics, that is, might claim a prized strategic advantage—certified quality—over purportedly more venal outsiders. Might this not translate into branding power?

Branding of educational products and services was, certainly, already underway. "The adult continuing-education student is looking for brands," declared John Kobara, CEO of OnlineLearning.net—which sought to partner with "name-brand universities," such as UCLA.[259] Duke University's online Global Executive MBA comprised one well-known provider that was able to charge a premium for delivering online education to well-connected distance learners. But branding promised to become more central than this. "It is conceivable," declared one survey, that "we will have celebrity professors with incomes and audiences comparable to those of some entertainers."[260] In turn, canny administrators were advised to identify viable market segments (that is, groups of students) and to attempt to hawk their brand on grounds of convenience or price.[261]

As the scale on which educational services could be "delivered" was enlarged, disparate institutional collaborations sought to exploit the new opportunities. Ventures developed, for example, among research libraries—long-time pillars of traditional university scholarship. The Digital Libraries Initiative was a federally sponsored effort to create tools to support construction and use of networked materials. But a raft of additional ventures was also apparent. Bringing together Big Ten universities with the University of Chicago and the leading vendor of library cataloguing services, OCLC, the Committee on Institutional Cooperation established a "virtual electronic library" to provide 500,000 students and 35,000 faculty with desktop access to library catalogs and other information stocks. Delivery would be available, significantly, "through traditional interlibrary loan, commercial document delivery, or online."[262] OCLC also joined with the community colleges and universities of Florida to build a "distance learning library" that would make use of the Internet to permit students to connect to online collections from homes, offices, or classrooms.[263]

The University of California, likewise, opened the California Digital Library—in effect, the nine-campus system's tenth general library. The venture's objective was to make full-text versions of 1,000 science and technology journals available to faculty, staff, and students via campus computers within a year. "In time, CDL hopes to create linkages with other universities and business and industry so that CDL holdings can be made available to a much broader clientele—though they must be willing to pay for such access." Prospectively even more significant, the CDL hoped to claw back "the scholarly product that our faculty give away to publishers," perhaps by serving itself as an online publisher for academics.[264] The University of Cincinnati, the University of Virginia, and Cornell took a slightly different tack, as they sought to leverage their rare books collections by turning them—and their librarians—into entrepreneurial marketers of digitized materials.[265]

Extended use of distance-learning technologies—including, preeminently, the Internet—tended to be rationalized as a measure compelled by a coming vast influx of students. In California, for example, "tidal wave II" referred to an expected deluge of enrollments around the millennium—an additional 488,000 annually by 2005, in one estimate.[266] Piggybacking on a high-speed network that already served the California State University system, all 107 of California's community colleges geared up for Internet videoconferencing, for example, in a full-scale effort to expand distance-education offerings.[267] But the institutional features of these emerging ventures cast doubt on the claim that they were simply intended to meet this projected demand. CSU trustees set about negotiating, largely in secret, with a group of high-tech corporations that included GTE, Fujitsu, Hughes, and Microsoft to launch the CETI (California Education Technology Initiative) Corporation in 1997. The governance structure of the consortium left some wondering whether corporate "equity stakeholders" might dominate it; and the proposal called for sale of CETI-controlled courses in general education and other areas as well as acquisition of educational materials from private industry.[268] By summer 1998, as protests mounted against CETI, the venture was pronounced dead.

Elsewhere, however, analogous attempts were underway. Fifteen Western state governors collectively established a new virtual university. But the venture, though technically nonprofit, was structured to go well beyond the provision of education to tens of thousands of expected new enrollments. The new institution, called Western Governors University, planned to transmit courses from traditional area colleges and universities as well as from organizations like Microsoft and Motorola. The WGU's role would be to contract for and coordinate the program and award degrees. This virtual university, wrote a skeptic, "describes itself as market-driven, competency-based, client-centered, accredited, high quality, and cost effective."[269] Anticipating a role in the WGU, Colorado's community college system unwrapped an associate-degree program that students anywhere could take entirely over the Internet—in partnership with Real Education, the Denver-based outsourcer.[270]

The scope of cyberschooling, territorially speaking, was unmistakably transnational. The flow of foreign science and engineering graduate students physically attending U.S. universities—what used to be called the "brain drain" from periphery to metropole—has risen to unprecedented levels. Between the late 1980s and 1996, the number of foreign students on temporary visas who earned doctorates at U.S. universities jumped 71 percent; by the latter date, the proportion of U.S. doctoral degree recipients on permanent or temporary non-U.S. visas was over 30 percent of the total awarded.[271] Overseas demand for U.S. degrees ran strong, however, at every curricular level. (Not least owing to improved job prospects: in one estimate, in 1990 nearly 12 percent of America's scientists and engineers were foreign-born.)[272] Why not serve at least some fraction of this student base through for-profit distance-learning programs?

The global dominance of English as a second language, its service as the lingua franca of contemporary business, science, and pop culture, added to the likelihood that vendors would succeed in selectively marketing educational products and services on a transnational scale—all the more so when, as we have seen, transnational corporations themselves were increasingly educators as well. And, finally, the emergence of serviceable forms of translation software was expected to broaden still further the geographic and cultural reach of the commercial learning industry.[273]

Even amid the economic crisis there, thus, the Apollo Group—parent of the University of Phoenix and the largest U.S. for-profit supplier of higher education—planned "an aggressive expansion" into China, the rest of Asia, and Europe. With a campus already set up in London, another being established in Mexico City, and some 3,300 students taking online courses in the United States, Apollo sought to move more heavily into information technology training.[274] Leading United States business schools alternatively explored franchising and building their own branch campuses in other countries.[275] An unprecedented educational institution—the so-called *mega-university*, enrolling more than 100,000 students—prepared to function as a broker of distance learning services on a world stage.[276]

Combined efforts by proprietary school chains, textbook publishers, information technology vendors, software companies, and universities themselves built powerful momentum behind for-profit education. The

very distinction between profit-making companies and educational institutions, indeed, was thrown into doubt, as James Traub explains, by vir-
tue of the emergence of "a new kind of institution . . . an alliance between
a state-university system, a 'content provider,' like Disney, and a technology firm, like Motorola." The corporate university was, in turn, "part
of a web, not of a pecking order—one of several kinds of 'providers'
filling in different aspects of a 'learner''s needs."[277] It was symptomatic
that, when a U.S. Distance Learning Association was created, its board
of directors sported representatives not only from universities, but from
companies such as Scientific Atlanta, GE Spacenet, and Bell Atlantic.[278]
Similarly, the National Learning Infrastructure Initiative launched in
1994 by Educom—itself a leading proponent of the trends sketched
here—joined the Universities of California, Iowa, Michigan, North Caro-
lina, Texas, Wisconsin, and other states, in cooperation with Addison-
Wesley, Eastman Kodak, IBM, International Thomson, John Wiley, the
Software Publishers Association, U.S. West, Times Mirror, and Taligent.
The initiative explicitly sought to establish a "market structure for development of interactive learning materials" and took portentous note that,
reputedly, 1 percent of all college courses—twenty-five titles—accounted
for over half of community college enrollments and about one-third of
baccalaureate enrollments.[279] Was a blockbuster orientation far behind?

Lobbyists successfully prevailed on legislators, meanwhile, to provide
funds with which to establish an enhanced Internet. With hefty corporate
support, the Next-Generation Internet proposal sought to grant access
to university-based programs to a speeded-up network and to spur multimedia service offerings.[280] A parallel, university-led effort—dubbed Internet 2—likewise aimed to create a testbed for advanced applications.
Internet 2 allied 130 colleges, each of which pledged $500,000 for infra-
structure and staff, with three major corporate partners—Quest communications, Nortel, and Cisco.[281] Utilizing Internet 2, researchers will be
able to cooperate on high-bandwidth experiments, students at different
campuses will be able to share the same interactive video lectures, and
entire university communities "will share online digital libraries of video
and audio content."[282] As so often, however, an apparently blameless
attempt to enhance common use actually served a less noble purpose.
Douglas S. Gale, assistant vice president for information systems and

services at George Washington University, related that Internet 2 would allow universities to teach more students with fewer faculty members and would permit institutions to reach new audiences via distance education. If universities did not embrace network provision, he asserted, students would turn to private companies that did—and that therefore could offer courses at lower prices. For-profit colleges, finally, seemed likely to drive many universities out of business. Concluded Gale: "The reason we need Internet 2 is, quite frankly, for the survival of education as we know it."[283]

Some readers may recall here the Vietnam War logic of burning the village in order to save it. But Gale was expressing what had already become the prevailing administrative wisdom. "If traditional colleges and universities do not exploit the new technologies," warned a widely cited Educom report, "other nontraditional providers of education will be quick to do so."[284] Instead of earning degrees in residence, student-customers would be enabled to "pick and choose Internet-based courses from a conglomeration of learning institutions to earn their degrees. Universities will somehow have to accommodate to the fact that "their students will be able to choose from courses at universities all over the globe."[285]

All Over but the Shouting?

Unfolding was a generalized process of institutional change. Management guru Peter Drucker declared, in a widely cited verdict, that universities on the old model "won't survive."[286] While textbooks ran chronically short in poor school districts,[287] and while some 200 traditional colleges shut their doors over the decade to 1997, politicos and corporate executives prattled on about the need to wire up additional "cyberschools."[288] "We want to redesign the entire learning process to fit the Information Age," summarized Newt Gingrich.[289]

The issue, however, was not a fight-to-the-finish struggle—either between business and academe or between brick-and-mortar and cyberspace. It was, rather, how and how far education will be transformed by the profit imperative. As I write, the process of creating market structures for educational provision remains nowhere near complete.

The critical question in turn is, Will that process continue to run largely free of real social opposition? Or will the creation of a vocational, for-profit learning industry begin to encounter more concerted resistance?

Those who would challenge the trend to market provision will find it difficult to avoid a defensive posture. In countless ways, they are asked if the sea change that is underway is not really an opportunity to introduce a consumer sovereignty that is long overdue. Popular hostility to long-established, top-down traditional teaching practices likely will prove more significant than some may prefer to acknowledge. Educators are easily caricatured as fustily out of date, resistant to change, intent on preserving prerogatives—above all, job security—that have been withdrawn from other workers. And, on the other hand, the job *in*security that now plagues a growing number of managers, as well as "ordinary" workers, only inflates the allure of vocationalism.

Furthermore, as I have already underlined, the academic labor force is itself of two minds about the trends that are underway. It is likely that most faculty—though by no means all—would reject the idea of market provision when presented as an explicit, considered institutional policy. But on vocationalism the verdict would be less certain; higher education, after all, has already long since begun to eschew the hegemony of the core curriculum and the liberal arts. Furthermore, an unknown but un-doubtedly large fraction of U.S. educators enthusiastically favors the infusion of technology into education. It is easy to point to faculty members—and to students—whose commitment to developing Web pages repulses critical scrutiny.

However, heightening anxiety among faculty and faculty unions will not be easy to dispel—especially as the trend toward digital capitalism in education continues to move rapidly from the periphery to the core of the enterprise. Already in 1996 the American Federation of Teachers called on its 100,000 higher-education members to oppose courses taught on the Internet, through videoconferencing, or with other technologies—unless they meet faculty members' standards of quality. The union also sought restrictions on the number of college credits that students may receive for distance education.[290] Another union, the National Education Association, likewise began to organize against the coupling of technology by virtual universities with low-paid, casualized instruction.[291] In late 1997, an AFT report spoke of the future this way:

What we may expect—and what unions should consider as they prepare for negotiation—is that a profession already afflicted with an extraordinarily high underemployment rate of its members—45 percent are part-time—will experience further decline. Thousands will retire and will not be replaced by younger members of the profession but by desktop workstations, courseware, "self-paced learning," large multisite distance learning classes, and a reengineered capital-to-labor ratio on their campuses.[292]

At York University in Toronto—as *Digital Diploma Mills*, a study by David Noble documents—a three-week strike by unionized faculty successfully gained contract language that afforded control by individual faculty members over the introduction of classroom technology.[293] In mid-1998, moreover, nearly 900 faculty members on the University of Washington campus signed a letter protesting to the governor the "frightening" and prospectively "disastrous" shift toward "a profit-driven, digitalized 'knowledge industry'" that seeks to supplant instructors with automated teaching tools.[294]

Within and around the university—the institution that Daniel Bell once hailed as the postindustrial economy's decisive node—conflict seems all but certain to increase over the terms on which network applications are deployed. Will such strife in turn portend a wider disunion as digital capitalism takes hold?

Conclusion: The Road Forward

When the Internet was still a fledgling, Simon Nora and Alain Minc asked of the overall process of computerization: "Are we headed, regardless of appearances and alibis, toward a society that will use this new technology to reinforce the mechanisms of rigidity, authority, and domination?"[1] A generation—an epoch—has passed, and as digital capitalism supplants its forbear, the question remains.

In chapters 1 and 2, we traced the overwhelmingly successful attempt made by transnational business users and independent equipment suppliers to reorganize telecommunications policy on neoliberal lines. Originating forty years ago within the giant U.S. market, new networking initiatives were encouraged by a series of piecemeal policy changes and system-development efforts over which federal agencies presided. Taking shape mainly at the margins of the regulated national telecommunications industry, network systems and applications were driven by a combination of private corporate demand and military strategic planning.

During the 1980s and 1990s, the push toward market-driven network development accelerated decisively. A series of events—unremitting U.S. pressure, supranational initiatives within the European Union and the World Trade Organization, shifting affinities among national elites after the fall of Soviet socialism, and, hardly least, the explosion of Internet systems themselves—cumulated in a new neoliberal paramountcy. As telecommunications privatizations occurred from Buenos Aires to Budapest, a system organized around nationally sovereign networks coupled, however inadequately, to welfarist social objectives began to give way. In its stead came network development efforts that favored integrated transnational production lines and business-to-business electronic commerce. The supply of residential access to services likewise metamorphosed. New market mechanisms privileged those with the resources to afford high-tech Internet and mobile applications.

In chapter 3, we followed a closely related vector of change, as the World Wide Web was refashioned into a novel consumer medium. Both as a prospective rival distributor and as a source of original content, the Web challenged newly arrived, vertically integrated megamedia firms. They duly jumped in, feet first, in an attempt to make the Web serve their own purposes. In increasing competition with upstart computer industry companies like Microsoft and Intel (and sometimes in competition with their own leading customers, giant consumer goods manufacturers) media powerhouses such as Time-Warner and Disney sought to harness the Web for advanced capitalism's most sacred social purpose: selling. Over a short interval, advertisers and advertising seized hold of the medium. Although the goal of reincarnating the Web as a stable system for reaching and teaching audiences remained incompletely realized, the sponsor system had unmistakably coopted it to its own needs.

But market development around networks—that is, digital capitalism—was not limited to the provision of familiar services such as commercial home entertainment. Nor did it entail merely market entry, moreover, but market creation as well. Would-be suppliers thus lined up to devise and sell a veritable raft of newly commercialized services. In chapter 4, we analyzed how this process was manifested in the vital and sensitive field of postsecondary education.

Faced with escalating needs for suitably trained workers, large U.S. companies began to furnish training and education as a private matter early in the twentieth century. Eventually, many of them began as well to sell training services to customers and suppliers. By the 1980s, it was apparent that this corporate "shadow system" was becoming a full-blown rival of formal higher education. Rather than seeking to challenge the trend to corporate educational provision, however, colleges and universities latched onto its coattails. Through an ongoing process of accommodation, higher-education institutions partnered with corporations to deliver instructional services. In this context, networks, including, in particular, the Internet, acquired an explosive significance. It was not only that, by deploying networks, educational vendors found means of reaching key target groups—employees, adult learners, existing student populations—on a newly cost-efficient basis. Networks also provided a venue or context within which the organization of the educational function itself could be radically transformed. Casualized labor policies, vocational objectives, and commercially oriented provision were the chief hallmarks of this emerging node of digital capitalism: a for-profit learning industry.

The common link between the domains we have traversed is a secular buildup of transnational corporate power to define and shape social institutions. A couple of thousand giant companies—as employers of workers laboring on networked production chains, as advertisers and, increasingly, as educators—today preside, not only over the economy but also over a larger web of institutions involved in social reproduction: business, of course, but also formal education, politics, and culture. Is this, however, a qualitatively new development?

In one sense, no. Loose corporate political hegemony over society at large comprised the ramifying achievement of a prior epoch. It took hold first, in the United States and Western Europe, in the events preceding and following World War I. Following the catastrophes of economic depression and global war, the institutional structure of corporate domination was successfully extended and enlarged, during the second half of the twentieth century, to encompass the nonsocialist world.

What *is* historically new, or so it seems to me, is a change in the sweep of corporate rule. For the first time since its emergence in the early twentieth century, the corporate-led market system no longer confronts a significant socialist adversary anywhere on the planet. Digital capitalism also is free to physically transcend territorial boundaries and, more important, to take economic advantage of the sudden absence of geopolitical constraints on its development. Not coincidentally, the corporate political economy is also diffusing more generally across the social field.

Over roughly a century, to be sure, big business has operated as a kind of senior partner in league with a variety of nonbusiness institutions—schools and universities, museums, professional societies, government agencies. Today, by contrast, corporations are committing themselves to a direct takeover of these key functions of social reproduction. This shift is not nominal but substantive. Activities long exempt from the direct workings of the for-profit market economy are being place on a true business basis.

A lengthening series of social practices through which we play, educate, and generally provide for one another are more or less rapidly being annexed by capital. Through this "march to the market," as the *Wall Street Journal* calls it, roughly one in twenty federal inmates in the U.S. is housed in a for-profit prison, and more than one in eight community-hospital beds is now an investor-owned hospital; even background checks on would-be federal employees are performed by a for-profit, privatized government agency.[2]

But if digital capitalism comprises a "purer" and more generalized form than the alloys with which we have lived in the past, then this change does not alleviate, and indeed may well increase, the volatility of the market system. Just one year ago, adherents of a so-called new economy grounded in networks trumpeted the news of a supposed "long boom" in which an unabating prosperity would flourish.[3] Even as their rosy forecasts hit the press, the Asian economic firestorm invalidated them. Pundits and columnists had to turn on a dime to engage questions of damage control: How to manage rampant speculative fevers? How to contain the effects of a secular buildup of industrial overcapacity? How to avert a full-scale global economic crisis?[4]

At somewhat longer range, perhaps, issues raised by deepening social inequality are hardly less grave. Disparities in socioeconomic well-being are more difficult to view as mere residues of a prior historical inclemency, when they are so obviously reproduced by the workings of digital capitalism itself.

Consider the trends within the United States, digital capitalism's generative historical locus and still its leading center. During the mid-1990s, U.S. corporations' average rate of profit enjoyed stellar growth. The profit record was such as to move the *Wall Street Journal* to gloat over "a five-year run of solid growth not seen since the mid-1960s."[5] One economist declared, indeed, that "no period in the postwar era has seen such rapid profit growth."[6] As we found in chapter 2, the redistribution of wealth has been such that the richest 1 percent of Americans today hold 21.4 percent of the country's wealth, while the number of Americans with gross assets of at least $600,000 has risen to 4.1 million.[7] A favored class of managers and professionals has fattened and prospered on stock options and a plethora of other new speculative instruments.

Their newfound luxury is, however, in major part a reflex of the redistribution of the social surplus from wage earners to property owners. This redistribution was accomplished via a relentless downward pressure on what some analysts called the social wage: the basket of available pay and benefits, both direct and indirect. Under the sign of "deregulation," severe cutbacks in government social programs were instrumental in ratcheting down these benefits, as were direct political attacks on trade unions. But two other linked initiatives were arguably paramount in reconfiguring the distribution of wealth. Aggressive corporate job cutting, well-publicized through the 1980s and 1990s as *downsizing* or *reengineering,* engendered a climate of pervasive anxiety and instability among the corporate workforce. Whereas, ten years before, the total employment of the top-ranked companies that make up the Standard & Poors 500 equaled 16 percent of the U.S. labor force, by 1997 it had declined to 14 percent.[8] The growing threat of capital flight, on the other hand—as companies gained the ability to invest with no loss of administrative control in offshore plants, offices, and factories—further enhanced corporate America's ability to demand concessions from employees.

Over the period from the 1970s to the 1990s, in turn, while middle-class earnings stagnated, the income gap between the wealthiest fifth and the poorest fifth of U.S. families increased. The percentage of children living in poverty in 1998 was up dramatically from what it was in 1969—to 20.5 percent (or 14.5 million) from 14 percent. In what one writer called "the new, ruthless economy," an estimated 25 percent of the population didn't even have checking accounts.[9] It was symptomatic that Microsoft, a corporate spearhead of digital capitalism, was "in the vanguard of a growing movement in corporate America, especially among high-tech companies: using full-time temp(orary) workers who save the company millions of dollars in benefits but who can be fired in the time it takes to boot up a computer." A business research group estimated that as many as one-fifth of U.S. companies use temps for more than 10 percent of their workforce; but 3,500 of Microsoft's 19,000 employees—or 18 percent—were temp workers in 1997. Among the Interactive Media Division, which creates Microsoft's Internet products, about half were temps.[10]

It can hardly be emphasized enough that accelerating corporate innovation around networks has been absolutely pivotal to this entire process of redistribution. Network-based automation itself comprises a major factor in the technologically induced layoffs that bulk so large in the "re-engineering" process. National, regional, and transnational networks, furthermore, are indispensable requirements of contemporary capital flight. As *permissive technologies* that are built to facilitate centralized control over far-flung corporate operations, networks permit transnational companies to elevate footloose profit hunger into what they seek to dignify with the term *globalization*. The result is to pit individual localities, states, and entire nations against one another in a competition to attract capital investment, and this rivalry predictably produces a "race to the bottom." Attaching conditions to continued or contemplated investments, companies demand lower corporate taxes, loosened environmental protections, diminished health and safety measures, and attenuated collective bargaining rights.[11] The decline in the social wage, in other words, and the redistribution of wealth that it has spurred are essentially functions of the neoliberal project that makes networks its centerpiece.

While commentators crow that Western Europe is enjoying economic recovery, double-digit unemployment rates persist there. Japan is in recession, and the vaunted Asian "Tigers" have mostly crashed into something worse still. In the United States, whose apparently buoyant economy more nearly approximates full employment than at any time over the past generation, mainstream commentators acknowledge that wage earners face "stagnant incomes, job instability, and economic anxiety."[12] For those on the fringes, life is indisputably harder. Welfare reform, notes a headline in the *Financial Times* "may push United States poor into squalor."[13] Throughout the less developed countries, where a significant band of middle-class strata has indeed emerged, general and chronic immiseration remains the general norm. The global economic crisis is unquestionably aggravating these deep stagnationist tendencies.[14]

When they are not trumpeting the wonders of digital networks, however, the stewards of digital capitalism remain basically complacent about their project's human face. Certainly, they have shown neither the ability nor the inclination to rekindle any widely shared prosperity. When asked to comment on the future, Intel's erstwhile CEO, the much-vaunted Andrew Grove, declares: "My view of the future is continuing the present."[15] At least he is straightforward. Just how far into difficulty the world's people are thrust, however, will clearly depend mainly on the quality of their own political response.

There is at least some ground for optimism. Uneasiness concerning unchecked capital flows is rising. In the United States, for the first time in decades, organized labor stirs with an unaccustomed rebelliousness, and serious debate about the economy is finding at least desultory expression—even if most audibly from the right: "Is the market penetrating too deeply into American life?" asks a front-page *Wall Street Journal* article?[16] Throughout much of the world, moreover, opposition to the institutional agents of neoliberal policy is apparent. In spring 1998, a World Trade Organization meeting in Geneva attracted thousands of demonstrators protesting globalization.[17] A global group of grassroots organizations opposed to the OECD's Multilateral Agreement on Investment—a secretive initiative that seeks to outlaw restrictions and controls that national governments might try to impose on supranational capital flows—publicized the campaign via the Internet itself and thereby momentarily checked its momentum.[18] In Puerto Rico, to cite another recent instance of resistance to digital capitalism, the prospective privatization and sale to foreign investors of the Puerto Rico Telephone Company provoked the largest demonstration in the island's history; a general strike opposing privatization shut down the economy there for a brief period in early July 1998.[19] Officials from nineteen countries, finally, met in Ottawa in hopes of forming a protective international cultural alliance through which to further national self-determination in the area of movies, television, music, and other entertainment.[20]

It is too soon to tell whether—and, if so, how—these disparate expressions of opposition to an untethered digital capitalism may come to cohere. No concerted or widespread social mobilization for a democratic reconstruction is, in truth, yet apparent. We may be confident, however, that digital capitalism has strengthened, rather than banished, the age-old scourges of the market system: inequality and domination. The road to redress begins from this recognition.

Notes

Introduction

1. Bill Gates, *The Road Ahead* (New York: Viking, 1995), 157.

2. Newt Gingrich, *To Renew America* (New York: HarperCollins, 1995), 56.

3. Richard B. DuBoff, "Global Something, but It's No Baloney," Manuscript, 1997, 1.

4. *The Unpredictable Certainty: Information Infrastructure Through 2000,* prepared by the NII 2000 Steering Committee; the Computer Science and Telecommunications Board; the Commission on Physical Sciences, Mathematics and Applications; and the National Research Council (Washington, D.C.: National Academy Press, 1996), 105.

Chapter 1

1. See Robert W. McChesney, "Off Limits: An Inquiry into the Lack of Debate over the Ownership, Structure and Control of the Mass Media in U.S. Political Life," *Communication 1992,* 13, 1–19.

2. See, for amplification, Robert Kuttner, *Everything for Sale: The Virtues and Limits of Markets* (New York: Knopf, 1997), 33–34; William Greider, *One World, Ready or Not: The Manic Logic of Global Capitalism* (New York: Simon & Schuster, 1997), 263. A work that illustrates the active historical role of government throughout the Industrial Revolution is Barry Supple, "The State and the Industrial Revolution 1700–1914," in Carlo M. Cipolla, *The Fontana Economic History of Europe: The Industrial Revolution* (Glasgow: Fontana/Collins, 1973), 301–357.

3. Dan Schiller, *Telematics and Government* (Norwood: Ablex, 1982), 24, 22.

4. Schiller, *Telematics and Government,* 22. I treat both the liberalization campaign and the early growth of corporate network applications in this work.

5. Telecommunications Reports, 5 December 1947, 21, 22, quoted in Alan Stone, *How America Got On-Line: Politics, Markets, and the Revolution in Telecommunications* (Armonk, N.Y.: Sharpe, 1997), 55.

6. Comment of the Automobile Manufacturers Association, 15 March 1957, 850–851, in U.S. Federal Communications Commission, Docket 11866, "In the Matter of Allocation of Frequencies in the Bands Above 890 Mc," NARA in Schiller, *Telematics and Government,* 11. See also Dan Schiller and RosaLinda Fregoso, "A Private View of the Digital World," *Telecommunications Policy,* June 1991, 195–208.

7. Anthony M. Rutkowski, "Factors Shaping Internet Self-Governance," in Brian Kahin and James H. Keller, eds., *Coordinating the Internet* (Cambridge: MIT Press, 1997), 98–99.

8. 77 FCC 2 384 (1980).

9. Rutkowski, "Factors Shaping Internet Self-Governance," 101.

10. "The Internet was designed . . . to determine how to build resilient computer networks that could survive physical attacks or malfunctions in portions of the network." *Critical Foundations: Protecting America's Infrastructures. The Report of the President's Commission on Critical Infrastructure Protection* (Washington, D.C.: USGPO, October 1997), 16–17.

11. Robert H. Reid, *Architects of the Web* (New York: Wiley, 1997), 4–5.

12. Katie Hafner and Matthew Lyon, *Where Wizards Stay Up Late: The Origins of the Internet* (New York: Simon & Schuster, 1996), 251.

13. Jeffrey K. MacKie-Mason and Hal R. Varian, "Economic FAQs About the Internet," in Lee W. McKnight and Joseph P. Bailey, eds., *Internet Economics* (Cambridge: MIT Press, 1997), 29.

14. Hafner and Lyon, *Where Wizards Stay Up Late,* 194, 214.

15. For example, see Aharon Kellerman, "The Diffusion of BITNET: A Communications System for Universities," *Telecommunications Policy,* June 1986, 88–92.

16. Schiller, *Telematics and Government;* Arthur L. Norberg and Judy E. O'Neill, *Transforming Computer Technology: Information Processing for the Pentagon, 1962–1986* (Baltimore: Johns Hopkins University Press, 1996), 39, 179.

17. Hafner and Lyon, *Where Wizards Stay Up Late,* 234.

18. John Markoff, "Long Before Microsoft's Internet War: A Peaceful Ethernet," *New York Times,* 18 May 1998, C1, C4.

19. Hafner and Lyon, *Where Wizards Stay Up Late,* 212.

20. *Critical Foundations,* 9.

21. Norberg and O'Neill, *Transforming Computer Technology,* 194.

22. Jack Rickard, "National Backbone Operators Internet Architecture," *Boardwatch Magazine Directory of Internet Service Providers,* July-August 1997, 6–8.

23. *Critical Foundations,* A-3.

24. Barney Warf, "Telecommunications and the Globalization of Financial Services," *Professional Geographer* (August 1989) 257–71; Pam Woodall, "A Survey of the World Economy: The Hitchhiker's Guide to Cybernomics," *Economist*, 4 October 1996, S15.

25. Seth Schiesel, "The No. One Customer: Sorry, It Isn't You," *New York Times*, 23 November 1997, sec. 3, pp. 1, 10.

26. Matt Murray, "Have You Noticed All of Those ATMs Suddenly Appearing?" *Wall Street Journal*, 7 October 1997, A1, A8; Emily Gest, "20–20 Visions," *Los Angeles Times*, 20 October 1995, E2, E7; Henry Fountain, "Ever Polite, Always Convenient, Superbly Efficient: The ATM," *New York Times*, 4 June 1998, D13.

27. Matt Murray, "Cost of Investing in New Technology Is a Growing Factor in Bank Mergers," *Wall Street Journal*, 20 November 1997, A4; Matt Murray and Raju Narisetti, "Bank Mergers' Hidden Engine: Technology," *Wall Street Journal*, 23 April 1998, B1, B9; Matt Murray, "Chase Manhattan Hopes to Expand Using Technology," *Wall Street Journal*, 27 May 1998, B4.

28. Lawrence H. Summers and Victoria P. Summers, "When Financial Markets Work Too Well: A Cautious Case for a Securities Transactions Tax," *Journal of Financial Services Research* 3, nos. 2 and 3 (December 1989): 261–286.

29. Greider, *One World, Ready or Not*, 227–258.

30. DuBoff, "Global Something."

31. U.S. Congress, Office of Technology Assessment, *Critical Connections: Communication for the Future*, OTA-CIT-407 (Washington, D.C.: USGPO, January 1990), 137.

32. Office of Technology Assessment, *Critical Connections*, 336–337; Frances Cairncross, "Telecommunications: The Death of Distance," *Economist*, 30 September 1995, 8.

33. John Evan Frook, "Boeing Intranet Takes Off," *Communications Week*, 27 January 1997, 1, 72; idem, "Big Three Race to Intranets," *Communications Week*, 10 March 1997, 1, 20; Walter Kuemmerle, "Building Effective R&D Capabilities Abroad," *Harvard Business Review* 75, no. 2 (March-April 1997): 61–70.

34. Andy Reinhardt with Peter Elstrom and Paul Judge, "Zooming Down the I-Way," *Business Week*, 7 April 1997, 87.

35. Robert D. Hershey, "The Law of Supply on Demand," *New York Times*, 28 December 1996, 23–24; Michael M. Phillips, "Retailers Rely on High-Tech Distribution," *Wall Street Journal*, 19 December 1996, A2.

36. Wendy Zellner, Louisa Shepard, Ian Katz, and David Lindorff, "Wal-Mart Spoken Here," *Business Week*, 23 June 1997, 138–144.

37. Bethan Hutton, "Japan's Seven-Eleven Sets Store by Computer Links," *Financial Times*, 17 March 1998, 20.

38. Brian Groom, "Call Centres Become a Jobs Phenomenon," *Financial Times*, 23 April 1998, S1.

39. Robert Frank, "A Stodgy Publisher Is Turning Electronic," *Wall Street Journal,* 11 August 1997, A10.

40. Laurence Zuckerman, "Do Computers Lift Productivity? It's Unclear, but Business Is Sold," *New York Times,* 2 January 1997, C15.

41. "Production Going Digital at Chrysler," *Los Angeles Times,* 12 May 1998, D13.

42. David Holley, "Toyota Heads Down a New Road," *Los Angeles Times,* 16 March 1997, A1, D12.

43. Peter Marsh and Nikki Tait, "Whirlpool's Platform for Growth," *Financial Times,* 26 March 1998, 8.

44. Bernard Wysocki, Jr., "Some Firms, Let Down by Costly Computers, Opt to 'De-Engineer,' " *Wall Street Journal,* 30 April 1998, A1, A6.

45. William Wolman and Anne Colamosca, *The Judas Economy: The Triumph of Capital and the Betrayal of Work* (Reading, Mass.: Addison-Wesley, 1997), 51; U.S. Department of Commerce, Secretariat on Electronic Commerce, *The Emerging Digital Economy* (Washington, D.C.: USGPO, 1998), 6, A1–A8. Available at http://www.ecommerce.gov.

46. Woodall, "A Survey of the World Economy," S15. And, almost certainly, neither information technology's occupational importance nor its preeminence in overall capital stock have yet peaked. At the height of the U.S. auto industry's economic power, from 1963 to 1966, highway transport industry jobs accounted for nearly one-fifth of total employment. At the height of late nineteenth-century U.S. industrialization, the railroads' contribution to overall U.S. capital stock was around twice as large as the information technology industry's today. Richard B. DuBoff, *Accumulation and Power: An Economic History of the United States* (Armonk, N.Y.: Sharpe, 1989), 32.

47. U.S. Department of Commerce, *The Emerging Digital Economy,* 4.

48. David C. Moschella, *Waves of Power: Dynamics of Global Technology Leadership 1964–2010* (New York: Amacom, 1997), 90, 218.

49. G. Pascal Zachary, "Intel CEO Says Asia Must Invest More in Information Technology for Growth," *Wall Street Journal,* 20 November 1997, A24.

50. U.S. Department of Commerce, *Survey of Current Business* 65, no. 7 (July 1985): 24, table 5.7; and 70, no. 6 (June 1990): 12, table 5.13; Ralph Winter, "Forecast for '86 Capital Outlays Improves," *Wall Street Journal,* 30 April 1986, 6.

51. G. Pascal Zachary, "High Tech Is Forming a Role as an Indicator," *Wall Street Journal,* 30 September 1996, A1; Woodall, "Survey of the World Economy," S13; U.S. Department of Commerce, *The Emerging Digital Economy,* 6, A1–7.

52. "New Thinking About the Economy" (editorial), *Business Week,* 19 May 1997, 150.

53. Steve Lohr, "Study Ranks Software as No. Three Industry," *New York Times,* 3 June 1997, C2.

54. Steve Lohr, "Information Technology Field Is Rated Largest U.S. Industry," *New York Times,* 18 November 1997, C12.

55. Michael J. Mandel, "The New Business Cycle," *Business Week,* 31 March 1997, 58, 59, 61; idem, "Just How Big Is High Tech?" *Business Week,* 31 March 1997, 68; DuBoff, *Accumulation and Power,* 102. For an opposing view, see Louis Uchitelle, "Computers Disappoint as Economic Force," New York Times News Service, in San Diego Union-Tribune Computerlink, 24 December 1996, 18.

56. "Computers to Lead Growth, Forecast Says," *Los Angeles Times,* 22 November 1997, D1, D3.

57. *Fortune,* Datamonitor, "Corporate Intranet and Extranet Strategies: The Business Implications," 1997, 1.

58. David Bollier, *The Networked Society: How New Technologies Are Transforming Markets, Organizations, and Social Relationships* (Washington, D.C.: Aspen Institute, 1997), 12–13.

59. Salvatore Salamone, "A T1 Resurgence," *Communications Week,* 21 April 97, 1, 73.

60. Norberg and O'Neill, *Transforming Computer Technology,* 155.

61. Norberg and O'Neill, *Transforming Computer Technology,* 154.

62. Norberg and O'Neill, *Transforming Computer Technology,* 192. I have substituted the word *employees* for *researchers.*

63. Rita Koselka, "The Hobby That Is Changing the Business World," *Forbes,* 6 October 1997, 104–108.

64. Mitch Irsfeld, "The 'Net Changes Everything," *Communications Week,* 30 June 1997, 57.

65. See "Oh, So That's An Intranet" (Microsoft advertisement), *Wall Street Journal,* 24 July 1997, B12.

66. Mary J. Cronin, "Tough Rules for Web Access," *Fortune,* 4 August 1997, 218–219.

67. Mary J. Cronin, "Intranets Reach the Factory Floor," *Fortune,* 18 August 1997, 208.

68. Michael Wiltshire, "Intranet Brings Big Savings for BT," *Financial Times,* 4 June 1997, FT-IT 5; George Black, "Final Call for Human Voice?" *Financial Times,* Review of the Telecommunications Industry, 10 September 1997, ix.

69. Mary J. Cronin, "Reinventing the Microsoft Intranet," *Fortune,* 23 June 1997, 142–143.

70. Margie Semlof, "Corporate Intranets and the Internet: Lines Blur," *Communications Week,* 15 July 1997, 1, 74.

71. Joseph B. White, "Chrysler's Intranet: Promise versus Reality," *Wall Street Journal,* 13 May 1997, B1, B7; Egil Juliussen, "Computers," *IEEE Spectrum* 34, no. 1 (January 1997): 52.

72. Michele Carlton and James R. Dukart, "How Reliable Are VPNs?" *Telephony* 233, no. 3 (21 July 1997): 28–35.

73. Moschella, *Waves of Power,* 221.

74. Mark Boslet, "Security-Software Market Is Razor Sharp," *Wall Street Journal,* 15 May 1998, B5A; Raju Narisetti, "IBM and Equifax Join Forces to Market Certification for Internet Transactions," *Wall Street Journal,* 8 June 1998, B9.

75. Mary J. Cronin, "Ford's Intranet Success," *Fortune,* 30 March 1998, 158; Haig Simonian, "Dealing with the Car Dealers," *Financial Times,* 4 March 1998, 13.

76. Irsfeld, "The 'Net Changes Everything," 57.

77. David Haskin, "The Extranet Team Play," *Internet World,* August 1997, 56–60.

78. Peter Marsh, "Raising Volume Around the World," *Financial Times,* 5 June 1998, 13.

79. Geoff Nairn, "Trading Places," *Financial Times,* 27 August 1997, 15.

80. Jube Shiver Jr., "The New Mark@place," *Los Angeles Times,* 14 September 1997, D1, D12.

81. Nairn, "Trading Places."

82. Shiver, "The New Mark@place," D12.

83. Patricia Nakache, "Cisco's Recruiting Edge," *Fortune,* 29 September 1997, 275.

84. Vanessa O'Connell, "Point, Click and Buy: On-Line Investing Draws Active Traders, Bargain Seekers," *Wall Street Journal,* 5 September 1997, C1, C17; Patrick McGeehan and Anita Raghavan, "On-Line Trading Battle Is Heating Up as Giant Firms Plan to Enter Arena," *Wall Street Journal,* 22 May 1998, C1, C21.

85. Rebecca Buckman, "Schwab Pushes Internet, Branch Service," *Wall Street Journal,* 23 March 1998, B9D.

86. Deborah Lohse, "E*Trade Bids to Be a Household Name," *Wall Street Journal,* 5 September 1997, B4.

87. Kimberley A. Strassel, "Citibank U.K. to Introduce Web Banking," *Wall Street Journal,* 5 June 1998, B9A.

88. Tracy Corrigan, "Banks Face Morgan Stanley Internet Challenge," *Financial Times,* 11 July 1997, 1, 22.

89. Tom Petruno, "What's Worthy on the Web," *Los Angeles Times,* 30 September 1997, D5.

90. Jeff Ubois, "The Next Opportunity," *Internet World* July 1997, 64.

91. Schiesel, "The No. One Customer," 1.

92. Vanessa Houlder, "Fear and Enterprise on the Net," *Financial Times,* 20 May 1998, 22.

93. Mitch Irsfeld, "The 'Net Changes Everything," *Communications Week,* 30 June 1997, 1, 57. See also James Flanigan, "Deals Show That GTE Got the

Wake-Up Call," *Los Angeles Times,* 11 May 1997, D1, D12. MCI's own research finding is that intranet services will account for more than half of the Internet industry's projected $43 billion in revenue by 2000; Jared Sandberg, "Microsoft Joins MCI-BT to Sell Intranet Services," *Wall Street Journal,* 14 November 1996, B8; Egil Juliussen, "Computers," *IEEE Spectrum* 34, no. 1 (January 1997): 52.

94. Steve Lohr, "Network Fails and Commerce Takes Big Hit," *New York Times,* 15 April 1998, C1, C22; Stephanie N. Mehta, "AT&T Is Seeking Cause of Big Outage in Data Network Used by Corporations," *Wall Street Journal,* 15 April 1998, B8; Penni Crabtree, "AT&T System Crash Is Wake-up Call for Business," *San Diego Union Tribune,* 15 April 1998, C1, C3.

95. Laurence Zuckerman, "Satellite Failure Is Rare, and Therefore Unsettling," *New York Times,* 21 May 1998, C3.

96. Robert L. Simison, "GM Sees Costs as High as $500 Million to Debug Year 2000 Computer Glitches," *Wall Street Journal,* 23 March 1998, A4.

97. "Fed Official Calls Year 2000 Bug 'Real and Serious,' " *Los Angeles Times,* 29 April 1998, D1, D9; David Wessel, "Year 2000 Is Costly, But Not Catastrophic," *Wall Street Journal,* 4 May 1998, A1.

98. *Critical Foundations.*

99. John Blau, "Telekom Prepares for Huge ATM Push," *Communications Week International,* 24 March 1997, 1.

100. Gautam Naik, "Demand for Phone Lines a Rising Tide," *San Diego Union-Tribune,* 9 November 1997, A37.

101. John J. Keller, "Lucent Agrees to Buy Yurie for $1 Billion," *Wall Street Journal,* 28 April 1998, A3, A6.

102. Paul Taylor, "Company Internet Use to Surge," *Financial Times,* 5 June 1998, 3.

103. Chairman Reed E. Hundt, FCC, "The Internet: From Here to Ubiquity," Paper presented before the Institute of Electrical and Electronics Engineers, 26 August 1997.

104. "UUNet Unveils Global Internet-Based Fax Service," *Telecommunications Reports Daily,* 9 July 1997.

105. Nicholas Denton, "Telecoms Set to Take Further Step into Cyberspace," *Financial Times,* 13 March 1998, 6.

106. David S. Isenberg, "The Rise of the Stupid Network," *Computer Telephony* 5, no. 8 (August 1997): 16–26; Renee Westmoreland and Richard Grigonis, "Real-Time Voice over IP Networks Explodes," *Computer Telephony* 5, no. 8 (August 1997): 70–97.

107. Thomas Kupper, "Pioneers in PC Phones," *San Diego Union-Tribune,* 24 March 1998, C1, C4.

108. Alan Cane, "Snared in the Net," *Financial Times,* 27 August 1997, 9; Larry Irving, "Voice on the Net: The Promise and the Challenge Ahead," Speech before Fall, 98: Voice on the Net Conference, Washington, D.C., 17 September 1998.

109. Stephanie N. Mehta, "ICG Joins Telephony Price Wars, Plans 5.9 Cents a Minute for Long Distance," *Wall Street Journal,* 11 March 1998, B4; Seth Schiesel, "Qwest Set to Acquire LCI for $4.4 Billion in Stock," *New York Times,* 10 March 1998, C2; David Diamond, "Building the Future-Proof Telco," *Wired* 6, no. 5 (May 1998): 124–127+.

110. Camille Mendler, "Carriers Wake Up to Intranet," *Communications Week International,* 24 March 1997, 2.

111. John J. Keller, "Data Traffic Helps MCI Beat Estimates," *Wall Street Journal,* 1 May 1998, B7. OECD research, tracing routes to the 100 most popular sites on the Net, showed that without any divestiture of Internet assets, a combined WorldCom and MCI would have been able to handle traffic to and from about fifty of the sites without relying on any other carrier. Sprint, the next biggest competitor, was able to do so for only eighteen of the sites. MCI/WorldCom would have needed to hand off to Sprint to reach only three of the top 100 sites, while Sprint would have to go to its competitor to gain access to twenty-six of them. Jennifer L. Schenker, "WorldCom, MCI Face Internet Objection," *Wall Street Journal,* 12 May 1998, B6.

112. See, for example, Paul Taylor, "Big Shake-up for Telecom Suppliers," *Financial Times,* 6 May 1998, 1; Nicholas Denton, "Mainstream.com," *Financial Times,* 3–4 January 1998, 6.

113. John J. Keller, "GTE Agrees to Buy BBN for $616 Million," *Wall Street Journal,* 7 May 1997, B7.

114. Seth Schiesel, "Internet Phone Calls, No Computer Necessary," *New York Times,* 16 April 1998, D1, D8; Seth Schiesel, "IBM Is Close to Deal on Phone Service over the Internet," *New York Times,* 18 May 1998, C1, C6.

115. Gautaum Naik, "Internet Phones Are Catching On as Global Experiment," *Wall Street Journal,* 24 November 1997, B4.

116. Chairman Reed E. Hundt, FCC, "Avoiding Digital Disruptions," Paper presented at International Engineering Consortium Network Reliability and Interoperability Comforum, Reston, Virginia, 16 September 1997.

117. Kenneth Cukier and Camille Mendler, "Technology or Ideology?" *Communications Week International,* 22 September 1997, 27–31; Deborah Claymon, "Father Knows Best," *Red Herring,* November 1997, 92–94.

118. G. Christian Hill, "Four Makers of Telecom Equipment Join to Invest in Project to Speed Up Internet," *Wall Street Journal,* 29 August 1997, B2; G. Christian Hill, "3Com Unveils New Switch as Firms Race to Increase Speed of Computer Networks," *Wall Street Journal,* 15 September 1997, B8.

119. Stephanie N. Mehta, "Lucent Unveils New Products to Expand Its Presence in Data-Networking Market," *Wall Street Journal,* 28 May 1998, B6; Andrew Kupfer, "Lucent Has a Brand-New Battle," *Fortune,* 25 May 1998, 89–92.

120. Alan Cane, "Faith Placed in Future of the Web," *Financial Times,* 12 May 1998, v; Seth Schiesel, "Phone Giant to Acquire Bay Networks," *New York Times,* 16 June 1998, C1, C4.

121. Brian E. Taptich, "The Intranet Mechanics," *Red Herring,* October 1997, 94.

122. Saul Hansell, "Now, Big Blue Is at Your Service," *New York Times,* 18 January 1998, sec. 3, pp. 1, 9.

123. Geoff Wheelwright, "Hidden Dimension to Historic Deal," *Financial Times,* 10 September 1997, Review of the Telecommunications Industry, vi.

124. Thomas E. Weber, "Sprint to Buy Paranet Inc. for $425 Million," *Wall Street Journal,* 21 July 1997, B10.

125. John J. Keller, "AT&T Profit Climbs 18 Percent; Stock Falters," *Wall Street Journal,* 21 April 1998, A3.

126. Rebecca Quick, "AT&T's Solutions Will Run Parent's Computer Network," *Wall Street Journal,* 10 September 1997, B8.

127. John J. Keller, "Lucent, in Big Expansion Move, Opens Network-Management Center for Clients," *Wall Street Journal,* 30 September 1997, B6.

128. Keller, "AT&T Profit Climbs."

129. Jared Sandberg, "AT&T Seeks Broad Marketing Technology Alliance with AOL," *Wall Street Journal,* 18 June 1998, B6.

130. "New Boss, New Man," *Business Week,* 2 February 1998, 122–132; Richard Poynder, "Internet Small Fry on the Road to Oblivion," *Financial Times,* 29 April 1998, 12.

131. Jack Rickard, Introduction, *Boardwatch Magazine Directory of Internet Service Providers,* July-August 1997, 5.

132. Henry Goldblatt, "AT&T Finally Has an Operator," *Fortune,* 16 February 1998, 79–82; "AT&T and Microsoft Internet-Access Plans Rethink 'Unlimited,'" *Wall Street Journal,* 1 April 1998, B4.

133. Jared Sandberg and Jon G. Auerbach, "AT&T Enters Marketing Pact with Lycos, Inc.," *Wall Street Journal,* 5 May 1998, B6.

134. Thomas E. Weber, "Sprint Plans Accord with EarthLink to Combine Internet-Access Businesses," *Wall Street Journal,* 11 February 1998, B10.

135. Rickard, Introduction, 5.

136. See Testimony of Scott C. Cleland, Legg Mason Wood Walker Inc., before the Communications Subcommittee Hearing of the U.S. Senate Committee on Commerce, Science, and Transportation, on "Wall Street's Perspective of 1996 Telecommunications Act Implementation," 18 March 1998, 2.

137. Nathan Newman, "The Hypocrisy of ISP Welfare and the Myth of the Cyber Free Market," *Enode* 2, no. 4 (July 1997), available from newman@garnet.berkeley.edu

138. Robert M. Entman, *Competition, Innovation, and Investment in Telecommunications: The Twelfth Annual Aspen Institute Conference on Telecommunications Policy* (Washington, D.C.: Aspen Institute, 1998), 6–7.

139. International Telecommunication Union, *World Telecommunications Development Report 1996–97,* (Geneva: ITU, February 1997), 70–71; Graham

Bowley, "CompuServe Services to Remain Separate," *Financial Times*, 11 September 1997, 18.

140. "Hitting Up the Internet," *Wall Street Journal*, 10 April 1998, A10 (editorial).

141. "Hitting Up the Internet"; U.S. FCC 98–67, In the Matter of Federal-State Joint Board on Universal Service, CC Docket No. 96–45, Report to Congress, 10 April 1998. See Seth Schiesel, "FCC Urges Policy Change in Cyberspace," *New York Times*, 11 April 1998, B1, B4; John Simons, "Internet Phone Calls Escape Full Force of FCC Regulation, But Face New Fees," *Wall Street Journal*, 13 April 1998, A24.

142. Stephanie N. Mehta, "Bell Atlantic Is Making Plans to Build Advanced Long-Distance Data Network," *Wall Street Journal*, 9 June 1998, B5.

143. Jared Sandberg, "How One Company Is Quietly Buying Up the Internet," *Wall Street Journal*, 9 September 1997, B1; Alan Cane, "Uunet in Dutch Internet Purchase," *Financial Times*, 3 September 1997, 22; John Greenwald, "WorldCom: Quiet Conqueror," *Time*, 22 September 1997, 50.

144. Jared Sandberg, "AT&T Is to Begin Offering Businesses High-Speed Connections to the Internet," *Wall Street Journal*, 9 October 1997, B8; "AT&T to Switch Data Traffic to Its Own IP-Based Backbone," *Telecommunications Reports*, 63, no. 41, (13 October 1997): 41–42.

145. Moschella, *Waves of Power*, 190.

146. Andrew Kantor and Michael Neubarth, "Off the Charts: The Internet 1996," *Internet World*, December 1996, 44–51; Seth Schiesel, "GTE Discloses Three Big Deals in Growth Bid," *New York Times*, 7 May 1997, C1, C4; Gordon Cook quoted by Steve Lohr, "The Internet as Commerce: Who Pays, Under What Rules?" *New York Times*, 12 May 1997, C1, C6.

147. Thomas K. Weber, "Baby Bells Versus the World: A Fight for Internet Fees," *Wall Street Journal*, 27 February 1997, B6; Lee Gomes, "UUNet Technologies Sparks an Outcry with Bid to Charge Internet Companies," *Wall Street Journal*, 1 May 1997, B7; Jennifer L. Schenker, "Internet Wars in Europe Scare Startup Firms," *Wall Street Journal*, 25 October 1996, A9A; Richard Poynder, "Internet Small Fry on the Road to Oblivion," *Financial Times*, 29 April 1998, 12.

148. Richard Waters, "U.S. Telecoms Groups in $19 Billion Deal," *Financial Times*, 27 August 1996, 1; Dan Schiller, *Bad Deal of the Century: The worrisome Implications of the WorldCom-MCI Merger*. Washington, D.C.: Economic Policy Institute, 1998.

149. John J. Keller, "The Old Phone System Is Facing an Overload, So Sprint Has a Plan," *Wall Street Journal*, 2 June 1998, A1, A8; Karen Kaplan and Elizabeth Douglass, "Nuts and Bolts Behind Sprint's New Network," *Los Angeles Times*, 3 June 1998, D1, D4.

150. Andrew Kupfer, "Son of Internet," *Fortune*, 23 June 1997, 120–122.

151. Seth Schiesel, "From a Supplier of Gas Comes a Digital Pipeline," *New York Times,* 12 January 1998, C8; John J. Keller, "Level Three Assails the WorldCom-MCI Deal," *Wall Street Journal,* 20 May 1998, B6; John J. Keller, "Qwest Plans to Buy Internet Provider EUnet of Europe," *Wall Street Journal,* 26 March 1998, B8.

152. Audrey Mandela, Chris Champion, Tony Dench, and Andrew Greenman, "It's Tough at the Top," *Communications Week International,* 25 November 1996, 20; Camille Mendler, "Making a Meal of Intranets," *Communications Week International,* 21 April 1997, 18–21; Gautam Naik, "Equant NVH as unusual Game Plan," *Wall Street Journal* 14 July 1998, B2.

153. Marsha Johnston, "Field of Dreams," *Communications Week International,* 22 September 1997, 18–24.

154. Jared Sandberg, "Microsoft Joins MCI-BT to Sell Intranet Services," *Wall Street Journal,* 14 November 1996, B8; Jeff Pulver, "When Worlds Collide," *Internet World,* May 1997, 80.

155. Kevin Werbach, "Digital Tornado: The Internet and Telecommunications Policy," U.S. Federal Communications Commission Office of Plans and Policy, OPP Working Paper Series no. 29, March 1997, 54.

156. "MCI, Cisco Offer Premium Net Service," *CCMI Telecom NewsFax Today,* 14, no. 61 (27 March 1997): 2.

157. Bruno Oudet, "Multilingualism on the Internet," *Scientific American* 276, no. 3 (March 1997): 77.

158. Camille Mendler and Nick Ingelbrecht, "Asia Unites Against FCC Rate Regime," *Communications Week International,* 17 February 1997, 1, 32; Kenneth Cukier, "Asian ISPs Band Together Against Internet Tariffing," *Communications Week International,* 21 April 1997, 6.

Chapter 2

1. International Telecommunication Union, *World Telecommunication Development Report 1998* (Geneva: ITU, March 1998), 14, fig. 1.2.

2. Eric Hobsbawm, *The Age of Extremes: A History of the World, 1914–1991* (New York: Pantheon, 1994), 205.

3. Edward Herman, "Globalization in Question?" *Z Magazine* 10, no. 4 (April 1997): 9; Du Boff, "Global Something," 8.

4. Joseph P. Quinlan, "Europe, Not Asia, Is Corporate America's Key Market," *Wall Street Journal,* 12 January 1998, A20.

5. Quinlan, "Europe, Not Asia."

6. The basic source on transnationalized economic activity is a serial publication, U.N. Conference on Trade and Development, *World Investment Report 1997, Transnational Corporations, Market Structure and Competition Policy* (New York: United Nations, 1997).

7. David Wessel, "Capital Flow to Developing Nations Surges 20 Percent," *Wall Street Journal,* 24 March 1997, B9; Du Boff, "Global Something," 7.

8. Robert Chote, "Capital Flow to Emerging Markets Falls," *Financial Times,* 30 January 1998, 7; Michael M. Phillips, "U.S. Firms Reassess Asian Joint Ventures," *Wall Street Journal,* 23 September 1998, A2, A10.

9. U.N. Conference on Trade and Development, *World Investment Report 1997,* xx; Fred R. Bleakley, "Developing Nations Attract Investment, Paced by Surge in China, Latin America," *Wall Street Journal,* 22 September 1997, B15A; Stephen Buckley, "Left Behind Prosperity's Door," *Washington Post,* National Weekly Edition, 24 March 1997, 8; David Wessel, "Capital Flow," B9A.

10. Paul J. Deveney, "Foreign Investment in Latin America Reaches a Record," *Wall Street Journal,* 5 May 1998, A16; Sylvia E. Bargas, "Direct Investment Positions for 1997," *Survey of Current Business* 78(7), July 1998, 35–45.

11. *Economic Report of the President 1997* (Washington, D.C.: USGPO, February 1997), 252. Thanks to Richard B. DuBoff for this point. Richard B. DuBoff, "Globalization and Wages: The Down Escalator," *Dollars and Sense,* September-October 1997, 36–40.

12. U.N. Conference on Trade and Development, *World Investment Report 1996* (New York: United Nations, 1996), xxiii.

13. William Lewis, "U.S. Mergers and Takeovers Set Record in First Six Months," *Financial Times,* 30 June 1998, 18.

14. Louise Lucas, "Way Is Paved for Cross-Border Deals," *Financial Times,* 27 April 1998, 29.

15. Steven Lipin, "Merger Activity Rose to Record Level in First Half," *Wall Street Journal,* 7 July 1997, A3, A5; David Whitford, "Sale of the Century," *Fortune,* 17 February 1997, 92.

16. Steven Lipin, "Corporations' Dreams Converge in One Idea: It's Time to Do a Deal," *Wall Street Journal,* 26 February 1997, A1, A8; Steven Lipin, "How Long Can Merger Boom Continue?" *Wall Street Journal,* 11 July 1996, C1, C6; Thomas Kamm and Matt Marshall, "Global Forces Push Europe's Firms, Too, into a Merger Frenzy," *Wall Street Journal,* 4 April 1997, A1, A4; Sarah Calian and Nicholas Bray, "Investment Banks Near M&A Record in Europe," *Wall Street Journal,* 14 October 1997, A16; Bill Spindle, "Merger Boomlet Takes Hold in Japan," *Wall Street Journal,* 13 April 1998, A18.

17. U.N. Conference on Trade and Development, *World Investment Report 1996,* 10; U.N. Conference on Trade and Development, *World Investment Report 1997,* xvii; Louis Uchitelle, "Some Cross-Border Mergers May Be Star-Crossed," *New York Times,* 8 May 1998, C1, C4.

18. U.N. Conference on Trade and Development, *World Investment Report 1997,* xvii.

19. Craig Torres, "Foreigners Snap Up Mexican Companies; Impact Is Enormous," *Wall Street Journal,* 30 September 1997, A1, A12.

20. Bleakley, "Developing Nations Attract Investment"; "25 Largest U.S. Acquisitions Overseas 1997" *Mergers and Acquistions* 32(5), March/April 1998, 59.

21. Tony Walker, "United States buys $8 Billion of Asian Businesses," *Financial Times*, 15 June 1998, 5; see also Nicholas D. Kristof, "Worsening Financial Flu in Asia Lowers Immunity to U.S. Business," *New York Times*, 1 February 1998, A1, A8; Michael Lewis, "The World's Biggest Going-out-of-Business Sale," *New York Times Magazine*, 31 May 1998, 34–41+.

22. Martin Wolf, "The Heart of the New World Economy," *Financial Times*, 1 October 1997, 12; Rebecca Blumenstein, "GM Is Building Plants in Developing Nations to Woo New Markets," *Wall Street Journal*, 4 August 1997, A1, A5.

23. ITU, *World Telecommunication Development Report 1996/97*, 2; ITU, *World Telecommunication Development Report 1998*, A–59.

24. U.N. Economic and Social Council, Commission on Transnational Corporations, "The Role of Transnational Corporations in Transborder Data Flows," 10th Session, 18–27 April 1984, E/C10/1984/14.

25. Peter John McMahon, "Technology and Social Control: The Role of Electronic Control Technology," Ph.D. dissertation, Murdoch University (Australia), 1996, 269–270; Gautam Naik "Unisource Expected to Merge Operations," *Wall Street Journal*, 4 June 1997, B5; Paul Taylor, "Company Internet Use to Surge," *Financial Times*, 5 June 1998, 3.

26. Quoted in Schiller, *Telematics and Government*, 104.

27. David Molony "Global Toll-Free to Swell Carrier Coffers," *Communications Week International*, 17 February 1997, 8.

28. Nanette Burns, "Dialing for Dinero," *Business Week*, 10 July 1995, 108.

29. William Wolman and Anne Colamosca, *The Judas Economy: The Triumph of Capital and the Betrayal of Work* (Reading, Mass.: Addison-Wesley, 1997), 33.

30. U.N. Conference on Trade and Development, *World Investment Report 1996*, 99; Harley Shaiken, *Mexico in the Global Economy: High Technology and Work Organization in Export Industries*, Monograph Series, 33 (San Diego: Center for U.S.-Mexico Studies, University of California, San Diego, 1990).

31. Michael Benson, "The Chips Are Down: California Loses Out on Semiconductor Plants," *Wall Street Journal*, 28 May 1997, CA1, CA3.

32. David Bank, "Cisco to Support Format to Ease Internet Traffic," *Wall Street Journal*, 9 December 1996, B7; "IBM Plans to Establish Research Center in India," *Wall Street Journal*, 23 July 1997, B3; "Cisco Sets Up Major Software Center in India," *Los Angeles Times*, 12 August 1997, D2; Mark Nicholson and Paul Taylor, "Microsoft in Plan for India Software Base," *Financial Times*, 15–16 November 1997, 4.

33. " 'Good Corporate Citizens' Today Must Address Universal Service, Worker Issues Globally," *Telecommunications Reports Journal* 1, no. 1, (1997), 53.

34. Mark L. Wilson, "Information Networks: The Global Offshore Labor Force," in Gerald Sussman and John A. Lent, eds., *Global Productions: Labor*

in the Making of the 'Information Society' (Cresskill, N.J.: Hampton Press, 1998), 42, 48.

35. John A. Lent, "The Animation Industry and Its Offshore Factories," in Sussman and Lent, eds., *Global Productions*: 239–254.

36. Harley Shaiken, "NAFTA Needs More Than Fine Tuning," *Los Angeles Times*, 7 July 1997, B5; "Five Billion Dollar Investment for 1997," *El Financiero*, 23 March 1997, 4, in *CCMI Telecom NewsFax Today* 14 (64) (1 April 1997): 2. In the projections of an Argentine think tank, roughly one-third of the total U.S. direct foreign investment into Argentina considered likely between 1997 and 2004—some $2.56 billion—would likewise be targeted at telecommunications. "U.S. Firms Target Argentine Telecoms," *Wall Street Journal*, 14 October 1997, A16.

37. ITU, *World Telecommunication Development Report 1996/97*, 3.

38. Telecommunications liberalization thus comprised a spur—alongside the attacks mounted by four successive Conservative Party administrations on British labor—to foreign investment. Britain was said in 1997 to draw about 40 percent of the new investment in the European Union. "Why Britain Is Voting Labour," *Toronto Globe and Mail*, 1 May 1997.

39. Paul J. Deveney, "U.K. Phone Regulator to Depart," *Wall Street Journal*, 24 September 1997, A15.

40. For a recent illustration of this continuing trend, Jennifer L. Schenker "Europe's Business Fumes over Phone Bills," *Wall Street Journal*, 16 April 1997, A13.

41. Anthony M. Rutkowski, "Factors Shaping Internet Self-Governance," in Brian Kahin and James H. Keller, eds., *Coordinating the Internet* (Cambridge: MIT Press, 1997), 95.

42. "G7 Meeting Maps Global Paths to Info Society/GII," *TR* 6 61, no. 9 (March 1995): 19; Ronnie Preiskel and Nicholas Higham, "Liberalization of Telecommunications Infrastructure and Cable Television Networks," *Telecommunications Policy* 19, no. 5 (1995): 381–390.

43. ITU, *World Telecommunication Development Report 1996/97*, 50–53, table 4.3.

44. ITU, *World Telecommunication Development Report 1996/97*, 2, figure 2.

45. ITU, *World Telecommunication Development Report 1996/97*, 45.

46. Joseph B. White, "Consulting Firms Break Revenue Records," *Wall Street Journal*, 3 March 1997, B2; Anita Raghavan, "Underwriting Fees Topped Record in '96," *Wall Street Journal*, 2 January 1997, R38.

47. Gautam Naik, Anita Raghavan, Douglas Lavin, and Sara Webb, "Tidal Wave of Global Telecom Offerings Builds," *Wall Street Journal*, 15 November 1996, A8; Lousie Kehoe, "Technology Mergers 'at record level,'" *Financial Times*, 29 July 1998, 16.

48. Vincent Boland, "Intense Competition Ends Banks' Privatisation Boom," *Financial Times*, 9 February 1998, 15.

49. John Blau, "Europe's Operators in Buying Spree," *Communications Week International,* 10 March 1997.

50. Silvia Ascarelli, "Deutsche Telekom Enters New World," *Wall Street Journal,* 18 November 1996, A9; Mary Williams Walsh, "High Marks," *Los Angeles Times,* 19 November 1996, D1, D15; "Telekom's Lesson" (editorial), *Wall Street Journal,* 25 November 1996, A18; Tom Burns, "Telefonica Sell-off Finds an Eager Home Market," *Financial Times,* 18 February 1997, 25; James Blitz, "Public Rushes to Buy Telecom Italia," *Financial Times,* 27 October 1997, 1, 16; Andrew Jack, "France Telecom Sell-off Hailed as 'Formidable,' " *Financial Times,* 18–19 October 1997, 24.

51. ITU, *World Telecommunication Development Report 1996/97,* 49.

52. Sara Webb, "Telecom Shares Deluge Foreign Markets," *Wall Street Journal,* 20 August 1997, C1, C19.

53. ITU, *World Telecommunication Development Report 1996/97,* 6, figure 5.

54. Paul Lewis, "The Stage May Soon Be Set for a Global Trade Pact on Computer and Software Products," *New York Times,* 20 November 1996, C19; Tyler Marshall and David Holley, "APEC Nations Endorse Cuts in Tariffs by 2000," *Los Angeles Times,* 26 November 1996, A1, A8; "EC Signals Approval of Technology Pact," *Telecommunications Reports,* 10 March 1997, 35.

55. John Alden, "Observers Hail Ground-Breaking Telecom Trade Pact: Examination of Fine Print Now Begins," *Telecommunications Reports,* 24 February 1997, 3.

56. Statement of Ambassador Charlene Barshefsky, Basic Telecom Negotiations, February 15, 1997.

57. Barshefsky, Basic Telecom Negotiations.

58. David E. Sanger, "Playing the Trade Card," *New York Times,* 17 February 1997, 1.

59. Alan Cane, "New Pact Must be Protected," *Financial Times,* 19 March 1997, "Survey of telecoms," 1.

60. Judy Dempsey, "Restructuring Costs Put Bezeq in the Red," *Financial Times,* 1 September 1997, 19; Justin Marozzi, "PLDT Upbeat on Revenues," *Financial Times,* 25 September 1997, 16; see Sean O'Siochru, "The ITU, the WTO and Accounting Rates: Limited Prospects for the South?" paper presented at the Twelfth Euricom Colloquium on Communication and Culture, 2–5 October 1997, Boulder, Colorado.

61. David P. Hamilton, "AT&T Unveils New 'Callback' Service in Japan That Could Cut Business Bills," *Wall Street Journal,* 29 November 1997, A4; Cynthia Beltz, "Global Telecommunications Rules: The Race with Technology," *Issues in Science and Technology* 13, no. 3(Spring 1997): 66.

62. David Owen, "New Round of Rate Cuts at France Telecom," *Financial Times,* 18 September 1997, 18; John R. Wilke and Gautam Naik, "International Phone Calls' Costs Are Cut," *Wall Street Journal,* 8 August 1997, A3, A6.

63. Frances Williams, "Developing Countries Urged to Update Phone Rates," *Financial Times,* 16 March 1998, 4.

64. John Alden, "FCC Puts Pin to International Settlements Bubble; Action Draws Fire as Protectionist," *Telecommunications Reports,* 11 August 1997, 1–4; Annie Turner, "Bell Tolls for Old System," *Financial Times,* 10 September 1997, Review of the Telecommunications Industry, vi.

65. Gary Silverman and Shada Islam, "Fax Americana," *Far Eastern Economic Review* 160, no. 9 (27 February 1997): 52.

66. Noam Chomsky, "The Passion for Free Markets," *Z Magazine,* May 1997, 27.

67. ITU, *World Telecommunication Development Report 1998,* A-87; ITU, *World Telecommunication Development Report 1996/97,* 3.

68. ITU, *World Telecommunication Development Report 1998,* A-71.

69. ITU, *World Telecommunication Development Report 1998,* A-10, A-40.

70. ITU, *World Telecommunication Development Report 1996/97,* A-76–A79.

71. Andrew Kupfer, "Transforming Telecom: The Big Switch," *Fortune,* 13 October 1997, 116.

72. Diana Lady Dougan, Foreword, in Milton Mueller and Zixiang Tan, *China in the Information Age: Telecommunications and the Dilemmas of Reform* (Westport: Praeger, 1997), xiii; Chris O'Malley, "Connecting China," *Popular Science,* August 1996, 75–78; Rone Tempest, "Wiring China," *Los Angeles Times,* 1 July 1996, D1, D6; Steve Glain, "How Beijing Officials Outnegotiated AT&T On Marine Cable Plans," *Wall Street Journal,* 23 July 1997, A1, A13; quote from Joseph Kahn, "Beijing Puts a Wall Around Its Thriving Phone System," *Wall Street Journal,* 28 August 1997, A11.

73. Dean E. Murphy, "Hungarians Light Up the Phones," *Los Angeles Times,* 28 August 1997, A1, A6.

74. ITU, *World Telecommunication Development Report 1998,* 15.

75. ITU, *World Telecommunication Development Report 1996–97,* table 2, A-8–9.

76. ITU, *World Telecommunication Development Report 1998,* 37–38.

77. ITU, *World Telecommunication Development Report 1998,* 15, 13.

78. ITU, *World Telecommunication Development Report 1998,* 22; also ITU, *World Telecommunication Development Report 1996–97,* 11.

79. ITU, *World Telecommunication Development Report 1998,* 37.

80. ITU, *World Telecommunication Development Report 1998,* 13.

81. Robin Wright, "Cellular Phones Answer Rural Areas' Needs," *Los Angeles Times,* 10 November 1997, D1, D3; Bernard Wysocki Jr., "Development Strategy: Close Information Gap," *Wall Street Journal,* 7 July 1997, A1; "The Last Frontier," *Business Week,* 18 September 1995, 99.

82. Sebastian Rotella, "Brazil of the Future Is Here, but Only for Some," *Los Angeles Times,* 12 October 1997, D1, D12. In Lima, where the top 50 percent of households (by income) enjoyed nearly universal telephone access in 1996, the bottom quarter of households subsisted on roughly an 8 percent subscribership level. ITU, *World Telecommunication Development Report 1998,* 31.

83. ITU, *World Telecommunication Development Report 1998,* 14; Lester R. Brown, Michael Renner, and Christopher Flavin, *Vital Signs 1998: The Environmental Trends That Are Shaping Our Future* (New York: Worldwatch Institute and Norton, 1998), 98.

84. Alexander Cockburn, "The '90s Boom Unmasked: It's a Wage Freeze," *Los Angeles Times,* 30 October 1997, B9.

85. Holly Sklar, "Boom Times for Billionaires, Bust for Workers and Children," *Z Magazine,* November 1997, 34–35.

86. David Leonhardt, "Two-Tier Marketing," *Business Week,* 17 March 1997, 82, 87. For the general picture, Herbert I. Schiller, *Information Inequality* (New York: Routledge, 1996).

87. Leslie Cauley, "BellSouth Net Up as Operating Profit Increases by 14 Percent," *Wall Street Journal,* 22 April 1997, B10; Greg Miller, "Tying Up the Phone Companies," *Los Angeles Times,* 21 January 1997, A1, A18.

88. Michael Antonoff, "An Internet Express Lane Just for Cliff Dwellers," *New York Times,* 3 April 1997, B1, B10; David Kushner, "Luxury Rentals Adding T–1 to Drmn and Hdwd Flrs," *New York Times,* 2 April 1998, D8; Lisa M. Collins, "Cyber-Friendly Digs," *San Diego Union-Tribune,* 12 April 1998, K-2.

89. G. Christian Hill, "It's War!" *Wall Street Journal Telecoms,* 16 September 1996, R4.

90. Melody Petersen, "New Jersey Phone Plan Neglects Poor, Critics Say," *New York Times,* 17 April 1997, A10.

91. Melanie Wells, "MCI Deal Rings in New Ad Strategy," *USA Today,* 6 November 1996, 1B.

92. Carla Hall, "Tiny Phone Rings Up Whopping Sales," *Los Angeles Times,* 4 September 1997, E1, E4.

93. John J. Keller, "AT&T Sets Bold New Business Strategy," *Wall Street Journal,* 18 September 1997, A3.

94. Jube Shiver, Jr., "New Rules Will Let Pay Phone Rates Climb," *Los Angeles Times,* 9 November 1996, A1, A19; "AT&T Sets Minimum of $3 for Monthly Long Distance," *Wall Street Journal,* 17 August 1998, B3.

95. Charisse Jones, "Internet Finds Its Way into Heart of Inner City," *New York Times,* 3 August 1996, 16; "Too Good to Last," *Economist,* 23 March 1996, 61–62; U.S. National Telecommunications and Information Administration, "Falling Through the Net II: New Data on the Digital Divide," Washington, D.C. U.S. Department of Commerce, 28 July 1998 http:www.ntia.doc.gov/ntiahome/net2/

96. Harry C. Katz, "Introduction and Comparative Overview," in idem., ed., *Telecommunications Restructuring Work and Employment Relations Worldwide.* (Ithaca: ILR Press, 1997), 1–27.

97. Steve Dubb, "The Logics of Resistance: Globalization and Telephone Unionism in Mexico and British Columbia," Ph.D. dissertation, University of California, San Diego, 1996, 169–221.

98. Dan Schiller, *Bad Deal of the Century: The Worrisome Implications of the WorldCom-MCI Merger* (Washington, D.C.: Economic Policy Institute, 1998), 19–20.

99. Sid Shniad and Charley Richardson, "Restructuring Global Telecommunications: The Telephone Workers' Response in British Columbia," in Sussman and Lent, eds., *Global Productions,* 265.

100. Carol J. Loomis, "AT&T Has No Clothes," *Fortune,* 5 February 1996, 77–80; "Fatal Attraction," *Economist,* 23 March 1996, 73–74.

101. Barney Warf, "Reach Out and Touch Someone: AT&T's Global Operations in the 1990s," *Professional Geographer* 50, no. 20 (1998): 258.

102. Terry Pristin, "Fearing Service Problems, Bell Atlantic Tries to Stop Exodus of Workers," *New York Times,* 31 May 1998, 24.

103. Pristin, "Fearing Service Problems"; Mark Landler, "For Nynex, Quality Is Suddenly Job No. 0ne," *New York Times,* 11 November 1996, C1, C8; Leslie Cauley, "Nynex Holders Clear Its Purchase, but State Again Fines Company," *Wall Street Journal,* 7 November 1996, B4.

104. Leslie Helm, "In Rush to Cyberspace, Local Phone Service Is Put on Hold," *Los Angeles Times,* 18 June 1995, D1, D3, D6.

105. Penni Crabtree, "All PacBell Offices to Be Shut in State," *San Diego Union-Tribune,* 18 March 1998, C1, C3.

106. Elizabeth Douglass, "PacBell Proposes Rate Hike for 411 and 'Cut-In' Calls," *Los Angeles Times,* 11 May 1998, D1, D8.

107. Steve Rosenbush, "More Complain of Phone-Service 'Slamming,' " *USA Today,* 4 August 1997, B1; John H. Cushman, Jr., "Con Artist Made Millions Off Phone 'Slamming,' " *New York Times,* 24 April 1998, A16.

108. John J. Keller, "How a Minister's Son Discovered 'Slamming' and Then Disappeared," *Wall Street Journal,* 23 April 1998, A1, A6.

109. John J. Keller, "It's Hard Not to Notice Phone Service Leaves a Lot to Be Desired," *Wall Street Journal,* 17 April 1998, A1, A6; Elizabeth Douglass, "Union Isn't Buying PacBell's Incentives for Sales Force," *Los Angeles Times,* 25 February 1998, D1, D7.

110. Jennifer Oldham, "L.A. Phone Sex Operation Accused of Deceptive Billing," *Los Angeles Times,* 23 April 1998, D1, D8; John M. Glionna, "Dial F for Fraud," *Los Angeles Times,* 7 May 1998, B1, B6.

111. Stephanie N. Mehta, "Telecommunications Companies Unite to Track Nonpaying Phone Customers," *Wall Street Journal,* 8 September 1997, A13A.

112. Jube Shiver, Jr. and Jonathan Peterson, "Phone Tax Complaints Get Congress Moving," *Los Angeles Times,* 6 June 1998, D1, D2.

113. Bryan Gruley, "FCC Likely to Offer Four Options to Fix Troubled Wireless Auction," *Wall Street Journal,* 24 September 1997, A2, A10.

114. Jube Shiver, Jr., "Bidding Firms Get FCC Relief in Wireless Deals," *Los Angeles Times,* 26 September 1997, D1, D12. As three successful bidders filed for bankruptcy protection, the debacle became a farce. NextWave, the largest defaulter sued the FCC, claiming that the agency had reduced the value of its licenses by withholding them until payment was made and by holding additional auctions in the interim. Scott Thurm, "NextWave Sues FCC over Licenses Won in Bidding," *Wall Street Journal,* 12 June 1998, B6.

115. Kenneth G. Robinson, "Foreign Ownership Restrictions: The U.S. and Its Allies Must Adapt," *Telecommunications Reports Journal* 1, no. 1 (1997): 23–29; Jube Shiver, Jr., "FCC Opens Phone Markets Further to Foreign Buyers," *New York Times,* 26 November 1997, D1, D15; Seth Schiesel, "FCC to Open Phone Market to Foreigners," *New York Times,* 25 November 1997, C1, C2; Matthew Petrillo, "Sen. Hollings Proposes Requiring Congress' Nod on USTR Agreements," *Telecommunications Reports,* 24 February 1997, 5–6. I have benefited from an unpublished paper by Roxanne Ho, "Liberalization Under the World Trade Organization Pact of February 15, 1997," University of California at San Diego, Spring 1998.

116. Canute James, "Puerto Rico Phone Sale Prompts Strike Threat," *Financial Times,* 3 June 1998, 5.

117. Barshefsky, Basic Telecom Negotiations.

118. Ralph T. King, Jr., "High-Tech Edge Gives U.S. Firms Global Lead in Computer Networks," *Wall Street Journal,* 9 September 1994, A1, A9; Daniel F. Burton, Jr., "The Brave New *Wired* World," *Foreign Policy,* no. 106 (Spring 1997): 23.

119. Reed E. Hundt, "Speech to Chamber of Commerce, Washington, D.C.," 29 May 1997, 3, and, for Hundt's comment on Greenspan, idem., "The Internet: From Here to Ubiquity," Paper presented to the Institute of Electrical and Electronic Engineers, The Symposium on Hot Chips, 26 August 1997; both available at http://www.fcc.gov.

120. Beltz, "Global Telecommunications Rules," 68, 64.

121. Beltz, "Global Telecommunications Rules," 64, 63.

122. Beltz, "Global Telecommunications Rules," 68.

123. Charles V. Bagli, "Conditions Are Right for a Takeover Frenzy," *New York Times,* 2 January 1997, C3; William Lewis, "U.S. Mergers and Takeovers Set Record in First Six Months," *Financial Times,* 30 June 1998, 18.

124. Mark Landler, "Communications Pact to Favor Growing Giants," *New York Times,* 18 February 1997, 1, 10; Alan Cane, "A Ringing Endorsement," *Financial Times*, 18 February 1997, 19.

125. Emily Nelson, "Corning Aims to Sell Off Its Pots, Pans," *Wall Street Journal,* 6 May 1997, B1; Rebecca Rohan, "Competing Claims Fuel Backbone Race," *Internet World* 8, no. 6, (June 1997): 16.

126. Timothy Aeppel, "Corning Warns of Slower Growth; Stock Plunges 12 Percent," *Wall Street Journal,* 12 September 1997, A8.

127. Jeffrey H. Keefe and Rosemary Batt, "United States," in Harry C. Katz, ed., *Telecommunications Restructuring Work and Employment Relations Worldwide* (Ithaca: ILR Press, 1997), 32.

128. John J. Keller and Steven Lipin, "The Battle for MCI Takes Another Twist: Now, It's GTE's Turn," *Wall Street Journal,* 16 October 1997, A1.

129. As they had periodically exerted influence throughout prior historical eras. Richard B. DuBoff and Edward S. Herman, "The Promotional-Financial Dynamic of Merger Movements: A Historical Perspective," *Journal of Economic Issues* 23, no. 1 (March 1989): 107–133.

130. Gautam Naik, Anita Raghavan, Douglas Lavin, and Sara Webb, "Tidal Wave of Global Telecom Offerings Builds," *Wall Street Journal,* 15 November 1996, A8.

131. Emma Tucker, Michael Lindemann, and Alan Cane, "Brussels Set to Allow Telecoms 'Supercarrier,' " *Financial Times,* 12 October 1995, 1; "Telmex Signs Data Pact," *CCMI Telecom NewsFax Today,* 14 no. 100 (21 May 1997): 2.

132. John J. Keller, "AT&T Defends Global Services Strategy as Rival MCI-BT Alliance Pulls Ahead," *Wall Street Journal,* 5 October 1995, A3, A4; Paul Betts, "Stet to Announce Ties with AT&T and Unisource," *Financial Times,* 2 July 1997, 15.

133. Warf, "Reach Out and Touch Someone," 259, 264.

134. "Wall Street Cheers BT-MCI Deal, Raises Stakes in Global Consolidation," *Telecommunications Reports* 62, no. 45 (11 November 1996): 13–15; "This Is the Idea Behind Concert" (advertisement), *Wall Street Journal,* 7 March 1997, A9; John J. Keller, "As MCI Changes Hands, a Gadfly Buzzes Off," *Wall Street Journal,* 3 April 1997, B1, B2; John J. Keller and Gautam Naik, "BT Secures Its Place Among Telecom Titans with MCI Takeover," *Wall Street Journal,* 4 November 1996, A1, A10; Douglas Lavin, "Merger Mania Is Spreading Among Big French Utilities," *Wall Street Journal,* 1 April 1997, B4; Gautam Naik, "Telefonica Deal Gives BT the Upper Hand in Industry Battle," *Wall Street Journal,* 18–19 April 1997, 1, 9; Alan Cane and Tom Burns, "Telefonica in BT, MCI Link," *Financial Times,* 19–20 April 1997, 1; Patrick McGeehan, "Adjustment in MCI Deal Is Reminder of the Perils for Takeover Speculators," *Wall Street Journal,* 25 August 1997, A8; Steven Lipin and John J. Keller, "BT-MCI Merger Deal's Value Reduced," *Wall Street Journal,* 22 August 1997, A3, A4.

135. Stephanie N. Mehta, "Bell Merger Bedevils Local-Service Rivals," *Wall Street Journal,* 12 May 1998, B1, B6.

136. William Lewis, "World Com Poised to Win MCI Battle with $37 Billion Bid," *Financial Times,* 11 November 1997, 1; Seth Schiesel, "MCI Accepts Offer

of $36.5 Billion; Deal Sets Record," *New York Times,* 11 November 1997, A1, C15; Anita Raghavan, "Salomon Net Jumps 84 Percent to $206 million as Bond Results Eclipse BT-MCI Loss," *Wall Street Journal,* 22 October 1997, B11; Patrick McGeehan, "GTE's Bold Bid Could Generate Whopping Fees," *Wall Street Journal,* 17 October 1997, C1; Peter Elstrom, Amy Barrett, Cathy Yang, and Julie Flynn, "The New World Order," *Business Week,* 13 October 1997, 26–33; Gautam Naik, "WorldCom Bid Worries Europe's Goliaths," *Wall Street Journal,* 6 October 1997, A18.

137. John J. Keller, "WorldCom Has Loss, but Revenue Soars," *Wall Street Journal,* 24 April 1998, B10.

138. Gautam Naik, "AT&T-BT Alliance Faces Bevy of Rivals," *Wall Street Journal,* 28 July 1998, B8.

139. Jong-Geun Oh, "Global Strategic Alliances in the Telecommunications Industry," *Telecommunications Policy* 20, no. 9 (1996): 714–715.

140. Moschella, *Waves of Power,* 84.

141. Jube Shiver, Jr., "MCI, BT Join Spanish Firm in New Alliance," *Los Angeles Times,* 19 April 1997, D1, D3; Gautam Naik and Jennifer L. Schenker, "AT&T Presence in Europe Is Questioned," *Wall Street Journal,* 30 May 1997, B5A.

142. Craig Torres, "Taking a Gamble, MCI Plunged into Mexico as AT&T Hesitated," *Wall Street Journal,* 18 November 1996, A1, A7; Julia Preston, "Mexican Rivals Campaign for Callers," *New York Times,* 14 January 1997, C9; Julia Preston, "A Telecom Revolucion in Mexico," *New York Times,* 14 November 1996, C1, C18; also see Jonathan Friedland, "Chile Is a Telecommunications Jungle," *Wall Street Journal,* 11 November 1996, A10.

143. "Qwest Deal Would Expand Fiber Network into Mexico," *Telecommunications Reports Daily,* 21 August 1997.

144. Henry Tricks, "SPC, Lucent in Mexican Wireless Deal," *Financial Times,* 19 May 1998, 21.

145. Torres, "Taking a Gamble," A1. Qwest Communications is likewise extending its fiber optic network to embrace fourteen Mexican cities in addition to the ninety-two U.S. cities it will serve. "Qwest Deal Would Expand Fiber Network into Mexico."

146. Christopher Price, "Acquisitions at Record $17 Billion," *Financial Times,* 26 March 1998, 6.

147. Tom Burns, "Telefonica Delays Decision on Global Partnership," *Financial Times* 18 February 1998, 16; David White, "Telefonica Joins Alliance with Two U.S. Groups," *Financial Times,* 10 March 1998, 24.

148. Douglas Lavin, "France Telecom's Privatization Spurs Service Makeover," *Wall Street Journal,* 21 April 1997, A15; Douglas Lavin, "France Telecom Is Seeking Ally in Italy with 49 Percent Stake in an Olivetti Venture," *Wall Street Journal,* 7 April 1997, A9C; Maureen Kline, Maria Sturani, and Gautam Naik, "Olivetti to Sell Big Telecom Stake to Mannesmann for $1.35 Billion," *Wall Street Journal,* 8 September 1997, A14.

149. John Blau and Glenn Manoff, "Telefonica's Key Role in Concert Plans," *CommunicationsWeek International*, 21 April 1997, 1, 27.

150. Maria Sturani, "Bell Atlantic Quits Telecom Venture with Olivetti SpA," *Wall Street Journal*, 2 September 1997, B6.

151. Gautam Naik, "MCI Losses Anger BT Shareholders; Merger Is Still On," *Wall Street Journal*, 17 July 1997, A18; Patrick McGeehan, "Adjustment in MCI Deal Is Reminder of the Perils for Takeover Speculators," *Wall Street Journal*, 25 August 1997, A8.

152. Paul Betts, "AT&T Link with Telecom Italia Close to Collapse," *Financial Times*, 23 March 1998, 1.

153. Gautam Naik and Matt Marshall, "Rivals of Deutsche Telekom Discover Apathy Is Biggest Hurdle to Winning New Customers," *Wall Street Journal*, 23 March 1998, A16, A19.

154. "Debitel and RSL of U.S. Join German Phone Fray," *Wall Street Journal*, 12 March 1997, A14.

155. Matt Marshall, "Mannesmann Takes on Germany's Phone Giant," *Wall Street Journal*, 26 January 1998, B6.

156. Owen, "New Round of Rate Cuts."

157. Victor Mallet, "Telecom Investors Prepare to Dial Africa's Number," *Financial Times*, 4 May 1998, 4.

158. Gautam Naik, "Hungary's Tough Call on Matav Pays Off," *Wall Street Journal*, 27 August 1997, A8.

159. William Kennard, "Three Steps to Heaven," *Financial Times*, 13 May 1998, 10.

160. Thomas Vogel, Jr., "Central America Goes from War Zone to Enterprise Zone," *Wall Street Journal*, 25 September 1997, A18.

161. Nicholas Bray, "European Projects and Profits in Doubt as Asian Pain Spreads," *Wall Street Journal*, 15 January 1998, A16.

162. John Ridding, "Crisis Could Act as a Stimulus," *Financial Times Telecoms*, 17 March 1998, vii; "Korea's SK Telecom to Meet Demands of Foreign Investors," *Wall Street Journal*, 20 March 1998, A13.

163. Sander Thoenes, "Telkom Hit by Threefold Rise in Forex Losses," *Financial Times*, 29 May 1998, 16; Jay Solmon, "Indonesia's Privatization Plans for 12 State Concerns Stumble," *Wall Street Journal*, 1 September 1998, A12.

164. Peter Fritsch, "Brazil Likely to Ease Foreign Limit on Telebras," *Wall Street Journal*, 11 May 1998, C1; Peter Fritsch, "Brazil Lifts All Foreign-Control Limits for Firms Created by Telebras Sell-Off," *Wall Street Journal*, 18 May 1998, A17.

165. James Kynge, "Chinese Telecoms May Open up Soon," *Financial Times*, 3 June 1998, 8; Ian Johnson, "China's Venture Ban Could Cost Foreign Firms," *Wall Street Journal*, 23 September 1998, A14, A17.

166. ITU, *World Telecommunication Development Report 1996/97*, 55.

167. "Taiwan Further Liberalizes Telecom Market with Mobile Phone, Paging License Awards," *East Asian Executive Reports* 18 (12) (15 December 1996): 8, 17.

168. "Airtouch Adds 2 Million International Customers," *CCMI Telecom NewsFax Today* 14, no. 91 (8 May 1997): 2; Richard Waters, "Wall Street Wakes Up to Airtouch's European Assets," *Financial Times,* 29 April 1998, 18.

169. Leslie Cauley and Matt Moffett, "BellSouth-Led Group Wins Wireless License in Brazil," *Wall Street Journal,* 10 July 1997, B4.

170. Christopher Price, "Privatisation Plan by Satellite Operators," *Financial Times,* 19 January 1998, 18; Nancy Dunne, "Intelsat Blasts Off for Privatisation," *Financial Times,* 1 April 1998, 5.

171. "India Has High Hopes for Satellite Launch," *Financial Times,* 12 September 1997, 6; "India Widens Net Access," *Financial Times,* 18 September 1997, 7.

172. Barry Miller, "Satellites Free Mobile Phones," *IEEE Spectrum* 35, no. 3 (March 1998): 26–35; Bruce V. Bigelow, "Lost in Space," *San Diego Union Tribune,* 21 June 1998, I-1, I-4; Karen Kaplan, "Space-Dust Buster," *Los Angeles Times,* 5 January 1998, D1, D8.

173. Ralph Vartabedian, "Commercial Satellite Boom Boosts Firms to New Heights," *Los Angeles Times,* 16 June 1998, A1, A22–23.

174. Merrill Lynch, Pierce, Fenner & Smith Inc., Global Securities Research and Economics Group, *Global Satellite Marketplace 98* (New York: Merrill Lynch, 22 April 1998), 3–4.

175. Jube Shiver, Jr., "Regulators OK Airwaves for Satellite Ventures," *Los Angeles Times,* 22 November 1997, D1, D2.

176. Marcon Antonio Cacers, "Satcoms Growth on Upswing," *Aviation Week and Space Technology,* 13 January 1997, 117–120; Jeff Cole, "New Satellite Era Looms Just over the Horizon," *Wall Street Journal,* 18 March 1997, B1, B12; Elizabeth Douglass, "Motorola Drops Satellite Project, Will Join Rival," *Los Angeles Times,* 22 May 1998, D1, D6.

177. Quentin Hardy, "Skybridge to Boost System of Satellites by Sixteen Units, to Eighty, as Price Tag Rises," *Wall Street Journal,* 2 June 1998, B4; Christopher Price, "Skybridge to Lift Capacity of System," *Financial Times,* 1 June 1998, 17.

178. Tim Smart, "Lockheed to Buy Comsat for $2.7 Billion," *Denver Post,* 21 September 1998, 1A, 9A.

179. Vicki Beard, "Iridium: The Revolution in Global Satellite Communications," March 1997, manuscript; Quentin Hardy, "Iridium Creates New Plan for Global Cellular Service," *Wall Street Journal,* 18 August 1997, B4.

180. Frederic M. Biddle, "Loral to Raise Globalstar Stake with Offer to System's Partners," *Wall Street Journal,* 27 April 1998, B4.

181. ITU, *World Telecommunications Development Report 1996–1997,* 65.

182. "Business Leaders Say Wireless Services Are Poised for Explosive Growth," *Telecommunications Reports,* 24 February 1997, 7. Overall, a U.S. IT industry growing by 15 percent each year saw more than 1,500 mergers and acquisitions during 1996, four or five transactions each day. Charles V. Bagli, "Conditions Are Right for a Takeover Frenzy," *New York Times,* 2 January 1997, C3.

183. Quentin Hardy, "Motorola Plans Vast Satellite Program That May Bolster Commercial Rocketry," *Wall Street Journal,* 15 October 1997, B8.

184. S. Karene Witcher, "Cell-Phone Firms May Be Damaged by Asian Economy," *Wall Street Journal,* 5 December 1997, B13C.

185. Price, "Skybridge to Lift Capacity."

186. Timothy Appel, "Why 'Too Much Stuff' Means Little Now," *Wall Street Journal,* 4 December 1997, A2, A8; Otis Port, "Through a Glass Quickly," *Business Week,* 7 December 1998, 96–98.

187. Clay Ryder, senior industry analyst at Zona Research, in Andrew Kantor and Michael Neubarth, "Off the Charts: The Internet 1996," *Internet World,* December 1996, 47.

188. *Reno V. American Civil Liberties Union,* No. 96–511, Decided 26 June 1997 (Slip Opinion); "The Framework for Global Electronic Commerce," Washington D.C.: The White House, 1 July 1997. http://www.ecommerce.gov/framework.htm.

189. In Edward Felsenthal and Jared Sandberg, "High Court Strikes Down Internet Smut Law," *Wall Street Journal,* 27 June 1997, B1.

190. Linda Greenhouse, "Decency Act Fails," *New York Times,* 27 June 1997, A1, A16.

191. "Presidential Message to Internet Users" and "Remarks by the President in Announcement of Electronic Commerce Initiative," Washington, D.C.: The White House, 1 July 1997. At http://www.ecommerce.gov.

192. Kevin Werbach, "Digital Tornado: The Internet and Telecommunications Policy," U.S. Federal Communications Commission Office of Plans and Policy, OPP Working Paper Series No. 29, March 1997.

193. Rajiv Chandrasekaran and John Schwartz, "White House Report Rejects New Laws on Internet Porn," *Los Angeles Times,* 17 June 1997, D1, D16.

194. Jeri Clausing, "Critics Contend U.S. Policy on the Internet Has Two Big Flaws," *New York Times,* 15 June 1998, C1, C5.

195. "The Framework for Global Electronic Commerce."

196. Herbert I. Schiller, *Communication and Cultural Domination* (White Plains: International Arts and Sciences Press, 1976), 45.

197. "Hands off the Internet," *Economist,* 5 July 1997, 15.

198. Beltz, "Global Telecommunications Rules," 66.

199. David R. Johnson and David G. Post, "The Rise of Law on the Global Network," in Brian Kahin and Charles Nesson, eds., *Borders in Cyberspace: In-*

formation Policy and the Global Information Infrastructure (Cambridge: MIT Press, 1997), 7.

200. Edmund L. Andrews, "Germany's Efforts to Police Web Are Upsetting Business," *New York Times,* 6 June 1997, A1, C2.

201. Milton L. Mueller, "The Battle Over Internet Domain Names: Global or National TLDs?" *Telecommunications Policy* 22, no. 2 (March 1998): 89–108.

202. *Reno v. ACLU* at 21, 22 (Slip Opinion).

203. Dan Schiller, "Les marchands a l'assaut d'Internet," *Le Monde Diplomatique,* March 1997, 1, 24. An English version is "O, What a Tangled Web We Weave," *Index on Censorship,* Spring 1997, 68–76. For radio, see http://www.ontheair.com.

204. "Remarks by the President in Announcement of Electronic Commerce Initiative."

205. Joseph Farrell, "Prospects for Deregulation in Telecommunications," 30 May 1997, 2, available at http://www.fcc.gov.

206. John M. Broder, "Let It Be," *New York Times,* 30 June 1997, D1, D9.

207. Of the Court's verdict, it was reported by the *New York Times:* "Companies that engage in electronic business applauded the decision, saying that the information revolution could not proceed without freedom of expression in cyberspace." John M. Broder, "Clinton Readies New Approach on Smut," *New York Times,* 27 June 1997, A17; see also Edward Felsenthal, "Supreme Court Gives Business Little to Cheer," *Wall Street Journal,* 30 June 1997, B1; and Rajiv Chandrasekeran, "Clinton to Call for Loose Reins on the Internet," *Los Angeles Times,* 30 June 1997, A1.

208. Linda Greenhouse, "Decency Act Fails" *New York Times,* 27 June 1997, A1, A16.

209. Broder, "Clinton Readies New Approach," A17.

210. Greg Miller, John-Thor Dahlburg, Vanora Bennett, and David Holley, "Countries Face Cyber Control in Their Own Ways," *Los Angeles Times,* 20 June 1997, D1, D4. See also Stephen Levy, "Bill and Al Get It Right," *Newsweek,* 7 July 1997, 80.

211. Miller, Dahlburg, Bennett, and Holley, "Countries Face Cyber Control," D1, D4.

212. "Remarks by the President in Announcement of Electronic Commerce Initiative."

213. "Remarks by the President in Announcement of Electronic Commerce Initiative."

214. Heather Bourbeau, "Momentum Grows for Internet Bill," *Financial Times,* 20 March 1998, 4; Joel Brinkley, "Way Is Cleared for House Bill on Internet Tax," *New York Times,* 20 March 1998, A12; John Simons, "White House to Unveil Plan to Expand Internet Projects in Developing Nations," *Wall Street Journal,* 3 December 1998, B7.

215. Bruce Clark, "'Step Towards Duty-Free Net,'" *Financial Times,* 10 December 1997, 6; Frances Williams, "WTO Weighs Duty-Free Trade on the Internet," *Financial Times,* 20 February 1998, 3; Jack Stephenson and Michael Zeisser, "Don't Tax the Internet—Yet," *Wall Street Journal,* 11 June 1998, A22.

216. Louise Kehoe, "U.S. Lays Out Governance for Internet," *Financial Times,* 6 February 1998, 7; Neil Buckley, "U.S. Bid to Calm Internet Fears," *Financial Times,* 27 May 1998, 9.

217. Raymond Lane, "The Information Age Is Not Yet Here," *New Perspectives Quarterly* 14, no. 2 (Spring 1997): 20.

218. Lester C. Thurow, "Needed: A New System of Intellectual Property Rights," *Harvard Business Review* (September-October 1997): 96.

219. Jared Sandberg, "Apache's Free Software Gives Microsoft, Netscape Fits," *Wall Street Journal,* 19 March 1998, B1, B7.

220. Bruce Lehman, "Multimedia Fair Use Guidelines: The Educational Gateway to the Information Age," Keynote speech presented by PBS Adult Learning Satellite Service, produced by Consortium of College and University Media Centers, 21 September 1995.

221. Thurow, "Needed: A New System," 98, 101.

222. Committee on Issues in the Transborder Flow of Scientific Data, National Committee for CODATA, U.S. National Research Council, *Bits of Power: Issues in Global Access to Scientific Data* (Washington, D.C.: National Academy Press, 1997), 142.

23. Committee on Issues in the Transborder Flow of Scientific Data, *Bits of Power,* 134.

224. Bill Holland, "U.S. WIPO Bill Is Entwined with Online Liability Issue," *Billboard,* 27 September 1997, 8, 110; "Europeans Push for Copyrights in Cyberspace," *New York Times,* 20 October 1997, C6; Ana Radelat, "Devil or Angel? Bruce Lehman, a Little-Known Commerce Department Bureaucrat, Takes the Lead in Regulating the Internet," *California Lawyer* 17, no. 6 (June 1997): 27–29+.

225. James Wilson, "U.S. Penalises Honduras," *Financial Times,* 1 April 1998, 7; Alice Rawsthorn, "HK Swoop on Software Pirates Nets $90 Million Haul," *Financial Times,* 29 April 1998, 1.

226. "Penalties Can Apply to Non-profit Postings; Clinton Signs Tough Digital Copyright Law," *San Jose Mercury News,* 18 December 1997, A4.

227. Jeri Clausing, "Legislation on On-Line Copyrights Advances," *New York Times,* 4 May 1998, C12; "Will Mickey Be the Mouse That Roared If Bill to Extend Copyright Fails?" *Wall Street Journal,* 6 February 1998, B7A; Goldie Blumenstyk, "Copyright Extension Approved by House," *Chronicle of Higher Education,* 3 April 1998, A36.

228. Denise Caruso, "Digital Commerce: The Clinton Administration Is Taking a Tough Stance on Cyberspace Copyrights," *New York Times,* 19 January 1998, C3.

229. "BMI's 'Robot' Scans the Web for Copyright Infringers," *Wall Street Journal,* 16 October 1997, B11.

230. Christopher Stern, "Biz Battles Web-Footed Foes," *Variety,* 16–22 June 1997, 24.

231. Nicholas Denton and Alice Rawsthorn, "Music Sales Offered Direct to PC," *Financial Times,* 12 September 1997, 4.

232. Matt Richtel, "Legal Situation Is Confused on Web Content Protections," *New York Times,* 9 June 1997, C5; Dan Trigeboff, "Gift Horse or Trojan Horse?" *Broadcasting and Cable,* 12 May 1997, 59.

233. David Shaw, "Fierce Battles Fought over Web Guides for Arts, Sports," *Los Angeles Times,* 18 June 1997, A1, A18–A19.

234. "WTO Rejects Canada's Appeal," *Los Angeles Times,* 1 July 1997, D23; quote from Bernard Simon, "Canada Scrambles to Protect Magazines," *Financial Times,* 2 July 1997, 6.

235. Rosanna Tamburri, "Canada Considers New Stand Against American Culture," *Wall Street Journal,* 4 February 1998, A18; Anthony De Palma, "Advertising," *New York Times,* 30 July 1998, C7.

236. Andrew Feenberg, "From Information to Communication: The French Experience with Videotex," in Martin Lea, ed., *Contexts of Computer-Mediated Communication* (New York: Harvester Wheatsheaf, 1992), 169.

237. Henry C. Lucas Jr., Hughes Levecq, Robert Kraut, and Lynn Streeter, "France's Grass-Roots Data Net," *IEEE Spectrum* (November 1995): 71–72.

238. Benjamin Tait, "French Revolution," *Communications International Reports,* 8 May 1998, retrieved at http://www.totaltele.com.

239. Kimberley A. Strassel, "Gallic Passion for Minitel Thwarts L'Internet in France," *Wall Street Journal,* 27 March 1998, B1, B8; Paul J. Deveney, "France Waves Flag for the Internet," *Wall Street Journal,* 19 January 1998, A10.

240. Robert Kagan, "The Benevolent Empire," *Foreign Policy,* no. 111 (Summer 1998): 26.

241. Charles William Maynes, "The Perils of (and for) an Imperial America," *Foreign Policy,* no. 111 (Summer 1998): 44.

242. David Rothkopf, "In Praise of Cultural Imperialism?" *Foreign Policy,* no. 107 (Summer 1997): 39, 43, 48–49.

243. Rothkopf, "In Praise of Cultural Imperialism?" 43.

244. Rothkopf, "In Praise of Cultural Imperialism?" 47; U.N. Conference on Trade and Development, *World Investment Report 1996,* 18–20; for more information, see U.S. Department of Commerce, International Trade Administration, *The Big Emerging Markets 1996 Outlook and Sourcebook* (Lanham, Md.: Bernan Press), 1995.

245. Rothkopf, "In Praise of Cultural Imperialism?" 47.

246. Rothkopf, "In Praise of Cultural Imperialism?" 47.

247. Johnson and Post, "Rise of Law," 27.

248. David C. Moschella, *Waves of Power: Dynamics of Global Technology Leadership 1964–2010* (New York: Amacom, 1997), 94–95.

249. Jim Barksdale, "Washington May Crash the Internet Economy," *Wall Street Journal,* 26 September 1997, A22.

250. Brent Schlender, "Microsoft First America, Now the World," *Fortune,* 18 August 1997, 214–218.

251. Matthew Rose and Brandon Mitchener, "Siemens to Quit PC Market, Sell Plants to Acer," *Wall Street Journal,* 24 April 1998, A13.

252. Michiyo Nakamoto and Julia Cuthbertson, "NEC to Adopt Global Standard for New PCs," *Financial Times,* 25 September 1997, 1, 14.

253. Michiyo Nakamoto, "Japan Sets 2000 for Terrestrial Digital TV," *Financial Times,* 11 June 1998, 4.

254. Moschella, *Waves of Power,* 216.

255. Lenny Mendonca and Greg Wilson, "Financial Megaplayers' Time Is Here," *Wall Street Journal,* 29 September 1997, A22.

256. Bill Spindle, "Japanese 'Big Bang' Is Leading to Big Boon for U.S. High-Tech," *Wall Street Journal,* 16 September 1997, A1, A13; Norihiko Shirouzu, "EDS, Benefiting From Japan's Turmoil, to Hire Six Hundred Staffers of Failed Yamaichi," *Wall Street Journal,* 2 December 1997, A17; Bill Spindle, "In a Matter of Months, Merrill Sets Itself Up as a Force in Japan," *Wall Street Journal,* 8 April 1998, A1, A10.

257. U.S. Department of Commerce, Bureau of Economic Analysis, "Selected Data on U.S. Direct Investment Abroad, 1950–76" (Washington, D.C.: USGPO, February 1982), iii.

258. Calculated from U.N. Conference on Trade and Development, *World Investment Report 1996,* 245, Annex table 4.

259. U.N. Conference on Trade and Development, *World Investment Report 1996, 16.*

260. "A New Breed of Blue Chips," *Business Week,* 7 July 1997, 53.

261. "U.S. Foreign Debt Rose 26.6 Percent in 1996; Strong Dollar Blamed," *Wall Street Journal,* 1 July 1997, A2.

262. For a landmark critical study, see Edward S. Herman and Robert W. McChesney, *The Global Media: The New Missionaries of Global Capitalism* (London: Cassell, 1997).

263. Jessica T. Matthews, "Are Networks Better Than Nations?" *New Perspectives Quarterly* 14, no. 2 (Spring 1997): 12.

264. "Group of Telecom, Information Industry Executives Urges Governments to Position Internet in Deregulatory Vanguard," *Telecommunications Reports Daily,* 28 May 1997.

265. "A European Initiative in Electronic Commerce," Communication to the European Parliament, the Council, the Economic and Social Committee, and the

Committee of the Regions, *Com* (97)157, April-May 1997, available at http://www.cordis.lu/esprit/src/ecomcom.htm; "Ministerial Declaration," Global Information Networks Ministerial Conference, Bonn 6–8 July 1997; Martin Bangemann, "A New World Order for Global Communications," speech presented at Telecom Inter@ctive '97, International Telecommunication Union, Geneva, 8 September 1997; European Commission, *Green Paper on the Convergence of the Telecommunications, Media and Information Technology Sectors, and the Implications for Regulation: Towards An Information Society Approach* (Brussels: EU, 3 December 1997), ch. V: 54–57; Ministry of Trade and Industry, Japan, "Toward the Age of the Digital Economy," May 1997; Samer Iskandar, "Businesses Agree to Tackle Electronic Commerce Pitfalls," *Financial Times*, 30 June 1998, 5.

266. "U.S. Cites Japan Aid in Limiting Privacy," *New York Times*, 15 May 1998, C2.

267. Levy, "Bill and Al Get It Right," 80.

268. Jagdish Bhagwati, "Free Trade Without Treaties," *Wall Street Journal*, 24 November 1997, A22.

269. "The Framework for Global Electronic Commerce."

270. Moschella, *Waves of Power*, 233; Steve Lohr, "Business to Business on the Internet," *New York Times*, 28 April 1997, C1, C9; Paul Taylor, "Two-Speed Digital Economy," *Financial Times*, 3 June 1998, 22; Christopher Price, "Bruised Netscape Angles for Corporate Users," *Financial Times*, 8 June 1998, 19.

271. "The Framework for Global Electronic Commerce."

272. Exports over imports by $1.2 billion from 1986 to 1994; sales by TNC affiliates by $6.1 billion between 1987 and 1993. Overall U.S. international trade in computer services for 1993 came to $17.908 billion, five-sixths of which was accounted for by affiliate as opposed to cross-border transactions. William C. Goodman, "The Software and Engineering Industries Threatened by Technological Change?" *Monthly Labor Review* 119, no. 8, (August 1996): 41. See also Claudia H. Deutsch, "Services Becoming the Goods in Industry," *New York Times*, 7 January 1997, C1, C4.

273. Edmund L. Andrews, "Germany's Efforts to Police Web Are Upsetting Business," *New York Times*, 6 June 1997, A1, C2.

274. Edward Herman, *The Triumph of the Market* (Boston: South End Press, 1995), 3.

Chapter 3

1. Robert R. Schaller, "Moore's Law: Past, Present, and Future," *IEEE Spectrum* 34, no. 6 (June 1997): 52–59.

2. Moschella, *Waves of Power*, 9.

3. Don Clark, "Intel's Tumble Underscores the Debate over Coming Changes in PC Hardware," *Wall Street Journal*, 25 August 1997, B2.

4. Vadim Zlotnikov, "Semiconductors," *Upside,* October 1997, 160; Greg Miller, "The Intel Hustle," *Los Angeles Times,* 7 September 1997, D12.

5. "Intel Cuts Prices on Pentiums for Portables," *Los Angeles Times,* 30 April 1998, D2.

6. Howard Anderson, "Target: Microsoft," *Upside,* April 1997, 68, 72–76; Don Clark, "How Microsoft Lost Cloak of Invincibility While Getting On-Line," *Wall Street Journal,* 5 November 1997, A1, A5.

7. Jared Sandberg, "PC Firms' Push for Home Use Seems to Falter," *Wall Street Journal,* 6 March 1997, B6.

8. Sharon Reier, "Why Europeans Lag in Using PCs," *International Herald Tribune,* 19 March 1998, 11; Matthew Rose, "Europeans Turn PC Buying into Boom, Increasing Sales 24 Percent in Fourth Quarter," *Wall Street Journal,* 4 February 1998, B6; "Asian PC Sales Drop by Nearly One-Third; Growth in China Slows," *Wall Street Journal,* 27 May 1998, B9.

9. Robert X. Cringely, "You Can Never Be Too Rich or Too PC," *Red Herring,* September 1997, 20; Paul Saffo quoted in James Flanigan, "Whether Apple Grows Anew Depends on Human Factor," *Los Angeles Times,* 10 August 1997, D1, D6.

10. Louise Kehoe and William Lewis, "TI May Sell Memory Chip Operation to Micron," *Financial Times,* 8 June 1998, 1; Andrew E. Serwer, "Michael Dell Turns the PC World Inside Out," *Fortune,* 8 September 1997, 76–86; David Kirkpatrick, "Now Everyone in PCs Wants to Be Like Mike," *Fortune,* 8 September 1997, 91–92; Evan Ramstad, "Compaq Posts a Profit But Warns of Difficulties," *Wall Street Journal,* 16 April 1998, B4; Raju Narisetti, "How IBM Turned Around Its Ailing PC Division," *Wall Street Journal,* 12 March 1998, B1.

11. Evan Ramstad, "Low-Cost PCs Made Gains over Holiday," *Wall Street Journal,* 31 December 1997, A3; Jim Carlton, "Cheaper PCs Start to Attract New Customers," *Wall Street Journal,* 26 January 1998, B1; Louise Kehoe and Paul Taylor, "Long and Winding Download," *Financial Times,* 12 March 1998, 11; Charles Piller, "Cyrix Is High on Low End of the PC Market," *Los Angeles Times,* 4 May 1998, D1, D6; Peter Burrows, Gary McWilliams, and Robert D. Hof, "Cheap PCs," *Business Week,* 23 March 1998, 28–32.

12. Burrows, McWilliams, and Hof, "Cheap PCs."

13. "Most Homes Have PC," *Windows User News,* September 1997; Raju Narisetti, "IBM to Revamp Struggling Home-PC Business," *Wall Street Journal,* 14 October 1997, B1, B14; Jim Carlton and Evan Ramstad, "New Cheap PCs Are Shaking Up the Industry," *Wall Street Journal,* 10 September 1997, B1, B8; Dean Takahashi, "How the Competition Got Ahead of Intel in Making Cheap Chips," *Wall Street Journal,* 12 February 1998, A1, A11.

14. "Intel Profit Warning Rattles Markets," *Wall Street Journal,* 6 March 1998, A3, A9.

15. Eva Ramstad and Dean Takahashi, "Compaq Unveils Two PCs for Under $1,000," *Wall Street Journal,* 1 July 1997, B6; Raju Narisetti, "IBM to Revamp

Struggling Home-PC Business," *Wall Street Journal,* 14 October 1997, B1, B14; G. Pascal Zachary, "PC Sales and Big Suppliers Show Strength," *Wall Street Journal,* 27 April 1998, B6.

16. Piller, "Cyrix Is High"; Dean Takahashi, "How the Competition Got Ahead of Intel in Making Cheap Chips," *Wall Street Journal,* 12 February 1998, A1, A11; Charles Piller, "Packard Bell to Use Cyrix's Low-Cost Chips," *Los Angeles Times,* 22 May 1998, D1, D12.

17. Gretchen Morgenson, "Inside Intel, Setbacks Bring Some Anxiety," *New York Times,* 28 May 1998, C1, C6.

18. Dean Takahashi, "Chip Firms Face Technological Hurdles That May Curb Growth, Report Suggests," *Wall Street Journal,* 1 December 1997, B8; "Intel Profit Expected to Rise Modestly," *Los Angeles Times,* 14 October 1997, D2; Takahashi, "How the Competition Got Ahead"; Dean Takahashi, "Intel Lowers Profit, Revenue Predictions," *Wall Street Journal,* 5 March 1998, A3, A16; Andy Reinhardt, Ira Sager, and Peter Burrows, "Intel: Can Andy Grove Keep Profits Up in an Era of Cheap PCs?" *Business Week,* 22 December 1997, 70–77; Lee Gomes and Bryan Gruley, "Intel Likely to Keep Pace Despite Expected FTC Action," *Wall Street Journal,* 29 May 1998, B6.

19. "Intel Unveils a Chip Specifically for PCs Costing Under $1,000," *Wall Street Journal,* 18 February 1998, B8.

20. Dean Takahashi, "Intel, Expecting Faster Growth, Lays Out Plans for New Products," *Wall Street Journal,* 22 April 1998, B6; Dean Takahashi, "Intel, Confronting New Market, Develops Own Design for Low-Cost PC Alternative," *Wall Street Journal,* 3 December 1997, B8.

21. See, for example, Joseph B. White and David Bank, "Computer Industry Races to Conquer the Automobile," *Wall Street Journal,* 23 February 1998, B1, B5; Michael Krantz, "The Ubiquitous Chip," *Time,* 29 December 97–5 January 1998, 78–81; Don Clark and David Bank, "Microsoft, Sony Agree to Work Together to Link Consumer-Electronics Devices," *Wall Street Journal,* 8 April 1998, B6.

22. David Kirkpatrick, "Intel's Amazing Profit Machine," *Fortune,* 17 February 1997, 62, 64; Dean Takahashi, "Intel Invests to Push Beyond the Usual Borders of PCs," *Wall Street Journal,* 14 April 1997, B8; Anthony Perkins, "Corporate entertainment," *Red Herring,* July 1997, 14; Greg Miller, "The Intel Hustle," *Los Angeles Times,* 7 September 1997, D1, D12; Karen Kaplan, "Chips, the Sequel," *Los Angeles Times,* 27 April 1998, D1, D6.

23. "Spending Its Billions," *New York Times,* 5 January 1998, C21.

24. Stephanie N. Mehta, "New Breed of Investor Brings More Than Cash to Hopeful Start-Ups," *Wall Street Journal,* 25 August 1997, A1; Nicholas Denton, "Venture Capital, Catalyst of the High-Tech Boom," *Financial Times,* 4 June 1997, FT-IT 2–3; "Venture Capital Investments Set Record," *Los Angeles Times,* 21 August 1997, D2; U.S. Department of Commerce, *The Emerging Digital Economy.* (Washington, D.C.: USGPO, April 1998), A2–A5.

25. Jube Shiver, Jr., "A Software Sell," *Los Angeles Times,* 23 August 1995, D4; Nikhil Hutheesing, "Who Needs the Middleman?" *Forbes,* 28 August 95, 110–111; Peter Lewis, "Technology," *New York Times,* 31 July 1995, D6.

26. Steve Lohr, "Who Uses Internet? 5.8 Million Are Said to Be Linked in U.S.," *New York Times,* 27 September 1995, C2.

27. John W. Verity, "Everyone's Rushing the Net," *Business Week,* 5 June 1995, 116–118.

28. Clark, "How Microsoft Lost Cloak of Invincibility," A1.

29. Jared Sandberg, "Inside AOL's Bid to Develop Its Own Hot Sites," *Wall Street Journal,* 21 November 1997, B1, B12.

30. Clark, "How Microsoft Lost Cloak of Invincibility," A1; Karen Kaplan, "Ready for Battle?" *Los Angeles Times,* 27 October 1997," D1, D6; Jared Sandberg, "AOL Swings to Profit, Beats Estimate," *Wall Street Journal,* 7 May 1998, B6; Thomas E. Weber, "AOL Sets Accord to Purchase Netscape in a Stock Transaction for $4.3 Billion," *Wall Street Journal,* 25 November 1998, A3, A6.

31. Menahem Blondheim, *News over the Wires: The Telegraph and the Flow of Public Information in America, 1844–1897* (Cambridge: Harvard University Press, 1994).

32. See, for example, Michele Hilmes, *Hollywood and Broadcasting from Radio to Cable* (Urbana: University of Illinois Press, 1990).

33. Jared Sandberg and Laura Johannes, "Kodak and AOL Are Expected to Unveil Pact Allowing Digitized Photos On-Line," *Wall Street Journal,* 19 May 1998, B5; George Cole, "A Projection for the Future of the Flicks," *Financial Times,* 27 April 1998, 12.

34. Chuck Philips, "Music Execs Gather to Ask: Is Radio Still Relevant?" *Los Angeles Times,* 11 June 1998, D1, D5.

35. Jim Carlton, "Amazon Posts Smaller Loss Than Forecast," *Wall Street Journal,* 28 April 1998, B4.

36. Alice Rawsthorn, "Internet Music Retailers Hear an Upbeat Tempo," *Financial Times,* 5 December 1997, 17.

37. Paul Karon, "Cybermalls Have Showbiz Salivating," *Variety,* 1–7 December 1997, 1, 87.

38. Heather Green, Gail DeGeorge, and Amy Barrett, "The Virtual Malls Gets Real," *Business Week,* 26 January 1998, 90–91; Louise Kehoe, "High Streets in Hyperspace," *Financial Times,* 18–19 April 1998, 6; Joel Kotkin, "When the Mall's Just a Keystroke Away, Should Retailers Worry?" *Los Angeles Times,* 3 May 1998, M1, M6.

39. Lisa Napoli, "Staying with the Pitch," *New York Times,* 23 February 1998, C1, C5; Shikhar Ghosh, "Making Business Sense of the Internet," *Harvard Business Review* 76, no. 2 (March-April 1998): 126–135; Kevin P. Coyne and Renee Dye, "The Competitive Dynamics of Network-Based Businesses," *Harvard Business Review* 76, no. 10 (January-February 1998): 99–109.

40. Thomas E. Weber, "TV-Station Web Sites Grab Classified Ads," *Wall Street Journal,* 27 August 1997, B1, B12.

41. Moschella, *Waves of Power,* 122.

42. Joseph Turow, *Media Systems in Society: Understanding Industries, Strategies, and Power* (New York: Longman, 1992), 242–243.

43. Beth Snyder, "Specter of Online Classifieds Spurs Papers to Experiment," *Advertising Age,* 20 April 1998, S16, S28; I. Jeanne Dugan, "New-Media Meltdown," *Business Week,* 23 March 1998, 70–71.

44. U.S. Department of Commerce, *The Emerging Digital Economy,* 24.

45. Richard Tedesco, "The Not Ready for Prime-Time Medium," *Broadcasting and Cable,* 25 May 1998, 22–23.

46. R. Lee Sullivan, "Radio Free Internet," *Forbes,* 22 April 1996, 44–45; Robert H. Reid, "Real Revolution," *Wired,* October 1997, 125, 174.

47. Christopher Parkes, "Walt Disney Nets Starwave to Boost Web Site Ambitions," *Financial Times,* 1 May 1998, 15; Mark Gimein with Laura Rich, "Disney's Net Play Could Be a Model for Media," *Industry Standard,* 1 June 1998, 22–26.

48. Debra Jo Immergut, "Webcast News," *Wall Street Journal,* 28 May 1998, A20.

49. Mark Lander, "Industries Agree on U.S. Standards for TV of Future," *New York Times,* 26 November 1996, A1, C6; Bryan Gruley, "Television and Computer Makers Reach an Accord on Design of Digital-TV Sets," *Wall Street Journal,* 26 November 1996, B10; Joel Brinkley, "Defining TVs and Computers for a Future of High Definition," *New York Times,* 2 December 1996, C1, C11.

50. David Bank and Don Clark, "Network Computers Fall Short in Context Against Cheap PCs," *Wall Street Journal,* 3 April 1998, A1, A6.

51. Moschella, *Waves of Power,* 148.

52. In Miller, "The Intel Hustle," D12.

53. Dean Takahashi, "Intel Breaks Ranks with PC Industry, Backing Broadcasters on Digital TV," *Wall Street Journal,* 5 December 1997, B7; Karen Kaplan, "Chips, the Sequel," *Los Angeles Times,* 27 April 1998, D1, D6.

54. Lisa Bransten, "Intel Develops Way to Speed Web Surfing," *Wall Street Journal,* 19 January 1998; Dean Takahashi, "Intel to Unveil Series of Computer-Networking Devices," *Wall Street Journal,* 24 February 1998, B4; Louise Kehoe, "Intel Tries to Net TV," *Financial Times,* 10 December 1997, 22.

55. Ken Auletta, "The Microsoft Provocateur," *New Yorker,* 12 May 1997, 71.

56. John R. Wilke and Don Clark, "Computer Firms Tell of Microsoft's Tough Tactics," *Wall Street Journal,* 23 October 1997, A3, A12.

57. Steve Hamm, "The Education of Marc Andreesen," *Business Week,* 13 April 1998, 84–92; Alex Gove, "Balancing Act," *Red Herring,* June 1998, 54–59.

58. "U.S. Expands Review of Four Microsoft Deals," *Los Angeles Times,* 20 August 1997, D2; Chuck Ross and Bradley Johnson, "PC Giants Offer Branded

Browsers," *Ad Age,* 17 November 1997, 3, 86; John R. Wilke, "Suit Against Microsoft by Justice Department Now Seems Imminent," *Wall Street Journal,* 8 May 1998, A1, A10; Charles R. Morris, "It's Time for Gates to Act Like a Grown-up," *Los Angeles Times,* 17 May 1998, M1, M6; Joel Brinkley, "U.S. and Twenty States File Suits Claiming Microsoft Blocks Competition over Internet: A Consumer Focus," *New York Times,* 19 May 1998, A1, C4; John R. Wilke, "U.S. Sues Microsoft on Antitrust Grounds," *Wall Street Journal,* 19 May 1998, A3; Amy Cortese, Susan B. Garland, Steve Hamm, "The Battle for the Cyber Future," *Business Week,* 1 June 1998, 38–42.

59. "Netscape to Unveil Technology in Race with Rival Microsoft," *Wall Street Journal,* 29 September 1997, B6.

60. Anya Sacharow, "Distribution Is King: Microsoft Looks for Outside Partners," *Ad Week,* 22 September 1997, 47; David Bank, "Microsoft May Face Battle over Content," *Wall Street Journal,* 13 February 1998, B20; David Bank, "Microsoft Weighs Killing 'Channels' on Web Browser," *Wall Street Journal,* 5 March 1998, B7; Steve Lohr, " 'Browser War' Limits Access to Web Sites," *New York Times,* 8 December 1997, C1, C13.

61. Steve Hamm, "Would You Pay to Read *Slate?*" *Business Week,* 23 February 1998, 120–121.

62. "MSNBC Site Redesign," *Windows User News,* September 1997; Kyle Pope, "As the Focus Shifts, the Picture Brightens at MSNBC," *Wall Street Journal,* 28 October 1997, B1, B13.

63. David Bank, "Microsoft Plans to Cut Back Web Services," *Wall Street Journal,* 27 February 1998, B6.

64. Nick Wingfield, "Microsoft to Buy E-Mail Start-Up in Stock Deal," *Wall Street Journal,* 2 January 1998, 12.

65. Nick Wingfield, "Microsoft Agrees to Buy Firefly Network in Move Toward Personal Web Searches," *Wall Street Journal,* 10 April 1998, B5.

66. Rebecca Blumenstein, "Haggling in Cyberspace Transforms Car Sales," *Wall Street Journal,* 30 December 1997, B1, B6; Bradley Johnson, "Microsoft Grows Sidewalk, Taking on Local Media," *Advertising Age,* 23 February 1998, 49.

67. Steve Hamm, Amy Cortese, and Susan B. Garland, "Microsoft's Future," *Business Week,* 19 January 1998, 58–67.

68. David Bank, "Clearing Microsoft's Path to Digital TV," *Wall Street Journal,* 14 April 1998, B1, B9; Carrie Lee, "Web Item Rings C-Phone's Bell as Shares Soar," *Wall Street Journal,* 18 May 1998, B11D; Michael Marriott, "WebTV Offers Cheap Web Access, but Consumers Are Wary," *New York Times,* 26 February 1998, D6; Diane Mermigas, "A passage to digital," *Electronic Media,* 30 March 1998, 1, 14.

69. Steve Hamm, "The Eight-Hundred-Pound Gorilla's New Toy," *Business Week,* 11 May 1998, 60–62; Kara Swisher, "A Web Pioneer Does a Delicate Dance with Microsoft," *Wall Street Journal,* 12 February 1998, B1, 10.

70. Peter Wayner, "Plugging in to the Internet: Many Paths, Many Speeds," *New York Times,* 2 July 1998, D11. Price data quoted below are taken from this source.

71. Nick Wingfield, "Publications Aimed at On-Line Users Face Shakeout After a Two-Year Boom," *Wall Street Journal,* 15 August 1997, A9A.

72. David Sweet, "When It's Baseball Versus the Bottom Line, Bosses Crack Down," *Wall Street Journal,* 7 July 1997, B3A; "Panic Button," *Wall Street Journal,* 14 October 1997, A1.

73. Alan Stone, *Public Service Liberalism* (Princeton: Princeton University Press, 1994).

74. Leslie Cauley, "US West's Plan to Split Up Reflects Failure in Strategy," *Wall Street Journal,* 28 October 1997, B4.

75. Saul Hansell, "Technology," *New York Times,* 29 June 1998, C4.

76. Jube Shiver, Jr., "FCC Sends 'Red Flare,' Says Cable Fees Up 8.5 Percent," *Los Angeles Times,* 14 January 1998, A1, A11.

77. Elizabeth Lesly and Ronald Grover, "Cable TV: A Crisis Looms," *Business Week,* 14 October 1996, 100–110; Mark Robichaux, "TCI Takes Back $125 Million Stake in Microsoft Network as Strategies Shift," *Wall Street Journal,* 15 November 1996: B19.

78. Eben Shapiro, "TCI Plans to Cut 6.5 Percent of Its Staff and Take Charge," *Wall Street Journal,* 6 December 1996, B9.

79. Eben Shapiro, "Time Warner Plans to Eliminate Staggered Terms of Its Directors," *Wall Street Journal,* 6 December 1996, B4.

80. Steve Lohr, "The Next Act for Microsoft," *New York Times,* 10 June 1997, C1, C5.

81. Katherine Stalter, "NBC, Intel Link to Channel TV to PC," *Variety,* 1–14 July 1996, 33.

82. Lee Hall, "Content to PCs via TV Signals?" *Electronic Media,* 23 February 1998, 5.

83. Diane Mermigas, "Microsoft Isn't a *Cable* Giant—Not Yet." *Electronic Media,* 4 May 1998, 54, 56.

84. Kara Swisher and Leslie Cauley, "Microsoft Co-Founder Puts Huge Bet on Cable-TV," *Wall Street Journal,* 7 April 1998, B12.

85. Don Clark, "Sun Microsystems Agrees to Buy Diba, Moving into Information Appliances," *Wall Street Journal,* 1 August 1997, B14.

86. Don Clark, "Oracle Plans to Integrate TV Programs with Data from the World Wide Web," *Wall Street Journal,* 13 August 1997, B7; Lee Hall, "WebTV Rival NetChannel Gives Up Ghost," *Electronic Media,* 4 May 1998, 30; "Oracle, Intel to Buy Stake in Net-Access Firm," *Los Angeles Times,* 5 May 1998, D2.

87. Joel Brinkley, *Defining Vision: The Battle for the Future of Television* (New York: Harcourt Brace, 1997); Richard Tedesco, "Set Makers Prepare for All of

the Above," *Broadcasting and Cable,* 8 September 1997, 15; Maribel Paredes Castaneda is developing a dissertation carrying political-economic analysis of digital television systems forward into the present.

88. Bradley Johnson, "Slow Start Is Anticipated for Digital TV products," *Advertising Age,* 12 January 1998, 4; Lee Hall, "Not All Can See Digital Big Picture," *Electronic Media,* 12 January 1998, 1, 118; Jim McConville and Michael Schneider, "Big Four Unifying Against Cable," *Electronic Media,* 30 March 1998, 1, 38; Doug Halonen, "Digital Tier Idea Irks Affiliates," *Electronic Media,* 4 May 1998, 1, 70; Joel Brinkley, "Cable Difficulties May Thwart HDTV Debut," *New York Times,* 8 June 1998, C3; P. J. Huffstutter, "The Dawning of the HDTV Era—Sort Of," *Los Angeles Times,* 8 January 1998, D1, D6; Joel Brinkley, "Questions over Demand as Digital TV's Network Premiere Nears," *New York Times,* 5 January 1998, C20.

89. Don Clark, "U.S. Reviews Microsoft Pact for Apple Stake," *Wall Street Journal,* 19 August 1997, B14; Don Clark and Jim Carlton, "Visions of PC and TV Firms Compete at Comdex," *Wall Street Journal,* 18 November 1997, B6; Don Clark, "Intel and Microsoft Split over Internet-TV Gear," *Wall Street Journal,* 3 October 1997, A3, A4; Dean Takahashi, "Motorola to Join Forces with Sarnoff on Low-Cost Chips for Digital TV Sets," *Wall Street Journal,* 10 November 1997, B6; Mark Robichaux, "Time Warner Inc. Is Expected to Order up to $450 Million of TV Set-Top Boxes," *Wall Street Journal,* 10 December 1996, B8; Andrew Kupfer, "How Hot Is Cable, Really?" *Fortune,* 16 February 1998, 70–76.

90. David Bank, "TCI Uses Hi-Tech 'Layer Cake' to Ward Off Microsoft," *Wall Street Journal,* 16 December 1997, B4; Leslie Cauley, "General Instrument Is Expected to Select Motorola, QED Chips for Set-Top Box," *Wall Street Journal,* 25 March 1998, B6; Leslie Cauley, "Sony Plans to Purchase a 5 Percent Stake in NextLevel," *Wall Street Journal,* 5 January 1998, A3, A14.

91. Don Clark and Matthew Rose, "Cable & Wireless PLC Chooses Software from Oracle Affiliate for Cable-TV Box," *Wall Street Journal,* 10 March 1998, B9.

92. Elizabeth Lesly and Amy Cortese, with Ron Grover, "Bill Gates: The Cable Guy," *Business Week,* 14 July 1997, 22–24; David Bank, "Why Microsoft Wants to Hook into Cable TV," *Wall Street Journal,* 16 October 1997, B1, B19; Mermigas, "Microsoft Isn't A *Cable* Giant"; Edward W. Desmond, "Malone Again," *Fortune,* 16 February 1998, 66–69; David Bank, "TCI Will Install Sun's Java Software in All TV Boxes, in Blow to Microsoft," *Wall Street Journal,* 7 May 1998, B14; David Bank, "Microsoft's Digital-TV Efforts Are Stymied," *Wall Street Journal,* 3 December 1998, B7.

93. Diane Mermigas, "Industry Stocks Zoom in 1997," *Electronic Media,* 12 January 1998, 48.

94. Leslie Cauley, "Time Warner's Results Beat Forecasts, and Levin Projects Strong Cash Flow," *Wall Street Journal,* 16 April 1998, B16; Ronald Grover, "Cable's Comeback Kid," *Business Week,* 11 May 1998, 86–88.

95. William E. Kennard, Chairman, Federal Communications Commission, speech presented to the National Cable Television Association, Atlanta, Ga., 5 May 1998, 2.

96. Jim Heid, "Getting a Grip," *Los Angeles Times*, 25 May 1998, D1, D6; Steven E. Brier, "Cable Modems: For a Few, Real Speed," *New York Times*, 21 May 1998, D6; Leslie Cauley, "Microsoft Is in Talks to Buy 20 Percent Stake in RoadRunner for About $400 Million," *Wall Street Journal*, 18 May 1998, B12.

97. Sallie Hofmeister and Elizabeth Douglass, "AT&T Will Buy Cable Power TCI in All-Stock Deal," *Los Angeles Times*, 24 June 1998, A1, A13; Leslie Cauley, "AT&T Appears Close to a Deal to Acquire TCI for $30 Billion," *Wall Street Journal*, 24 June 1998, A1, A8.

98. Joel Brinkley, "Ready or Not, Here Comes HDTV," *New York Times*, 6 April 1998, C1, C4; Kyle Pope and Leslie Cauley, "Duel Threatens to Delay Debut of Digital TV," *Wall Street Journal*, 20 April 1998, B1, B6.

99. Seth Schiesel, "Venture Promises Far Faster Speeds for Internet Data," *New York Times*, 20 January 1998, A1, C7.

100. "Lucent Unveils DSL Chip Sets for Home Phone Lines," *Telecommunications Reports Daily*, 20 January 1998; Elizabeth Douglass, "PacBell Plans High-Speed Internet Lines for Southland," *Los Angeles Times*, 28 May 1998, D1, D5.

101. "Bell Atlantic to Launch Commercial ADSL in Fall," *Telecommunications Reports Daily*, 3 June 1998.

102. "UUNet Targets Larger Masses with Multicasting Service," *Telecommunications Reports*, 29 September 1997, 19.

103. Saul Hansell, "Hooking Up the Nation," *New York Times*, 25 June 1998, A1, C5; Scott Thurm, "Computer-Industry Group to Pursue Home Networking," *Wall Street Journal*, 22 June 1998, B4.

104. "Telco, CATV Broadband Race Picks Up Steam," *Telecommunications Reports Daily*, 4 September 1997.

105. David Bank, "Microsoft, Time Warner and US West Discuss High-Speed Internet Service," *Wall Street Journal*, 6 November 1997, B10; Cauley, "Microsoft Is in Talks to Buy 20 Percent Stake," B12; Dan Fost, "Cable for Geeks," *Ad Week*, 4 May 1998, 36–41; David Bank and Leslie Cauley, "Microsoft, Compaq Make Net-Access Bet," *Wall Street Journal*, 16 June 1998, A3, A8.

106. Diane Mermigas, "Web Services Near Big Deal," *Electronic Media*, 2 March 1998, 3, 31.

107. Amy Cortese, "Not @Home Alone: Bill Comes Knocking," *Business Week*, 14 July 1997, 24; "Cablevision, @Home Network Ink Internet Alliance," *Telecommunications Reports Daily*, 3 October 1997.

108. G. Christian Hill, "Major Investors in @Home Network to Supply Another Round of Financing," *Wall Street Journal*, 11 April 1997, B7C; John Markoff, "Canadian Cable TV Operators in Internet Deal with @Home," *New York Times*, 10 April 1997, C6.

109. Tim Jackson, "Internet Profits Begin @Home," *Financial Times,* 18 May 1998, 11.

110. Leslie Cauley, "TCI and AT&T Look to Enter Venture With Cable TV Firms on Phone Service," *Wall Street Journal,* 24 September 1998, B14.

111. James Kraft, *Stage to Studio* (Baltimore: Johns Hopkins University Press, 1996).

112. Steve Hamm, with Amy Cortese and Cathy Yang, "Microsoft Refines Its Net Game," *Business Week,* 8 September 1997, 126.

113. Marc Gunther, "The Internet Is Mr. Case's Neighborhood," *Fortune,* 30 March 1998, 69–80; William M. Bulkeley, "Parable Will Make *South Park* One of Those Things," *Wall Street Journal,* 4 June 1998, B6.

114. Kyle Pope, "NBC Set to Give Viewers Access to Digital Data," *Wall Street Journal,* 30 June 1997, B6.

115. Chuck Ross, "*Seinfeld* Tries to Set Ad Record on Web Site, Too," *Advertising Age,* 23 March 1998, 4, 48.

116. Chuck Ross, "Disney Eyes Stake in Excite as Part of Bold Web Strategy," *Advertising Age,* 1 June 1998, 1, 52; Saul Hansell, "Disney Will Invest in a Web Gateway," *New York Times,* 19 June 1998, A1, C3; Kyle Pope and Kara Swisher, "NBC Stakes Out an Entry Point onto the Web," *Wall Street Journal,* 10 June 1998, B1, B6; Bruce Orwall and Kara Swisher, "Disney to Buy Infoseek Stake for Web Help," *Wall Street Journal* 19 June 1998, A3, A6.

117. Eben Shapiro and John Lippman, "Murdoch Sells TV Guide to an Affiliate of TCI," *Wall Street Journal,* 12 June 1998, B1, B8.

118. "TCI's Malone Seeks Summit with Agencies," *Advertising Age,* 18 May 1998, 11–12.

119. For an illuminating discussion, see Matthew P. McAllister, *The Commercialization of American Culture* (Thousand Oaks, CA: Sage, 1996).

120. Edwin L. Artzt, "The Future of Advertising," *Vital Speeches of the Day* 60, no. 22, (1 September 1994): 686.

121. Artzt, "The Future of Advertising," 686–687.

122. Artzt, "The Future of Advertising," 688.

123. John W. Verity, "Planet Internet," *Business Week,* 3 April 1995, 118–124.

124. Sheila Muto, "Web Firms Start Tussling as L.A. Market Heats Up," *Wall Street Journal,* 18 March 1998, CA1; Robin Frost, "Digital Artists Link Up with Talent Agencies," *Wall Street Journal,* 16 March 1998, B5B.

125. David Zgodzinksi, "Click Here to Pay," *Internet World,* September 1997, 61–68.

126. Matej Vipotnik, "U.S. Ruling May Aid Net Encryption Software Exports," *Financial Times,* 27 August 1997, 1, 10.

127. Elizabeth Veomett, "Just Add Watermark," *Business Week,* 1 September 1997, 35.

128. Kate Maddox, "Forrester Study Says Users Ready For E-Commerce," *Advertising Age,* 23 March 1998, 34; Peter Clemente, *The State of the Net* (New York: McGraw-Hill, 1998), 88–89.

129. Jane Greenstein, "Advertisers Still Trying to Get a Line on Net Users," *Los Angeles Times,* 2 December 1996, D5; Kyle Pope, "Nielsen, Lucent Sign Deal to Track Digital TV Viewers," *Wall Street Journal,* 30 June 1997, B6; Sally Goll Beatty, "Firms Vie to Tally Those Snagged on Web," *Wall Street Journal,* 16 September 1997, B12; Russell Shaw, "At Least There Are No Web Sweeps (Yet)," *Electronic Media,* 2 March 1998, 17, 21.

130. Rex Weiner, "Nielsen Soldiers March on Net," *Variety,* 11–17 September 1995, 39.

131. Joan Voight, "Beyond the Banner," *Wired,* December 1996, 196, 204.

132. Denis F. Beausejour, Vice President–Advertising, Worldwide, Procter & Gamble Company, "Branding and Bonding Beyond the Banner," Paper presented at Ad-Tech Conference, 7 May 1998, 4–5, http//www.pg.com/speech.html.

133. Janice Maloney, "Dave Dornan: The Push PointCast Needs to Go Public?" *Industry Standard,* 11 May 1998, 26–30.

134. Peter Storck of Jupiter Communications, in Kate Maddox, "Don't Push It, Say Users and Web Marketers," *Advertising Age,* 10 November 1997, S1, S30.

135. Steve Hamm, "Dwats, Dat Wabbit Wuvs Micwosoft," *Business Week,* 6 October 1997, 8.

136. Paul Taylor, "Microsoft Launches New Web Browser," *Financial Times,* 1 October 1997, 22.

137. David Bank, "Microsoft Nabs About Twelve Providers of 'Content' for Its Web Software," *Wall Street Journal,* 22 May 1997, B8; Don Clark, "Microsoft, Netscape Prepare to Launch New Browser Battle," *Wall Street Journal,* 4 June 1997, B6; "Netscape Releases Push Services," *Advertising Age,* 18 August 1997, 19. See Bradley Johnson, "Netscape, Microsoft Continue Their Battle with Push Services," *Advertising Age,* 10 November 1997, S2.

138. Stuart Elliott, "Advertising," *New York Times,* 20 November 1996, C5.

139. David Haskin, "A Push in the Right Direction," *Internet World,* September 1997, 75–83; David Bank, "New Web Browsers Play Down TV-Channel Approach," *Wall Street Journal,* 30 September 1997, B1, B12.

140. David Bank, "How Net Is Becoming More Like Television to Draw Advertisers," *Wall Street Journal,* 13 December 1996, A1, A8.

141. Don Clark, "Microsoft's On-Line Service Goes to a TV Format," *Wall Street Journal,* 9 December 1996, B7.

142. Walter S. Mossberg, "Here's an Easy Way to Free Yourself from Browser Promos," *Wall Street Journal,* 21 August 1997, B1.

143. In one report, the most thorough search engine only finds about one-third of the pages on the Web. Thomas E. Weber, "Web's Vastness Foils Even Best Search Engines," *Wall Street Journal,* 3 April 1998, B1, B7.

144. Randall E. Stross, "How Yahoo! Won the Search Wars," *Fortune,* 2 March 1998, 148–154; see also Nicholas Denton, "Yahoo Extends Net Lead," *Financial Times,* 15 January 1998, 18.

145. Kara Swisher, "The Two Grown-Ups Behind Yahoo!'s Surge," *Wall Street Journal,* 10 April 1998, B1, B10; Walter Mossberg, "Yahoo! Challenges AOL as a Portal to World Wide Web," *Wall Street Journal,* 19 March 1998, B1.

146. Kara Swisher, "This Time, It's the Barbarians at the Web," *Wall Street Journal,* 22 May 1998, B1, B5.

147. Christopher Price, "Creating a New Sense of Community," *Financial Times,* 7 May 1998, 18.

148. David Bank, "Microsoft Again Revamps Its Network Strategy," *Wall Street Journal,* 10 July 1997, B9; Steve Lohr, "America Online Turns to TV as a Model," *New York Times,* 6 October 1997, C6.

149. Saul Hansell, "A Reorganization Is Expected at America Online," *New York Times,* 6 February 1998, C1, C3; "Meet Prime Time's Hottest New Network" (advertisement), *Ad Age,* 20 April 1998, 51; Beth Snyder, "AOL's Partners Put Up Millions, Wait for Payoff," *Advertising Age,* 20 April 1998, 30; Saul Hansell, "America Online Posts Profit as Subscriber Base Surges,"*New York Times,* 7 May 1998, C2; Jared Sandberg, "AOL Swings to Profit, Beats Estimates," *Wall Street Journal,* 7 May 1998, B6; Kimberley A. Strassel, "AOL Launches New Assault in Europe by Building System of Local Alliances," *Wall Street Journal,* 27 February 1998, B9C; Jon G. Auerbach and Jared Sandberg, "America Online to Buy Stake in Boston Firm," *Wall Street Journal,* 30 April 1998, B9.

150. Leslie Heim, "Microsoft to Unite Web Sites," *Los Angeles Times,* 2 February 1998, D1, D10; Kara Swisher, "Microsoft Readies New Home Page for the Internet," *Wall Street Journal,* 3 February 1998, B7.

151. Don Clark, "Netscape Says Revenue Rose 80 Percent in Quarter," *Wall Street Journal,* 23 July 1997, B3; Kara Swisher, "Netscape Uses Browser to Beef Up Web Business," *Wall Street Journal,* 1 June 1998, B5; Kara Swisher, "Netscape Jolts Web by Allying with Excite, Inc.," *Wall Street Journal,* 5 May 1998; B1, B8; Kara Swisher, "Netscape Posts Profit, Beats Expectations," *Wall Street Journal,* 27 May 1998, A3, A10; Saul Hansell, "Excite, a Web Directory Service, in a Two-Year Deal with Netscape," *New York Times,* 5 May 1998, C1, C11; Ira Sager, Catherine Yang, Linda Himelstein, and Neil Gross, "A New Cyber Order," *Business Week,* 7 December 1998, 27–31.

152. Nicholas Denton, "Online Media Face Heavy Job Losses," *Financial Times,* 12 March 1998, 6.

153. Hunter Madsen, "Reclaim the Deadzone," *Wired,* December 1996, 206–220.

154. Jeff Harrington, "P&G's Programming Push," *USA Today,* 25 November 1996, 12B; Patricia Riedman, "ParentTime First family channel for PointCast," *Advertisting Age,* 18 August 1997, 19; Bradley Johnson, "Microsoft Exec Sounds Off on Net," *Advertising Age,* 1 September 1997, 23.

155. Wendy Goldman Rohm, "Going for Broke," *Upside,* October 1997, 120, 119.

156. Beausejour, "Branding and Bonding Beyond the Banner."

157. For an elegant and sophisticated historical elaboration of this claim, see Richard Ohman, *Selling Culture* (London: Verso, 1996).

158. Betsy Morris, "The Brand's the Thing," *Fortune,* 4 March 1996, 82. Test marketing a new product costs an average of $1 million; rolling out the new product nationally can cost over $20 million, though on average for a grocery store product upward of $5 million. Typically it takes at least three years for a new product to pay back original investment, and the failure rate is 80 to 90 percent.

159. Stephen Kreider Yoder, "Japan's Smokestack Industries Pin Hopes on Research," *Wall Street Journal,* 25 March 1987, 26; Betsy Morris, "Food Items Proliferate, Making Grocery Aisles a Corporate Battlefield," *Wall Street Journal,* 17 August 1984, 1, 6.

160. Dana Canedy, "Where Nothing Lasts Forever," *New York Times,* 24 April 1998, C1, C3.

161. "Introducing Advertising and Marketing," *Los Angeles Times,* 4 September 1997, D1.

162. Brian Lowry, "ABC Abruptly Pulls the Plug on *The Dana Carvey Show,*" *Los Angeles Times,* 7 May 1996, D6.

163. C. Bruce Knecht, "Magazine Advertisers Demand Prior Notice of 'Offensive' Articles," *Wall Street Journal,* 30 April 1997, A1, A9; Robin Pogrebin, "Magazine Publishers Circling Wagons Against Advertisers," *New York Times,* 29 September 1997, C1, C6.

164. G. Bruce Knecht, "Magazine Publishers, Editors Take Stand Against Advance Disclosure," *Wall Street Journal,* 24 September 1997, B10.

165. B. Bruce Knecht, "Chrysler Drops Its Demand for Early Look at Magazines," *Wall Street Journal,* 15 October 1997, B1, B17.

166. Michael Schudson, "A Lot More Apologies Are in Order," *Los Angeles Times,* 30 August 1995, B9; Mark Landler, "ABC News Settles Suits on Tobacco," *New York Times,* 22 August 1995, A1, C6.

167. G. Bruce Knecht, "Vanity Fair Guide Raises Selection Issues," *Wall Street Journal,* 22 August 1997, B10.

168. Russ Baker, "The Squeeze," *Columbia Journalism Review* (September-October 1997): 30–36.

169. Robin Pogrebin, "Magazine Marketing Raises Question of Editorial Independence," *New York Times,* 4 May 1998, C1, C9.

170. Chuck Ross, "History Channel Signs Up Marketers as Co-producers," *Advertising Age,* 27 May 1996, 16; Sally Goll Beatty, "History Channel Blurs the Line with Sponsors," *Wall Street Journal,* 3 June 1996, B1, B4.

171. James Sterngold, "A Growing Clash of Visions at the *Los Angeles Times*," *New York Times*, 13 October 1997, 1, 8; Peter Gumbel and Frederick Rose, "*Times Mirror* Carves Out New Beat for Flagship Paper," *Wall Street Journal*, 13 October 1997, B4; David Shaw, "Cooperation Within *Times* Viewed with Trepidation," *Los Angeles Times*, 30 March 1998, A1, A10; David Shaw, "An Uneasy Alliance of News and Ads," *Los Angeles Times*, 29 March 1998, A1, A28.

172. Doug Underwood, "It's Not Just in L.A.," *Columbia Journalism Review* (January-February): 1998, 24–27.

173. Bill Carter, "In About-Face, NBC Is Marketing Its Wares with Toll-Free Number," *New York Times*, 1 May 1998, A1, C4.

174. Marla Matzer, "More Film Directors Finding a Spot in TV Ads," *Los Angeles Times*, 12 March 1998, D1, D5.

175. Diane Seo, "Ads Using Alternative Music to Grab Trendy Youth," *Los Angeles Times*, 7 May 1998, D1, D4.

176. Jeff Harrington, "P&G's Programming Push," *USA Today*, 25 November 1996, 12B; Patrick M. Reilly, "Virginia Slims Gets Its Own Record Label," *Wall Street Journal*, 15 January 1997, B1, B2; Patrick M. Reilly, "*Times* Are a-Changin'; Rockers Do Industry Gigs," *Wall Street Journal*, 28 April 1997, B1, B3.

177. Suein L. Hwang and John Lippman, "Hollywood to Antismoking Activists: Butt Out," *Wall Street Journal*, 17 March 1998, B1, B8.

178. Carol Marie Cropper, "Fruit to Walls to Floor, Ads Are on the March," *New York Times*, 26 February 1998, A1, C8; "Cosmonauts on Mir Become QVC Pitchmen," *Los Angeles Times*, 8 February 1998, A8.

179. "Industry Spotlight: Advertising," *Industry Standard*, 29 June 1998, 47.

180. "Digits," *Wall Street Journal*, 26 March 1998, B6.

181. For those wishing to learn more about the role of advertising in television itself, check out Erik Barnouw's classic book, *The Sponsor* (New York: Oxford University Press, 1978).

182. Sreenatj Sreemovassan, "Web Retailers Finding Allies at Sites with Nothing to Sell," *New York Times*, 14 April 1997, C4.

183. Robert W. McChesney, *Telecommunications, Mass Media and Democracy* (New York: Oxford University Press, 1993).

184. Rebecca Quick, "Measures to Rid Cyberspace of 'Spam' Run into Snags," *Wall Street Journal*, 18 May 1998, B1, B10.

185. Thomas S. Mulligan, "Match Proves Internet Can Be King," *Los Angeles Times*, 15 May 1997, D1, D5.

186. Elizabeth Lesly and Robert D. Hof, with Peter Elstrom, Amy Cortese, and Amy Barrett, "Is Digital Convergence for Real?" *Business Week*, 23 June 1997, 42–43.

187. "TCI's Malone Seeks Summit with Agencies," *Advertising Age*, 18 May 1998, 11–12.

188. John Andrews, "The World of Sport," *Economist,* 6 June 1998, S14.

189. Thomas S. Mulligan, "Media Firms Find Winning Strategy in Owning Teams," *Los Angeles Times,* 21 March 1998, A1, A19; Ronald Grover, "Online Sports: Cyber Fans Are Roaring," *Business Week,* 1 June 1998, 155; Johanna Bennett, "Golfers Go for Green in On-Line Game Based on Pro Tour," *Wall Street Journal,* 20 February 1998, B9A.

190. Richard Tedesco, "Microsoft Speeds Toward Oblivion," *Broadcasting and Cable,* 1 June 1998, 38.

191. Dean Takahashi, "Can Riven, Sequel to Myst, Live up to Expectations?" *Wall Street Journal,* 25 August 1997, B1.

192. Stuart Elliott, "Advertising," *New York Times,* 1 June 1998, C12.

193. Stefan Fatsis, "NFL Raises Price to ESPN to Build Its Internet Site," *Wall Street Journal,* 27 May 1998, B9.

194. Dean Takahashi, "Internet Transforms the Way PC Games Are Developed," *Wall Street Journal,* 19 June 1997, B4; Mark Hyman, "Do You Love the Orioles and Live in L.A.?" *Business Week,* 12 May 1997, 108; Tish Williams, "If They Build It, Will Mom Come?" *Upside,* October 1997, 109–113, 134–139; also see Karen Kaplan, "The Digital Fan," *Los Angeles Times,* 7 July 1997, D1, D8; "Today, of All Days, IBM Is Staging a Public Demonstration of E-Business. Are we nuts?" (advertisement), *Los Angeles Times,* 25 January 1998, A11; Stephen H. Wildstrom, "Super Bowl Loser? The Web," *Business Week,* 9 February 1998, 23.

195. Jane Greenstein, "Advertisers Still Trying to Get a Line on Net Users," *Los Angeles Times,* 2 December 1996, D5; Seth Schiesel, "Payoff Still Elusive in Internet Gold Rush," *New York Times,* 2 January 1997, C17.

196. Peter C.T. Elsworth, "Internet Advertising Growing Slowly," *New York Times,* 24 February 1997, C5.

197. Kate Maddox, "Internet Ad Sales Approach $1 Billion," *Advertising Age,* 6 April 1998, 32, 34; Robert J. Coen, "Ad Revenue Growth Hits 7 Percent in 1997 to Surpass Forecasts," *Advertising Age,* 18 May 1998, 50.

198. Bradley Johnson, "Microsoft Web Ad Spending to Explode," *Advertising Age,* 11 August 1997, 1, 27.

199. Linda Himelstein, Ellen Neuborne, and Paul M. Eng, "Web Ads Start to Click," *Business Week,* 6 October 1997, 128–138.

200. Jared Sandberg, "Retailers Pay Big for Prime Internet Real Estate," *Wall Street Journal,* 8 July 1997, B1, B6.

201. Joelle Tessler, "Advertising Is Driving Growth at Internet Firms," *Wall Street Journal,* 6 October 1997, B11A; Himelstein, Neuborne, and Eng, "Web Ads Start to Click," 128.

202. Sheila Muto, "Web Firms Start Tussling as L.A. Market Heats Up," *Wall Street Journal,* 18 March 1998, CA1.

203. Robert H. Reid, *Architects of the Web* (New York: Wiley, 1997), 236–237.

204. Kate Maddox, "Jupiter Unveils Brand Action Marketing Plan," *Advertising Age,* 12 January 1998, 24.

205. Ellen Neuborne, "Saatchi Takes the Net Plunge," *Business Week,* 6 October 1997, 138.

206. Kate Maddox, "Information Still Killer App on the Internet," *Advertising Age,* 6 October 1997, 42, 48.

207. Kate Maddox, "Don't Push It, Say Users and Web Marketers," *Advertising Age,* 10 November 1997, S1, S3; Maddox, "Jupiter Unveils Brand Action Marketing Plan," 24.

208. Beausejour, "Branding and Bonding Beyond the Banner," 3.

209. Maddox, "Internet Ad Sales Approach $1 Billion," 32, 34.

210. Joseph Turow, *Breaking Up America: Advertisers and the New Media World* (Chicago: University of Chicago Press, 1997), 137; Richard P. Adler, *The Future of Advertising: New Approaches to the Attention Economy* (Washington, D.C.: Aspen Institute, 1997).

211. Sir Michael Perry, Chairman, Unilever, "Advertising: The Link in the Chain of Supply and Demand," *International Advertising Association Perspectives,* February 1996, 2.

212. Reid, *Architects of the Web,* xliv, 213–214.

213. "Digits," *Wall Street Journal,* 9 April 1998, B6.

214. Don Clark, "Facing Early Losses, Some Web Publishers Begin to Pull the Plug," *Wall Street Journal,* 14 January 1997, A1, A9; Seth Schiesel, "Web Publishers Start to Feel Lack of Advertising," *New York Times,* 25 March 1997, C1, 5; Tim Jackson, "War of Portals Starts Here," *Financial Times,* 9 February 1998, 9.

215. Nick Wingfield, "Publications Aimed at On-Line Users Face Shakeout After a Two-Year Boom," *Wall Street Journal,* 15 August 1997, A9A.

216. John Geirland and Eva Sonesh-Kedar, "PointCast Chief Describes the Pull of 'Push' Media," *Los Angeles Times,* 6 April 1998, D3, D4.

217. Thomas E. Weber, "Web Sites Say: Your Ads Sells or It's on Us," *Wall Street Journal,* 27 June 1997, B5; Thomas E. Weber, "Red Flags from Leading Web-Ad Seller," *Wall Street Journal,* 18 December 1997, B1, B4; Diane Seo, "DoubleClick Sees Commercial Potential on Web," *Los Angeles Times,* 26 March 1998, D5, D13.

218. "Advertising on the Internet Number Four" (advertisement), *Red Herring,* September 1997, 51; David Bank, "Venture Capitalists Open Their Wallets for the Internet," *Wall Street Journal,* 22 August 1997, B5.

219. Robert D. Hof, with Seanna Browder and Peter Elstrom, "Internet Communities," *Business Week,* 5 May 1997, 64–85.

220. Bernhard Warner, "Web-Bound Electronic Arts: It's in the Net," *Ad Week,* 12 May 1997, 52.

221. Lisa Bransten, "Companies Are Talking Up Chat Rooms as Way to Improve Customer Service," *Wall Street Journal,* 15 December 1997, B9B; Jennifer Oldham, "Small Talk, Big Results," *Los Angeles Times,* 1 June 1998, D1, D6.

222. Bob Herbold, "If You're Constantly Changing, How Can People Be Sure It's Still You?" (advertisement), *Wall Street Journal,* 10 June 1998, CA6.

223. Herbold, "If You're Constantly Changing," CA6.

224. Edward S. Herman and Robert McChesney, *The Global Media* (London: Cassell, 1997).

225. "—D" (advertisement), *New York Times,* 27 January 1997, A7; Eleanor Randolph, "*New York Times* Aims Beyond Its Home Base," *Los Angeles Times,* 15 June 1997, A18-A20.

226. Louise Kehoe and Nick Denton, "Accidental Advertising Campaigns," *Financial Times,* 17 October 1997, 12.

227. Linda Himelstein, Ellen Neuborne, and Paul M. Eng, "Web Ads Start to Click," *Business Week,* 6 October 1997, 134; Kimberley A. Strassel, "Swedish Search Engine Firm Powers Ahead," *Wall Street Journal Europe,* 18–19 April 1997, 4; "A Lycos-Bertelsmann European Venture," *New York Times,* 13 May 1997, C21.

228. Bradley Johnson, "IDG to Launch Giant Tech Site," *Advertising Age,* 9 June 1997, 38.

229. "Hi Ho, Hi Ho, Down the Data Mine We Go," *Economist,* 23 August 1997, 47.

230. Christina Binkley, "Harrah's Builds Database About Patrons," *Wall Street Journal,* 2 September 1997, B1, B10.

231. Kyle Pope and Leslie Cauley, "In Battle for TV Ads, Cable Is Now the Enemy," *Wall Street Journal,* 6 May 1998, B1, B13; Robert J. Coen, "Ad Spending Tops $175 Billion During Robust '96," *Advertising Age,* 12 May 1997, 20; Robert J. Coen, "Ad Revenue Growth Hits 7 Percent in 1997 to Surpass Forecasts," *Advertising Age,* 18 May 1998, 50.

232. "Hi Ho, Hi Ho, Down the Data Mine We Go," 47.

233. Turow, *Breaking Up America,* 153.

234. Yumiko Ono, "Kraft Foods, TCI Plan to Target Cable-TV Ads to Specific Viewers," *Wall Street Journal,* 5 February 1998, B10.

235. Andrew Ross Sorkin, "Targeted Advertising on *Times* Web Site," *New York Times,* 14 July 1997, C12.

236. Rebecca Quick, "Don't Expect Your Secrets to Get Kept on the Internet: Privacy Is Always at Risk as You Surf," *Wall Street Journal,* 6 February 1998, B5; Peter H. Lewis, "Forget Big Brother," *New York Times,* 19 March 1998, D1, D6; Ira Teinowitz, "FTC Study Gives Fuel for Backers of Internet Regs,"

Advertising Age, 18 May 1998, 61; Amy Harmon, "FTC to Propose Laws to Protect Children on Line," *New York Times,* 4 June 1998, C1, C6.

237. Alice Z. Cuneo, "Advertisers Target Women, but Market Remains Elusive," *Advertising Age,* 10 November 1997, 1, 24, 26.

238. "InterViews," *Advertising Age,* 13 March 1995, S-26.

239. Steve Lohr, "It Takes a Child to Raze a Village," *New York Times,* 5 March 1998, D1, D7.

240. Bill Carter, "A Top Female Executive Leaves Disney/ABC," *New York Times,* 29 May 1998, C5.

241. Andrew Kantor and Michael Neubarth, "Off the Charts: The Internet 1996," *Internet World,* December 1996, 44–51; Beth Snyder, "New Networks, Site Upgrades Target Women," *Ad Age,* 15 September 1997, 52; Peter Clemente, *The State of the Net* (New York: McGraw-Hill, 1998), 53, 57–60; Amy Harmon, "Guess Who's Going On Line," *New York Times,* 26 March 1998, D1, D7; Tim Race, "Building Girls Cyber Rooms of Their Own," *New York Times,* 5 March 1998, D3.

242. Beausejour, "Branding and Bonding Beyond the Banner," 2.

243. "Women on the Web, We've Captured Their Attention" (advertisement), *Ad Week,* 18 August 1997, Interactive Quarterly, 7.

244. Don Clark, "Microsoft's On-Line Service Goes to a TV Format," *Wall Street Journal,* 9 December 1996, B7.

245. Patricia Rieman, "Women's Forum Debuts Female Ad Network," *Advertising Age,* 11 August 1997, 18.

246. "Where to Find Her Online" (advertisement), *Ad Week,* 18 August 1997, Interactive Quarterly, 21.

247. Alice Z. Cuneo, "Levi Strauss Sponsors Splam Site in Effort to Target Girls," *Advertising Age,* 1 September 1997, 25.

248. Bradley Johnson, "Microsoft Exec Sounds Off on Net," *Advertising Age,* 1 Sept 1997, 23; Beth Snyder, "New Networks, Site Upgrades Target Women," *Advertising Age,* 15 September 1997, 52.

249. Jack Neff, "P&G Reaches Out to Women At Work," *Advertising Age,* 10 November 1997, S4.

250. Cuneo, "Advertisers Target Women, but Market Remains Elusive," 26.

251. "Hi Ho, Hi Ho, Down the Data Mine We Go," 47.

252. Oscar Gandy, *The Panoptic Sort.* (Boulder: Westview, 1996).

253. David Leonhardt, "Two-Tier Marketing," *Business Week,* 17 March 1997, 82, 87. See also Herbert I. Schiller, *Information Inequality* (New York: Routledge, 1996).

254. Terry Pristin, "When Revenues Don't Match Ratings," *New York Times,* 18 May 1998, C7.

255. Robin Pogrebin, "A *Mademoiselle* for the Senorita Set Gives Its Readers Practical Information," *New York Times*, 6 November 1996, A23.

256. James Katz and Philip Aspden, "Motivations and Barriers to Internet Usage: Results of a National Public Opinion Survey," Manuscript, 25 February 1997; Robert Lee Hotz, "Study Finds Racial Divide Among Internet Users," *Los Angeles Times*, 17 April 1998, A26; Amy Harmon, "Blacks Found to Trail Whites in Cyberspace," *New York Times*, 17 April 1998, A1, A18; National Telecommunications and Information Administration, "Falling Through The Net II: New Data on The Digital Divide." Washington, D.C.: U.S. Department of Commerce, 28 July 1998.

Chapter 4

1. U.S. Congress, Office of Technology Assessment, *Informational Technology and Its Impact on American Higher Education*, OTA-CIT–187 (Washington, D.C.: USGPO, November 1982), 69.

2. Jacques Attali, "School the Day After Tomorrow," *New Perspectives Quarterly* 14, no. 2 (Spring 1997): 24.

3. *The Fourth Revolution: Instructional Technology in Higher Education. A Report and Recommendations by the Carnegie Commission on Higher Education* (New York: McGraw-Hill, 1972), 94.

4. Joan O'C. Hamilton and Heidi Dawley, "Welcome to the World Wide Lab," *Business Week*, 30 October 1995, 66–67.

5. Committee on Issues in the Transborder Flow of Scientific Data, U.S. National Committee for CODATA, National Research Council, *Bits of Power: Issues in Global Access to Scientific Data* (Washington, D.C.: National Academy Press, 1997), 31.

6. Thomas J. DeLoughry, "An Upheaval in the Structure of the Internet," *Chronicle of Higher Education*, 20 January 1995, A19, A20.

7. David L. Wilson, "Traffic Jams Are Decreasing the Internet's Usefulness, Say Many in Higher Education," *Chronicle of Higher Education*, 11 October 1996, A30–A31; Committee on Issues, *Bits of Power*, 36.

8. Eric Hobsbawm, *The Age of Empire, 1875–1914* (New York: Pantheon, 1987), 345, table 5.

9. Frank A. Vanderlip, *Business and Education* (New York: Duffield, 1907), 6, 10–11, argued in 1905 for creation of "a great central fund," whose "mighty impress" would induce "co-ordination of our whole system of higher education" so as to improve its "efficiency."

10. David Smith, *Who Rules the University?* (New York: Monthly Review, 1974); Laurence Veysey, *The Emergence of the American University* (Chicago: University of Chicago Press, 1965); Richard Hofstadter and C. DeWitt Hardy, *The Development and Scope of Higher Education in the United States* (New

York: Columbia University Press, 1952); Michael B. Katz, *Reconstructing American Education.* Cambridge: Harvard, 1987, 160–183; David Nasaw, *Schooled to Order* (New York: Oxford, 1979); Roger L. Geiger, *To Advance Knowledge: The Growth of American Research Universities, 1900–1940* (New York: Oxford University Press, 1986).

11. Clark Kerr, *The Uses of the University*, 3d ed. (Cambridge: Harvard University Press, 1982), 154.

12. Ira Shor, *Culture Wars: School and Society in the Conservative Restoration 1969–1984* (Boston: Routledge & Kegan Paul, 1986), 44; Arthur M. Cohen and Florence Brawer, *The American Community College* (San Francisco: Jossey-Bass, 1982), 24; Steven Brint and Jerome Karabel, *The Diverted Dream: Community Colleges and the Promise of Educational Opportunity in America, 1900–1985* (New York: Oxford, 1989), 5–6. See also Martin Carnoy and Henry M. Levin, *Schooling and Work in the Democratic State* (Stanford: Stanford University Press, 1985).

13. Sheila Slaughter and Larry L. Leslie, *Academic Capitalism: Politics, Policies, and the Entrepreneurial University* (Baltimore: Johns Hopkins University Press, 1997).

14. Lloyd S. Steinmetz, "The History of Training," in Robert L. Craig, ed., *Training and Development Handbook*, 2d ed. (New York: McGraw-Hill, 1976), 3–14, at 6; Robert L. Craig and Christine J. Evers, "Employers as Educators: The 'Shadow Education System,' " in Gerald G. Gold, ed., *Business and Higher Education: Toward New Alliances* (San Francisco: Jossey-Bass, 1981), 34; Berenice M. Fisher, *Industrial Education: American Ideals and Institutions* (Madison: University of Wisconsin Press, 1967), 85–137, sees the rise of corporate trade education as a key weapon directed against controls over apprenticeship still exercised by organized labor, a view echoed in I. Shor, *Culture Wars*, 45–47.

15. Craig and Evers, "Employers as Educators."

16. Gregory B. Smith, "Employer-Sponsored Programs of Recurrent Education," *Education and Urban Society* 14, no. 3 (May 1982): 301–329, at 302–304. Some corporate education also grew directly from wartime production needs, at Northrup and General Motors, for example. Nell Eurich, *Corporate Classrooms: The Learning Business* (Princeton: Carnegie Foundation for the Advancement of Teaching, Princeton University Press, 1985), 41.

17. Craig and Evers, "Employers as Educators," 35.

18. Steinmetz, "History of Training," 11.

19. Steinmetz, "History of Training," 12.

20. Steinmetz, "History of Training," 13.

21. Craig, *Training and Development Handbook,* xiii (original emphasis).

22. Lewis M. Branscomb and Paul C. Gilmore, "Education in Private Industry," *Daedalus* 104 (1975): 222–233, at 223–224, offer a cogent analysis; see also Ray S. Abu Zayyad, "The Right People at the Right Time," *Training and Development Journal* 39 (September 1985): 14, 18.

23. Andrew Pollack, "IBM: A Giant Among Giants in the Classroom as Well," *New York Times*, 30 August 1981, Survey of Continuing Education, sec. 12, pp. 20–21; Abu Zayyad, "The Right People," 14.

24. Craig and Evers, "Employers as Educators," 30; Gene I. Maeroff, "Business Is Cutting into the Market," *New York Times*, 30 August 1981, l; Beverly T. Watkins, "Higher Education Now Big Business for Big Business," *Chronicle of Higher Education*, 13 April 1983, 1; "Retraining Displaced Workers: Too Little, Too Late?" *Business Week*, 19 July 1982, 183.

25. Watkins, "Higher Education Now Big Business," 1.

26. Craig and Evers, "Employers as Educators," 30; "Change in America," *Chronicle of Higher Education*, 17 September 1986, 1.

27. Arthur J. Oettmeier, in Cheryl M. Fields, "Education 'Brokers' Are Helping Two-Year Colleges Train Workers to Fill Needs of Local Businesses," *Chronicle of Higher Education*, 11 March 1987, 30.

28. Laura Landro, "GE's Wizards Turning from the Bottom Line to Share of the Market," *Wall Street Journal*, 12 July 1982, 1, 12.

29. John J. McGarraghy and Kevin P. Reilly, "College Credit for Corporate Training," in Gold, *Business and Higher Education*, 85–96 at 88–89.

30. Kate Murphy, "Pitfalls versus Promise in Training by CD-ROM," *New York Times*, 6 May 1996, C3; Charles Bermant, "For the Latest in Corporate Training, Try a CD-ROM," *New York Times*, 16 October 1995, C5.

31. Nell P. Eurich, *The Learning Industry: Education for Adult Workers* (Princeton: Carnegie Foundation for the Advancement of Teaching, 1990), 87–88, 94.

32. Watkins, "Higher Education Now Big Business."

33. "1998 Survey of Corporate University Future Directions: Corporate Universities Transform Management Education," *Corporate Universities International* 4, no. 1 (January-February 1998): 1.

34. Jeanne C. Meister, *Corporate Universities: Lessons in Building a World-Class Work Force*, rev. ed. (New York: McGraw-Hill, 1998), 255–262, xi.

35. John Authors, "Motorola Leads the Way in the Corporate University Sector," *Financial Times*, 18 June 1998, 7.

36. Lionel V. Baldwin, "Instructional Television," *IEEE Spectrum*, (November 1984), 114; Eurich, *Learning Industry*, 166, 193.

37. Eurich, *Learning Industry*, 218.

38. Eurich, *Corporate Classrooms*, 98.

39. Peter David, "The Knowledge Factory: A Survey of Universities," *Economist*, 4 October 1997, 19.

40. Eurich, *Learning Industry*, 215; Stan Davis and Jim Botkin, *The Monster Under the Bed* (New York: Simon & Schuster, 1994), 129.

41. Ray Marshall and Marc Tucker, *Thinking for a Living: Education and the Wealth of Nations* (New York: Basic Books, 1992), 51.

42. Shuichi Hayashi, "NEC: Focus Overseas," *Journal of Japanese Trade and Industry,* no. 5, (1991): 12–13; see also Kaoru Kobayashi, "Corporate In-house Education," *Journal of Japanese Trade and Industry,* no. 5 (1991), 8–12.

43. Kenta Mnuakata, "Fuji Xerox: Marketing Know-How," *Japanese Journal of Trade and Industry,* no. 5 (1991), 16–17.

44. David, "The Knowledge Factory," 19.

45. "Home-Made Universities," *Financial Times,* 6 October 1997, 11.

46. Eurich, *Learning Industry,* 18; Craig and Evers, "Employers as Educators," 31; Harold L. Hodgkinson, "Preface," in Gold, *Business and Higher Education,* 1–2; Business–Higher Education Forum, "The Chairman's Report 1984–1986," Washington, D.C., n.d., 22; U.S. Department of Commerce, *1987 U.S. Industrial Outlook* (Washington, D.C.: USGPO, January 1987), 62–63.

47. Eurich, *Learning Industry,* 18, 35.

48. Eurich, *Corporate Classrooms,* 52; Howard R. Bowen and Jack H. Schuster, *American Professors: A National Resource Imperiled* (New York: Oxford University Press, 1986), 13; by 1992, there were 528,000 full-time U.S. faculty members and 376,400 part-timers. Jack H. Schuster, "Reconfiguring the Professoriate: An Overview," *Academe* (January-February 1998), 49.

49. http://www.astd.org/who/research/benchmar/96stats/graph13.gif.

50. Victoria Griffith, "Firm Approach to Education," *Financial Times,* 29 May 1998, 22.

51. Gerald G. Gold, "Toward Business-Higher Education Alliances," in Gold, *Business and Higher Education,* 9; Hodgkinson, "Preface."

52. Maeroff, "Business Is Cutting into the Market," 19; Kenneth B. Noble, "The Corporate Halls of Ivy Grow," Survey of Continuing Education, *New York Times,* 30 August 1981, 21.

53. Watkins, "Higher Education Now Big Business," 6.

54. Davis and Botkin, *Monster Under the Bed,* 147.

55. Kelly McCollum, "Accreditors Urged to Prepare for Distance Learning," *Chronicle of Higher Education,* 15 May 1998, A34.

56. Gary W. Peterson and Robert G. Stakenas, "Performance-Based Education," *Journal of Higher Education* 52, no. 4 (July-August 1981): 352–368, at 356; "Bennett Calls on Colleges to Assess Their Own Performance, Publish Results," *Chronicle of Higher Education,* 6 November 1985, 25.

57. "How Business Is Joining the Fight Against Functional Illiteracy," *Business Week,* 16 April 1984: 94, 98; Maeroff, "Business Is Cutting into the Market," 19; Newt Gingrich, *To Renew America* (New York: HarperCollins, 1995), 142.

58. Gingrich, *To Renew America,* 143.

59. Craig and Evers, "Employers as Educators," 36.

60. Eurich, *Learning Industry,* 137, 159.

61. U.S. Department of Commerce, Bureau of the Census, *Statistical Abstract of the U.S., 1990* (Washington, D.C.: USGPO, 1991), 582; Bernard Wysocki, Jr., "As Innovation Revives, Some See Complacency," *Wall Street Journal,* 23 March 1998, A1.

62. James P. Miller, "R&D Budgets to Rise 4.66 Percent in 1998, Continuing Change from Flat Outlays," *Wall Street Journal,* 30 December 1997, A2; Louis Uchitelle, "Companies Reported Spending More on Research," *New York Times,* 7 November 1997, C8.

63. Elyse Tanouye and Robert Langreth, "Cost of Drug Research Is Driving Merger Talks of Glaxo, SmithKline," *Wall Street Journal,* 2 February 1998, A1, A8; Wysocki, "As Innovation Revives."

64. Raju Narisetti, "Xerox Files Suit Against H-P Over Patent," *Wall Street Journal,* 15 May 1998, B6; Raju Narisetti, "IBM Wins 1,724 Patents for No. One Spot on '97 List, but Fruits of R&D Fall 8 Percent," *Wall Street Journal,* 12 January 1998, B14.

65. Clive Cookson, "The R&D Scoreboard: Advantages to the Scientists," *Financial Times,* 25 June 1998, 13.

66. Andrew C. Revkin, "Victor Mills Is Dead at 100; Father of Disposable Diapers," *New York Times,* 7 November 1997, A15.

67. Ronald Alsop, "Business Bulletin," *Wall Street Journal,* 15 January 1998, A1.

68. Betsy Morris, "The Brand's the Thing," *Fortune,* 4 March 1996, 82. See David Harvey, *The Limits to Capital.* (Oxford: Basil Blackwell, 1982), 119–125.

69. Eurich, *Learning Industry,* 195.

70. Michael Useem, "Corporate Education and Training," in Carl Kaysen, ed., *The American Corporation Today* (Oxford: Oxford University Press, 1996), 292–326.

71. Tessa Morris-Suzuki, "Robots and Capitalism," *New Left Review,* 147 Sept/Oct 1984, 120; for amplification, see Jim Davis, Thomas Hirschl, and Michael Stack, eds., *Cutting Edge: Technology, Information, Capitalism and Social Revolution* (London: Verso, 1997).

72. "Training: A Built-In Market Worth Billions," *Business Week,* 1 November 1982, 84–85; Catalog of Professional Development Seminars, Institute for Advanced Technology, Control Data Corporation, January 1985 through June 1985, advertising brochure; Institute for Communications and Information Management, brochure, n.p. n.d.

73. David Bank, "Microsoft Emphasizes Its Role as a Partner at Comdex," *Wall Street Journal,* 19 November 1997, B4.

74. Drew Cullen, "Users Face Training Costs Dilemma," *Communications Week International,* 22 September 1997, 10.

75. Eurich, *Learning Industry,* 29.

76. Control Data Corporation, "Author System," brochure, 1983.

77. Eurich, *Corporate Classrooms*, 135.

78. Branscomb and Gilmore, "Education in Private Industry," 228.

79. Eurich, *Corporate Classrooms*, 135.

80. Eurich, *Learning Industry*, 5, 8.

81. Gingrich, *To Renew America*, 145.

82. James Flanigan, "More Than Credits Needed for Colleges," *Los Angeles Times*, 31 August 1997, D1, D12.

83. Keith H. Hammonds, Susan Jackson, Gail DeGeorge, and Kathleen Morris, "The New U," *Business Week*, 22 December 1997, 97.

84. Peter Schmidt, "State Appropriations for Colleges Increase at Highest Rate Since 1990," *Chronicle of Higher Education*, 14 November 1997, A30–A31; Peter Schmidt, "More Money for Public Higher Education," *Chronicle of Higher Education*, 12 June 1998, A30.

85. Normon Solomon, "What's Out of the Question for Debates," *Creators Syndicate*, 26 September 1996; Hammonds, Jackson, DeGeorge, and Morris, "The New U," 97.

86. "Tuition Is Up, and So Is Family Debt," *Financial Times on Campus*, November 1997, 3.

87. "More High School Grads Are Going to College," *Financial Times on Campus*, November 1997, 2.

88. Arthur Levine, "How the Academic Profession Is Changing," *Daedalus* 126, no. 4 (Fall 1997): 6.

89. Business Higher Education Forum, "1986 Chairman's Report."

90. Peter Applebome, "A Corporate Agenda," *New York Times*, 28 March 1996, A11.

91. David, "The Knowledge Factory," 12, 16.

92. Goldie Blumenstyk, "Conflict-of-Interest Fears Rise as Universities Chase Industry Support," *Chronicle of Higher Education*, 22 May 1998, A41–A43.

93. Richard Waters, "Academic Frustrations," *Financial Times*, 18 November 1997, 27.

94. Davis and Botkin, *Monster Under the Bed*, 150; Robert Cwiklik, "Ivory Tower Inc.: When Research and Lobbying Mesh," *Wall Street Journal*, 9 June 1998, B1, B13.

95. David, "The Knowledge Factory," 19.

96. Michael Schrage, "To All Ph.D.s: A Fifty-Cent Dollar for Your Thoughts," *Los Angeles Times*, 23 November 1997, D4.

97. "UC Tallies License Revenues," *San Diego Union-Tribune*, 4 April 1998, C2; Robert Ovetz, "Turning Resistance into Rebellion: Student Movements and the Entrepreneurialization of the Universities," *Capital and Class*, no. 58 (Spring

1996): 113–152; Bruce V. Bigelow, "UC Leads in Royalty Race," *San Diego Union-Tribune,* 9 February 1996, C1, C3; Paul Jacobs, "UC Relishes Power of the Patent," *Los Angeles Times,* 14 February 1996, A1, A23. On the general subject, see David Dickson, *The New Politics of Science* (New York: Pantheon, 1984).

98. Goldie Blumenstock, "High-Stakes Patent Fight Features Big Money, Cancer Research, Politics, and Public Relations," *Chronicle of Higher Education,* 27 June 1997, A37–39; Goldie Blumenstock, "Arizona Patent Policy Aims to Spur Collaboration with Businesses," *Chronicle of Higher Education,* 16 August 1996, A34.

99. Martin Kenney, *Biotechnology: The University-Industrial Complex* (New Haven: Yale University Press, 1986). Also see Thomas W. Langfitt, Sheldon Hackney, Alfred P. Fishman, and Albert V. Glowasky, *Partners in the Research Enterprise: University Corporate Relations in Science and Technology* (Philadelphia: University of Pennsylvania Press, 1983).

100. Paulette Walker Campbell, "Pacts Between Universities and Companies Worry Federal Officials," *Chronicle of Higher Education,* 15 May 1998, A37; Blumenstock, "Conflict-of-Interest Fears Rise," A41.

101. Lawrence K. Altman, "Secrecy Hurting Research, Official Says," *New York Times,* 10 February 1996, 7.

102. Cwiklik, "Ivory Tower Inc."

103. George Keller, *Academic Strategy: The Management Revolution in American Higher Education* (Baltimore: Johns Hopkins University Press, 1983), 121.

104. Office of Technology Assessment, *Informational Technology,* 20.

105. Richard Attiyeh, "A New Look at the Economics of Higher Education," *Minerva* 11, no. 3 (July 1973): 341.

106. Marshall and Tucker, *Thinking for a Living,* xvi.

107. "Campus Research Funds Will Now Come from UC Patents," *Notice,* Publication of the Academic Senate, University of California, 22, no. 2 (November 1997): 2.

108. Alison Schneider, "Recruiting Academic Stars: New Tactics in an Old Game," *Chronicle of Higher Education,* 29 May 1998, A12–A14; Victoria Griffith, "Staff Find Halls of Academe Are Paved With Gold—but Only for the Star Performers," *Financial Times,* 3 June 1998, 4.

109. Griffith, "Staff Finds Halls of Academe."

110. Courtney Leatherman, "Growing Use of Part-Time Professors Prompts Debate and Calls for Action," *Chronicle of Higher Education,* 10 October 1997, A14.

111. Courtney Leatherman, "Do Accreditors Look the Other Way When Colleges Rely on Part-Timers?" *Chronicle of Higher Education,* 7 November 1997, A12–A14.

112. Robin Wilson, "Contracts Replace the Tenure Track for a Growing Number of Professors," *Chronicle of Higher Education,* 12 June 1998, A12.

113. William Zumeta, "Anatomy of the Boom in Postdoctoral Appointments During the 1970s: Troubling Implications for Quality Science?" *Science, Technology, and Human Values* 9 no. 2 (1984): 23–37; Judith M. Gappa, *Part-Time Faculty: Higher Education at a Crossroads,* ASHE-ERIC Higher Education Research Report No. 3 (Washington, D.C.: Association for the Study of Higher Education, 1984); Alison Schneider, "Universities Urged to Improve Quality of Postdoctoral Education," *Chronicle of Higher Education,* 29 May 1998, A14; Denise K. Magner, " 'Postdocs,' Seeing Little Way into the Academic Job Market, Seek Better Terms in the Lab," *Chronicle of Higher Education,* 7 August 1998, A10–A12.

114. Peter Schmidt, "Govenors Want Fundamental Changes in Colleges, Question Place of Tenure," *Chronicle of Higher Education,* 19 June 1998, A38.

115. Jack H. Schuster, "Reconfiguring the Professoriate: An Overview," *Academe* (January-February 1998): 48–53.

116. Emily M. Bernstein, "SUNY Trustees Proposing Sliding Scale for Tuitions," *New York Times,* 22 November 1995, B11.

117. Karen W. Arenson, "Struggling Campuses Will Try Off-Peak Pricing Experiment," *New York Times,* 28 September 1996, 1, 20.

118. See Pamela J. Tate, "Measuring Learning from Life and Work Experience," R. B. Ekstrom, ed., *Measurement, Technology, and Individuality in Education,* New Directions for Testing and Measurement, No. 17 (San Francisco: Jossey-Bass, March 1983), 55–67.

119. Jacqueline E. King, "Too Many Students Are Holding Jobs for Too Many Hours," *Chronicle of Higher Education,* 1 May 1998, A72.

120. Beverly T. Watkins, "Contracts to Provide Courses for Workers Can Be a 'Win-Win Deal,' Universities Are Learning," *Chronicle of Higher Education,* 27 June 1984, 1, 10; Daniel T. Hayes and Paul R. Heath, "Contracting with Industry for Delivery of Instruction," *Proceedings of Applying New Technologies in Higher Education Conference,* Sponsored by the Division of Continuing Education, Kansas State University, 6 (March 1982): 178–183.

121. Gold, "Toward Business–Higher-Education Alliances," 23; Shor, *Culture Wars,* 30–58.

122. Gold, "Toward Business–Higher-Education Alliances," 23–24.

123. Cheryl M. Fields, "Education 'Brokers' Are Helping Two-Year Colleges Train Workers to Fill Needs of Local Businesses," *Chronicle of Higher Education,* 11 March 1987, 30.

124. "Adult Students Flock to Classes," *Wall Street Journal,* 4 September 1997, A1.

125. Cheryl M. Fields, "Need to Retrain People," *Chronicle of Higher Education,* 17 September 1986, 39; Eurich, *Learning Industry.*

126. Thomas J. Meyer, "Fast-Food Gobblers, Here's Your Future: Turkeyburgers by Prof. Buergermeister," *Chronicle of Higher Education,* 13 August 1986, 1, 14.

127. W. Norton Grubb, "The Bandwagon Once More: Vocational Preparation for High-Tech Occupations," *Harvard Educational Review* 54, no. 4 (1984): 429–451.

128. Carnoy and Levin, *Schooling and Work,* 88.

129. Cheryl M. Fields, "Doubts Raised over Tax Break for Employer-Paid Tuition," *Chronicle of Higher Education,* 17 September 1986, 37–38.

130. *The Fourth Revolution: Instructional Technology in Higher Education,* 9.

131. Office of Technology Assessment, *Informational Technology,* iii.

132. Peter Drucker, "The Second Information Revolution," *New Perspectives Quarterly* 14, no. 2 (Spring 1997): 21.

133. Lewis M. Branscomb and Paul C. Gilmore, "Education in Private Industry," *Daedalus* 104 (1975): 231–232.

134. Jack H. Schuster, "Whither the Faculty? The Changing Academic Labor Market," *Educational Record* 76, no. 4 (Fall 1995): 28–33.

135. David F. Noble, *American by Design* (New York: Oxford, 1979); George Emmerson, *Engineering Education: A Social History* (New York: Crane, Russak, 1973), 267; Newman Hall, ed., *Britannica Review of Developments in Engineering Education* (Chicago: Encyclopedia Britannica, 1970), 70–71.

136. Phil Norgren and Aaron Warner, "Obsolescence and Updating of Engineers' and Scientists' Skills," Final Revised Report for Office of Manpower Policy, Evaluation and Research, U.S. Department of Labor, 1966; R. L. Whiting, "Continuing Education: The Key to Minimizing Obsolescence of Engineers," *Journal of Petroleum Technology* 17 (April 1965): 405–408.

137. Emmerson, *Engineering Education,* 267.

138. In Don Tapscott, *The Digital Economy: Promise and Peril in the Age of Networked Intelligence,* (New York: McGraaw. Hill, 1996), 198–99.

139. University of California Engineering Advisory Council, "An Engineering Master Plan Study for the University of California," n.p., 1965, 105; W. A. Conwell, "Continuing Education: What ASCE Is Doing," *Civil Engineering* 35 (May 1968): 32.

140. American Society for Engineering Education, "Goals of Engineering Education: Final Report of the Goals Committee," 1968, 59; D. Allison, "Engineer Renewal," *International Science and Technology* 30 (June 1964): 48–54.

141. Niels Krebs Ovesen, *Advances in the Continuing Education of Engineers,* Studies in Engineering Education 6 (Paris: UNESCO, 1980), 98.

142. Beverly Watkins, "Notes on Continuing Education," *Chronicle of Higher Education,* 23 May 1984, 3; Eurich, *Learning Industry,* 188.

143. Lionel V. Baldwin, "Instructional Television," *IEEE Spectrum,* November 1984, 108–114.

144. "MIT Adopts Stanford's Video Tutor Program," *Computerworld*, 1 November 1982, 20.

145. Baldwin, "Instructional Television," 114.

146. Marc S. Tucker, "The Turning Point: Telecommunications and Higher Education," *Journal of Communication*, 33, no. 1 (Winter 1983): 118–130, at 123.

147. Baldwin, "Instructional Television," 113.

148. Baldwin, "Instructional Television," 108.

149. Baldwin, "Instructional Television," 109; Eurich, *Learning Industry*, 196–197.

150. Eurich, *Learning Industry*, 196–197; Edward B. Fiske, "Engineers to Get Course by Satellite," *New York Times*, 5 February 1985, Cl, Cll; Lionel V. Baldwin, "A National Cooperative Program: The NTU/AMCEE Satellite Network," in Lawrence P. Grayson and Joseph M. Biedenbach, eds., *1986 World Conference on Continuing Engineering Education Proceedings, May 7–9 1986, Lake Buena Vista, Florida*, 2 vols. (n.p., n.d.), Vol. 2: 527–534.

151. Tapscott, *Digital Economy*, 211–212.

152. http://www.ntu.edu. "Institution Forms a for-Profit Company," *Chronicle of Higher Education*, 24 July 1998, A30.

153. Philip Condit and R. Byron Pipes, "The Global University," *Issues in Science and Technology* 14, no. 1 (Fall 1997): 27–28.

154. Eurich, *Corporate Classrooms*, 2, 47.

155. Eurich, *Learning Industry*, 67.

156. Eurich, *Corporate Classrooms*, 9, 50.

157. Eurich, *Corporate Classrooms*, 74.

158. Eurich, *Learning Industry*, 69.

159. Davis and Botkin, *Monster Under the Bed*, 129.

160. John A. Byrne, "Virtual B-Schools," *Business Week*, 23 October 1995, 64–68.

161. Byrne, "Virtual B-Schools," 64–68.

162. Ron Winslow, "Baylor, Williams Unit Launch Channel Offering Medical Education to Doctors," *Wall Street Journal*, 26 August 1997, B2.

163. http://www.astd.org/who/research/benchmar/96stats/graph13.gif.

164. Wendy Webb, "The New One-Room Schoolhouse," *Web Guide Magazine*, September-October 1997, 21–22.

165. Mary B.W. Tabor, "Investors Look to Education as Possibility for High Flier," *New York Times*, 29 May 1996, B8.

166. E. S. Browning, "Stocks of Education, Health, Environmental and TV Firms May Be Postelection Winners," *Wall Street Journal*, 8 November 1996, C2; Deborah Lohse, "Investors Mulling Education Stocks Hit the Books," *Wall Street Journal*, 6 September 1997, C1, C9.

167. Steven Stecklow, "Businesses Scramble to Run Charter Schools," *Wall Street Journal*, 21 August 1997, B1, B8; Michael Janofsky, "Principal's Suspension Saves a School," *New York Times*, 7 November 1997, A8.

168. Peter Applebome, "Company That Runs Schools Gets Capital," *New York Times*, 20 November 1996, B8; Peter Applebome, "For-Profit Education Venture to Expand," *New York Times*, 2 June 1997, A8.

169. "Educational Software: Why It's a Hard Sell," *Business Week*, 29 October 1984, 121–126; Andrew Pollack, "Slugging It Out on the Software Front," *New York Times*, 16 October 1983, sec. 3, pp. 1, 8; "Keeping Home Computer Owners Turned On," *Business Week*, 13 June 1983, 109; "New Learning Games Make the Grade," *Business Week*, 24 January 1983, 81.

170. Paul Desruisseaux, "Lack of Computer Programs Slows Use, Humanists Say," *Chronicle of Higher Education*, 23 February 1983, 10; see also Marilyn J. Chartrand and Constance D. Williams, *Educational Software Directory* (Littleton, Colo.: Libraries Unlimited, 1982).

171. Douglas D. Noble, "Jumping Off the Computer Bandwagon," *Education Week*, 3 October 1984, 19, 24; "Serious Software Helps the Home Computer Grow Up," *Business Week*, 11 June 1984, 114, 118; "Software: The New Driving Force," *Business Week*, 27 February 1984: 74–98; "Software Publishing and Selling," *Publishers Weekly*, 21 December 1984, 29–61; Pollack, "Slugging It Out"; William M. Bulkeley, "Computer Software for Younger Children Garners Big Share of Home Education Sales," *Wall Street Journal*, 22 August 1984: 27. Sixty percent of those purchasing computers costing over $500 had incomes over $40,000 in the early 1980s, and no less than 93 percent of home users were males, in one report. Constance Holden, "Will Home Computers Transform Schools?" *Science* 225 (20 July 1984): 296.

172. *Gulf + Western Industries, Inc., 1984 Annual Report*, 6, 10, 17, 44; *Gulf+ Western Industries, Inc., 1985 Annual Report*, 7, 21, 23; *Gulf+Western Industries, Inc., 1986 Annual Report*, 14–16, 29; Peter W. Barnes and Roger Lowenstein, "Harcourt Brace to Buy CBS's Book Division," *Wall Street Journal*, 27 October 1986, 4; *Harcourt, Brace, Jovanovich 1984 10-K Report to the SEC*, 2–7; *Harcourt, Brace, Jovanovich 1986 Annual Report*, 21–22, 52.

173. *Addison-Wesley 1984 Annual Report*, 15.

174. *John Wiley 1983 Annual Report*, 1, 5, 7, 8; *John Wiley 1984 Annual Report*, 9, 12–13; *John Wiley 1986 10-K Report to the SEC*, n.p.

175. *Macmillan Annual Report 1985*, 27, 28.

176. Denyse Forman, "Search of the Literature" *The Computing Teacher* (January 1982): 37–51, at 37; *McGraw-Hill 1983 Annual Report*, 8, 9, 20; *McGraw-Hill 1984 Annual Report*, 23–25; *McGraw-Hill 1985 Annual Report*, 15–16; *SFN 1983 Annual Report*, 2, 3, 8, 10, 12, 15, 18; SFN Co. *1984 Annual Report*, 2–4, 29–30; *SFN Co. 1985 10-K Report to the SEC*, 1–2, 5, 82–83; *Addison-Wesley 1983 Annual Report 1983*, 1, 18–19; *Addison-Wesley 1984 10-K Report to the SEC*; *Addison-Wesley 1984 Annual Report*, 15, 17; *Addison-Wesley 1985*

10-K Report to the SEC, 4–6; *Addison-Wesley 1985 Annual Report,* 2, 18, 30; Richard W. Stevenson, "Xerox to Sell Its Publishing Units," *New York Times,* 23 April 1985, D20; Laura Landro, "SFN to Sell Unit to *Time* for $520 Million," *Wall Street Journal,* 15 October 1986, 2; J. Kendrick Noble, Jr., "Book Publishing," in Benjamin Compaine, *Who Owns the Media?* 2d ed. (White Plains: Knowledge Industry Publications, 1982), 95–142, esp. 134–135.

177. *Scholastic 1983 Annual Report* 5, 13, 2; *1984 Scholastic, Inc. 10-K Report to the SEC,* 4, 7; *1985 Scholastic, Inc. 10-K Report to the SEC,* 4, 7.

178. Timothy L. O'Brien, "Scholastic Corp. Learns It's Best to Be Prepared for Class," *Wall Street Journal,* 8 July 1997, B4.

179. G. Bruce Knight, "Viacom Sets $4.6 Billion Pearson Pact," *Wall Street Journal,* 18 May 1998, A3, A8.

180. Geraldine Fabrikant, "Publishing: Why a Number of Leveraged Buyout Firms Are Now Interested in Simon & Schuster," *New York Times,* 27 April 1998, C8; G. Bruce Knight, "Five Buyers, Including Michael Milken, Consider Purchase of Simon & Schuster," *Wall Street Journal,* 21 April 1998, B24; G. Bruce Knight, "Milken's Company Believed to Be Suitor of Simon & Schuster," *Wall Street Journal,* 14 May 1998, B15; Laura Sandler, "Milken Builds a New Empire in Education," *Wall Street Journal,* 15 May 1998, C1, C2.

181. Jeffrey Selingo, "British Publisher to Buy Simon & Schuster Unit," *Chronicle of Higher Education,* 29 May 1998, A42.

182. Lawrie Mifflin, "Joint Venture Would Create New Network," *New York Times,* 29 April 1998, C1, C6.

183. Leslie Helm, "That's Edutainment," *Los Angeles Times,* 31 January 1996, D1, D4; "Computers and the Family," *Newsweek Extra,* Winter 1997, 26–51.

184. Laurence Zuckerman, "IBM to Buy Ailing Edmark for $110 Million," *New York Times,* 14 November 1996, C4.

185. Jon G. Auerbach, "Learning Co. Agrees to Buy Broderbund," *Wall Street Journal,* 23 June 1998, A3.

186. Jon G. Auerbach, "Learning Co. Keeps Getting Caught Behind the Curve," *Wall Street Journal,* 4 August 1997, B4; for Disney, see Heim, "That's Edutainment!" D1, D4.

187. http://www.wiley.com/about/corpnews/template.html.

188. William M. Bulkeley, "Back to School," *Wall Street Journal Reports Technology,* 13 November 1995, R6; Lillian Salazar Leopold, "Schools Boldly Embrace the Computer Age," *San Diego Union-Tribune,* 17 November 1997, B1, B5; Consortium for School Networking Third Annual Conference, 21 November 1997 (announcement) from owner-benton-compolicy@cdinet.com

189. Leslie Helm, "High Tech Sales Goals Fuel Reach into Schools," *Los Angeles Times,* 9 June 1997, A1, A20.

190. Victoria Griffiths, "Jobs Pins Hopes on Education Market," *Financial Times,* 7 August 1997, 12.

191. "Gateway Overtakes Apple in Education Field," *Los Angeles Times,* 21 August 1997, D2.

192. Consortium for School Networking Third Annual Conference.

193. Jay D. Geer, "Sponsoring Educational Software," *Public Relations Journal* (December 1985): 15–16.

194. Consumers Union Education Services, *Captive Kids: Commercial Pressures on Kids at School,* (New York: Consumers Union 1995), vol. 1.

195. William M. Bulkeley, "Channel One Taps Principals as Promoters," *Wall Street Journal,* 15 September 1997, B1, B10.

196. Luise Lee, "School's Back, and So Are the Marketers," *Wall Street Journal,* 15 September 1997, B1, B10.

197. Bruce Orwall, "Why Are School Kids Eating Dimitri's Fudge?" *Wall Street Journal,* 24 November 1997, B1, B10.

198. Denise Gellene, "Consumer Education," *Los Angeles Times,* 4 June 1998, D1, D6.

199. Zev Barrow, "Buyer Learning," *Spin* 12, October 1996, 38.

200. Barrow, "Buyer Learning," 38.

201. Karen Kaplan, "Teachers' Pet," *Los Angeles Times,* 3 November 1997, D6.

202. Nina J.A. Davis, "Netting a Profit," *Red Herring,* September 1996, 114–115.

203. Patricia Riedman, "College Web Ad Networks Compete for Marketers," *Advertising Age,* 20 April 1998, 34.

204. Henry M. Brickell and Carol B. Aslanian, "The Colleges and Business Competition," *New York Times* survey, 30 August 1981, 37.

205. Office of Technology Assessment, *Informational Technology, 91.*

206. http://www.devry.com/aboutinc.htm.

207. "Bell & Howell: Sharpening Its Focus on Video, Technical Schools, and Office Machines," *Business Week,* 16 April 1984, 104–105.

208. http://www.devry.com/aboutinc.htm; http://www.sec.gov/Archives/edgar/data/730464/0000950137–97–001173.txt.

209. "National Education: Trade Schools Go High Tech," *Business Week,* 4 July 1982, 85–86; *National Education Corporation 1997 10-K Report to SEC,* 22.

210. *NEC 1997 10-K,* 4–6.

211. *NEC 1997 10-K,* 8, 4, 2, 13.

212. *NEC 1997 10-K,* 22, 21.

213. U.S. Department of Commerce, *1987 U.S. Industrial Outlook* (Washington, D.C.: USGPO, January 1987), 62–66; idem., *1985 U.S. Industrial Outlook* (Washington, D.C.: USGPO, January 1985), 65–65; Nellie Henderson, "A Vocational Big Business," *New York Times,* Education Winter Survey, 9 January 1983, sect. 12, p. 8.

214. *NEC 1997 10-K*, 3, 6.

215. *Sylvan Learning Systems Inc. 1997 10-K Report to SEC*, 2, 9.

216. Amy Barrett, "Lessons for the Tutors," *Business Week*, 17 November 1997, 91, 94.

217. Richard Lee Colvin, "District Hires Tutors, Raising Questions," *Los Angeles Times*, 23 February 1998, A1, A16.

218. *Sylvan Learning 1997 10-K*, 6–7; "School Privatizers, in Retreat," *New York Times*, 12 February 1996, A12.

219. Jocelyn Y. Stewart, "Schools, Companies Team Up," *Los Angeles Times*, 14 May 1998, B1, B6.

220. *Sylvan Learning 1997 10-K*, 7.

221. *Sylvan Learning 1997 10-K*, 5, 6.

222. "Growing Market" (advertisement), *Wall Street Journal*, 28 May 1998, B14.

223. *Sylvan Learning Systems 1997 10-K*, 2–4.

224. *Sylvan Learning 1997 10-K*, 3.

225. Eurich, *Corporate Classrooms*, 130.

226. "Control Data: Is There Room for Change After Bill Norris?" *Business Week*, 17 October 1983, 121.

227. Judith Axler Turner, "Private Company to Offer 170 Courses by Computer in 'Electronic University,' " *Chronicle of Higher Education*, 21 September 1983, 18.

228. "A Wizard's Plan for an 'Electronic University,' " *Business Week*, 19 March 1984, 60; Lisa B. Stahr, "The Electronic University," *PC World*, January 1984, 248.

229. Turner, "Private Company to Offer 170 Courses," 18.

230. Stahr, "Electronic University," 248.

231. Thomas J. DeLoughry, "Reaching a 'Critical Mass,' " *Chronicle of Higher Education*, 26 January 1996, A17, A20; Thomas J. Deloughry, "Science Foundation Giving Fourty-Three Colleges Access to Its New, High-Speed Computer Network," *Chronicle of Higher Education*, 6 September 1996, A37.

232. William F. Massy and Robert Zemsky, "Using Information Technology to Enhance Academic Productivity," 1995, at http://www.educom.edu.

233. Pamela Mendels, "Report Examines How Technology May Change Higher Education," at http://www.NewYorkTimes.com/library/tech/98/05/cyber/education/27education.html.

234. Dennis Kelly, "IBM to Help Colleges Expand Cybercampuses," *USA Today*, 10 October 1996, D1. See also Melissa Lee, "Leading the Way," *Wall Street Journal Reports Technology*, 13 November 1995, R28; Kelly McCollum, "Magazine Ranks Colleges on How 'Wired' They Are; MIT Comes Out on Top," *Chronicle of Higher Education*, 25 April 1997, A24.

235. Jennifer Croshaw, "Distance Learning It's Closer Than You May Think," *San Diego Union-Tribune Computer Link,* 21 October 1997, 4, 19; Deborah Solomon, "Online Students Number 5 Million-Plus," *San Diego Union-Tribune* Computer Link, 21 October 1997, 21.

236. Lisa Guernsey, "E-Mail Is Now Used in a Third of College Courses, Survey Finds," *Chronicle of Higher Education,* 17 October 1997, A30; Reed Hundt, "Better Education @Email.com," *Wall Street Journal,* 31 March 1998, A22.

237. "On Line," *Chronicle of Higher Education,* 17 October 1997, A27.

238. Thomas J. Deloughry, "New School for Social Research Bolsters Flagging Enrollment with Ninety On-Line Courses," *Chronicle of Higher Education,* 20 September 1996, A27, A28.

239. Goldie Blumenstyk, "Some Elite Private Universities Get Serious About Distance Learning," *Chronicle of Higher Education,* 20 June 1997, A23-A24; Dellas Bradshaw, "Education On Line," *Financial Times,* 4 May 1998, 10.

240. NEA Higher Education Research Center, *Update* 4, no. 1 (February 1998), 1.

241. Jeffrey R. Young, "Wave of the Future or a Waste? UCLA Requires Web Page for Every Class," *Chronicle of Higher Education,* 1 August 1997, A21–A22; Jeffrey R. Young, "A Year of Web Pages for Every Class," *Chronicle of Higher Education,* 15 May 1998, A29-A31.

242. David Noble, "Digital Diploma Mills, Part II: The Coming Battle Over On-line Instruction," available from rre@lists.gseis.ucla.edu.

243. Todd Woody, "Higher Earning: The Fight to Control the Academy's Intellectual Capital," *Industry Standard,* 29 June 1998, 22.

244. Robert A. Gorman, "Intellectual Property: The Rights of Faculty as Creators and Users," *Academe* (May-June 1998): 14–18; M. M. Scott, "Intellectual Property Rights: A Ticking Time Bomb in Academia," *Academe* (May-June 1998): 22–26; Lisa Guernsey and Jeffrey R. Young, "Who Owns On-Line Courses?" *Chronicle of Higher Education,* 5 June 1998, A21–A23.

245. Kelly McCollum, "A New Industry Sprouts Up to Help Professors Put Courses On Line," *Chronicle of Higher Education,* 31 October 1997, A33–A34.

246. Mark Fiore, "Colleges That Hire Companies to Create Their Web Sites Face Many Tough Decisions," *Chronicle of Higher Education,* 19 September 1997, A29–A30.

247. Woody, "Higher Earning," 22.

248. Thomas J. Deloughry, "A California Company Finds Success with Computerized Mathematics Courses," *Chronicle of Higher Education,* 25 October 1996, A27–28.

249. Amy Hession, "Team Creates Electronic Law-School Materials," *Chronicle of Higher Education,* 12 January 1996, A21 William M. Bulkeley, "Kaplan Plans A Law School Via the Web," *Wall Street Journal,* 16 September 1998, B1, B16.

250. Dennis Kelly, "IBM to Help Colleges Expand Cybercampuses," *USA Today,* 10 October 1996, D1; Walter S. Baer, "Will the Internet Transform Higher Education?" in Institute for Information Studies, *The Emerging Internet* (Nashville: Nortel, 1998), 94.

251. http://www.athena.edu/athena/html.

252. Baer, "Will the Internet Transform Higher Education?" 92–93.

253. Kim Strosnider, "An Aggressive, For-Profit University Challenges Traditional Colleges Nationwide," *Chronicle of Higher Education,* 6 June 1997, A32–A33; Bulkeley, "Kaplan Plans a Law School," B1.

254. James Traub, "Drive-Thru U," *New Yorker,* 20–27 October 1997, 114.

255. *Chronicle of Higher Education,* 3 July 1997, A5.

256. "Join the Leader in Online Education over the Internet," (advertisement), *Chronicle of Higher Education,* 19 June 1998, B23; Woody, "Higher Earning," 22.

257. Vikas Bajaj, "U. of Southern California Plans Cinema Class on the Internet," *Chronicle of Higher Education,* 13 September 1996, A31.

258. Eurich, *Corporate Classrooms,* 131.

259. Woody, "Higher Earning," 22; Keith H. Hammonds, Susan Jackson, Gail DeGeorge, and Kathleen Morris, "The New U," *Business Week,* 22 December 1997, 97.

260. John A. Byrne, "Virtual B-Schools," *Business Week,* 23 October 1995, 64–68.

261. Hammonds, Jackson, DeGeorge, and Morris, "The New U," 97.

262. "The Committee on Institutional Cooperation and OCLC Are Building . . . a Virtual Electronic Library" (advertisement), *Chronicle of Higher Education,* 27 June 1997, A2.

263. "The Community Colleges and Universities of Florida and OCLC Are Building . . . a Distance Learning Library" (advertisement) *Chronicle of Higher Education,* 7 November 1997, A18–A19.

264. "Mission of University's 'Digital Library' Extends to Reshaping Academic Publishing," *Notice,* Publication of the Academic Senate, University of California, 22, no. 20 (November 1997): 1, 4.

265. Lisa Guernsey, "Digital Presses Transform Librarians into Entrepreneurs," *Chronicle of Higher Education,* 22 May 1998, A27.

266. "Higher Education: Staying Afloat in a 'Tidal Wave,' " Editorial, *Los Angeles Times,* 1 July 1996, B4.

267. "OnLine," *Chronicle of Higher Education,* 18 July 1997, A21.

268. Dr. Mark Hanna, "CSU, Corporations Rush to Technology 'Partnership,' " *California Faculty,* 1998, 7.

269. Perry Robinson, "Awash in Technology," *Financial Times on Campus,* 17 (November 1997): 7–8. See also Peter Applebome, "Governors Try to Map New

Education Era," *New York Times,* 26 March 1996, A15; John H. Cushman, Jr., "Ten Governors in West Agree to Create On-Line College," *New York Times,* 25 June 1996, A9; Amy Wallace, "State May Launch Own Online College," *Los Angeles Times,* 10 July 1996, A3.

270. Lisa Guernsey, "Colorado Community Colleges Plan Degree to Be Offered Entirely over the Internet," *Chronicle of Higher Education,* 28 November 1997, A25.

271. Denise K. Magner, "The Number of Minority Ph.D.s Reached an All-Time High in 1996," *Chronicle of Higher Education,* 21 November 1997, A10–A11.

272. Catherine Yang, "Give Me Your Huddled . . . High-Tech Ph.D.s," *Business Week,* 6 November 1995, 161–164.

273. Martin du Bois, "Microsoft to Give Lernout $45 Million for Development of Speech Technologies," *Wall Street Journal,* 12 September 1997, B9C.

274. John Authers, "Apollo to Expand into China," *Financial Times,* 9 January 1998, 21.

275. John Authers, "A Fork in the Road to Global Enlightenment," *Financial Times,* 20 April 1998, 28.

276. John S. Daniel, *Mega-Universities and Knowledge Media: Technology Strategies for Higher Education* (London: Kogan Page, 1996).

277. Traub, "Drive-Thru U.," 121, 122.

278. http://www.usdla.org/board/html.

279. "NLII Call to Participate," November 1, 1994, and "Creating a Market Structure for Development of Interactive Learning Materials," both at http://www.educom.edu/program/nlii.

280. Thomas J. Deloughry, "Computing Officials at Thirty-four Universities Seek to Create a Network for Higher Education," *Chronicle of Higher Education,* 11 October 1996, A29–A30; Jeffrey R. Young, "Gore Announces Plans for New Fiber-Optic Network to Serve Researchers," *Chronicle of Higher Education,* 24 April 1998, A36.

281. Jeffrey Young, "Key Lawmaker Blasts Administration on Budget Plan for Next-Generation Internet," *Chronicle of Higher Education,* 19 September 1997, A31; Jeffrey R. Young, "Indiana University Is Chosen to Run Nerve Center for Internet 2," *Chronicle of Higher Education,* 14 August 1998, A23.

282. Gerry Blackwell, "Tomorrow's Net Today," *Internet World,* September 1997, 20; Jeffrey R. Young, "Some Participants in Internet 2 Fear It Is Becoming Too Large," *Chronicle of Higher Education,* 27 June 1997, A23, A24.

283. "EDUCOM Notebook: Merger Plans, High-Tech Colleges, and the Death of the Book," *Chronicle of Higher Education,* 7 November 1997, A29.

284. William F. Massy and Robert Zemsky, "Using Information Technology to Enhance Academic Productivity," Washington, D.C.: Interuniversity Communication Council, Inc., (c) Educomreg, 1995.

285. Webb, "The New One-Room Schoolhouse," 22.

286. Lisa Gubernick and Ashlea Ebeling, "I Got My Degree Through E-Mail," *Forbes*, 16 June 1997, 84–92.

287. Amy Pyle, "Textbook Fee Fails to Solve Shortage—and It's Illegal," *Los Angeles Times*, 14 November 1997, A1, A26.

288. Kim Strosnider, "An Aggressive, For-Profit University Challenges Traditional Colleges Nationwide," *Chronicle of Higher Education*, 6 June 1997, A32–A33.

289. Gingrich, *To Renew America*, 152.

290. Goldie Blumenstyk, "Faculty Group Calls for Caution and Curbs on Distance Education," *Chronicle of Higher Education*, 26 January 1996, A20.

291. Peter Monaghan, "Union Leaders Raise Concerns About Technology," *Chronicle of Higher Education*, 15 March 1996, A26–A27.

292. Perry Robinson, "Awash in Technology," *Financial Times on Campus*, November 1997, 8.

293. David Noble, "Digital Diploma Mills, "Available at rre@lists.gseis.ucla.edu.

294. Peter Monaghan, "U. of Washington Professors Decry Governor's Visions for Technology," *Chronicle of Higher Education*, 19 June 1998, A23, A26.

Conclusion

1. Simon Nora and Alain Minc, *The Computerization of Society* (Cambridge: MIT Press, 1980), 10–11.

2. David Wessel and John Harwood, "Capitalism Is Giddy with Triumph: Is It Possible to Overdo It?" *Wall Street Journal*, 14 May 1998, A1, A10.

3. Art Pine, "Economists See Rosy Long-Term U.S. Future," *Los Angeles Times*, 10 June 1997, A1, A22; Peter Schwartz and Peter Leyden, "The Long Boom," *Wired*, July 1997, 115–129+.

4. Nancy Dunne, "U.S. Wholesale Prices Fall Sparks Deflation Debate," *Financial Times*, 19 February 1998, 5; Robert L. Simison, "Fears of Overcapacity Continue to Grow," *Wall Street Journal*, 2 March 1998, A2, A8; Bernard Wysocki Jr., "Even High Tech Faces Problems with Pricing," *Wall Street Journal*, 13 April 1998, A1; Greg Ip, "Some Analysts Seek Signs of Speculative Excess," *Wall Street Journal*, 18 May 1998, C1, C2; William Greider, "When Optimism Meets Overcapacity," *New York Times*, 1 October 1997, A19; idem, *One World, Ready or Not: The Manic Logic of Global Capitalism* (New York: Simon & Schuster, 1997).

5. G. Pascal Zachary, "Global Growth Attains a New, Higher Level That Could Be Lasting," *Wall Street Journal*, 13 March 1997, A1, A8; Fred R. Bleakley, "Companies' Earnings Rocket 61 Percent, Capping Five-Year Winning Streak,"

Wall Street Journal, 18 February 1997, C13; Greg Ip, "Stocks of Big Multinationals Just Keep Rolling Along," *Wall Street Journal,* 28 April 1997, C1; Jacob M. Schlesinger, "Corporate Profits Stay Aloft Despite Tight Labor," *Wall Street Journal,* 28 November 1997, A2.

6. John Simons, "Profits Fell 2.3 Percent in the Fourth Quarter of 1997," *Wall Street Journal,* 27 March 1998, A2.

7. Jacob M. Schlesinger, "Rise in Inequality of Wealth in 1980s Slowed in Early 1990s, IRS Study Shows," *Wall Street Journal,* 27 March 1998, A2.

8. Greg Ip, "The Outlook: Why the Stock Market Isn't the Economy," *Wall Street Journal,* 22 September 1997: A1.

9. Richard Perez-Pena, "New York's Income Gap Largest in Nation," *New York Times,* 17 December 1997, A14; "Child Poverty Statistics Hold Firm in South Despite Boom," *Los Angeles Times,* 5 May 1998, A17; Simon Head, "The New, Ruthless Economy," *New York Review of Books,* 29 February 1996, 47–52; Deborah Vrana, "Whose Interest?" *Los Angeles Times,* 18 January 1998, D1, D6.

10. Leslie Helm, "Microsoft Testing Limits on Temp Worker Use," *Los Angeles Times,* 7 December 1997, D1, D14.

11. Barry Bluestone and Bennett Harrison, *The Deindustrialization of America* (New York: Basic Books, 1982); Bennett Harrison and Barry Bluestone, *The Great U-Turn: Corporate Restructuring and the Polarizing of America* (New York: Basic Books, 1988).

12. William Wolman and Anne Colamosca, *The Judas Economy: The Triumph of Capital and the Betrayal of Work.* (Reading: Addision-Wesley, 1997) 23.

13. Nicholas Timmins, "Reform May Push U.S. Poor into Squalor," *Financial Times,* 23 November 1997, 1.

14. International Labour Organization, *World Employment Report 1998.* Geneva: ILO, 1998.

15. In David E. Kalish, "Intel CEO Seems to Relish a Fight," *San Diego Union-Tribune,* 19 October 1997, I2.

16. Wessel and Harwood, "Capitalism Is Giddy with Triumph."

17. Bhushan Bahree, "As WTO Marks Fiftieth Birthday, Event Attracts Opponents to Globalization," *Wall Street Journal,* 18 May 1998, B11A.

18. George Monbiot, "A Charter to Let Loose the Multinationals," *Guardian,* 15 April 1997, 9; William Lucy, "Web Traps Mighty Foe," *American Federation of State County and Municipal Employees Public Employee* 63, no. 3 (May-June 1998) at http://www.afscme.org.

19. Mireya Navarro, "More Unions Set to Join Strike over Puerto Rico Phones," *New York Times,* 30 June 1998, A14.

20. Craig Turner, "Nations Wary of U.S. Culture Plan Alliance," *Los Angeles Times,* 1 July 1998, A1, A15.

Index